Stoicism and the Art of Happiness

Donald Robertson

Donald Robertson is a cognitive-behavioural psychotherapist who specializes in evidence-based approaches to the treatment of anxiety, and the relationship between ancient philosophy and modern psychotherapy, particularly Stoicism and cognitive-behavioural therapy (CBT). He is the author of five books on philosophy and psychotherapy, including *Build your Resilience* (Hodder & Stoughton, 2012) in the *Teach Yourself* series and *The Philosophy of Cognitive-Behavioural Therapy: Stoic Philosophy as Rational and Cognitive Psychotherapy* (Karnac, 2010). Donald was born in Scotland, and lived in England for many years where he ran a busy Harley Street therapy practice, before emigrating to Nova Scotia in Canada.

Stoicism and the Art of Happiness

Donald Robertson

First published in Great Britain in 2013 by Hodder & Stoughton. An Hachette UK company.

First published in US in 2013 by The McGraw-Hill Companies, Inc.

This edition published 2018

Copyright © Donald Robertson 2013

The right of Donald Robertson to be identified as the Author of the Work has been asserted by him in accordance with the Copyright, Designs and Patents Act 1988.

Database right Hodder & Stoughton (makers)

The *Teach Yourself* name is a registered trademark of Hachette UK.

All rights reserved. No part of this publication may be reproduced, stored in a retrieval system or transmitted in any form or by any means, electronic, mechanical, photocopying, recording or otherwise, without the prior written permission of the publisher, or as expressly permitted by law, or under terms agreed with the appropriate reprographic rights organization. Enquiries concerning reproduction outside the scope of the above should be sent to the Rights Department, Hodder & Stoughton, at the address below.

You must not circulate this book in any other binding or cover and you must impose this same condition on any acquirer.

British Library Cataloguing in Publication Data: a catalogue record for this title is available from the British Library.

Library of Congress Catalog Card Number: on file.

10 9 8 7

The publisher has used its best endeavours to ensure that any website addresses referred to in this book are correct and active at the time of going to press. However, the publisher and the author have no responsibility for the websites and can make no guarantee that a site will remain live or that the content will remain relevant, decent or appropriate.

The publisher has made every effort to mark as such all words which it believes to be trademarks. The publisher should also like to make it clear that the presence of a word in the book, whether marked or unmarked, in no way affects its legal status as a trademark.

Every reasonable effort has been made by the publisher to trace the copyright holders of material in this book. Any errors or omissions should be notified in writing to the publisher, who will endeavour to rectify the situation for any reprints and future editions.

Cover image © Beboy – Photoalia

Typeset by Cenveo® Publisher Services.

Printed and bound in Great Britain by CPI Group (UK) Ltd., Croydon, CRO 4YY.

Hodder & Stoughton policy is to use papers that are natural, renewable and recyclable products and made from wood grown in sustainable forests. The logging and manufacturing processes are expected to conform to the environmental regulations of the country of origin.

Hodder & Stoughton Ltd

338 Euston Road

London NW1 3BH

www.hodder.co.uk

Also available in ebook

Acknowledgements

I'd like to dedicate this book to my wife, Mandy, and to our beautiful daughter, Poppy Louise Robertson. I love you both.

I'd also like to thank everyone involved with Stoic Week and the projects initiated by Professor Christopher Gill and Patrick Ussher at the University of Exeter, for their advice, support, and ideas.

The Metaphor of the Tree

Why, then, do you wonder that good men are shaken in order that they may grow strong? No tree becomes rooted and sturdy unless many a wind assails it. For by its very tossing it tightens its grip and plants its roots more securely; the fragile trees are those that have grown in a sunny valley. It is, therefore, to the advantage even of good men, to the end that they may be unafraid, to live constantly amidst alarms and to bear with patience the happenings which are ills to him only who ill supports them.

Seneca, *On Providence*

Contents

Note on terminology and citations

I've chosen to retain conventional translations of certain key terms employed in ancient Stoic literature, while sometimes offering alternative translations. My aim has been to make this book more contemporary in feel and accessible to a modern reader, without compromising too much on meaning. *Eudaimonia*, I've translated using the conventional 'Happiness', although this is problematic and I've chosen to address that in the book; it's also capitalized, therefore, to highlight the special sense of the word.

Referencing, Translations and Further Reading

I've deliberately omitted many references because the typical format of the *Teach Yourself* series is geared towards general readability and practical application. Where I've referenced primary sources I've often abbreviated the citation by leaving out specific passage numbers, etc. – again, for the sake of simplicity and readability. In many cases, I've quoted or paraphrased ancient sources without including the specific reference.

Throughout this book I've quoted from many different ancient sources, most of which are available in many different English translations. For the sake of consistency, I've typically retranslated passages from the original Greek myself, often drawing on several existing translations in doing so. The main English translations I've quoted from, or consulted, are listed below:

► Seneca, *Dialogues and Essays* (trans. John Davie, 2007). Oxford: Oxford University Press. [Includes selections from *On Anger, On Clemency/Mercy*, the *Consolations to Marcia and Helvia*, and *On Earthquakes*, etc.]

► Seneca, *Selected Letters* (trans. Elaine Fantham, 2010). Oxford: Oxford University Press.

- Cicero, *On the Good Life* (trans. Michael Grant, 2005). Middlesex: Penguin.

- Cicero, *On Moral Ends* (trans. Raphael Woolf, 2001). Cambridge: Cambridge University Press.

- Musonius Rufus, *Lectures and Sayings* (trans. Cynthia King, 2010). Lulu.

- Marcus Aurelius, *The Meditations* (trans. C.R. Haines, 1989). The Loeb Classical Library. Cambridge: Harvard University Press.

- Epictetus, *The Discourses & Handbook* (trans. W.A. Oldfather, 1925). The Loeb Classical Library. Cambridge: Harvard University Press.

- Lucan, *The Civil War* (trans. Susan H. Braund, 1992). Oxford: Oxford University Press.

- Diogenes the Cynic, *Sayings and Anecdotes* (trans. Robin Hard, 2012). Oxford: Oxford University Press.

- Cicero, *On Moral Ends* (*De Finibus*) (trans. Raphael Woolf, 2001). Cambridge: Cambridge University Press.

- Cicero, *On the Good Life* (trans. Michael Grant, 1971). Middlesex: Penguin. [Includes *Tusculan Disputations*, *On Duties*, Laelius: *On Friendship*, and *The Dream of Scipio*, etc.]

- Diogenes Laertius, *Lives of Eminent Philosophers* (trans. R.D. Hicks, 1925). The Loeb Classical Library. Cambridge: Harvard University Press.

The two main translations of early Greek Stoic fragments are:

- *The Hellenistic Philosophers (Vol 1): Translations of the Principal Sources with Philosophical Commentary.* (1987). (A.A. Long & D.N. Seldey, Trans.). Cambridge: Cambridge University Press.

- *The Stoics Reader: Selected Writings and Testimonia.* (2008). (B. Inwood, & L. P. Gerson, Trans.) Cambridge: Hackett.

Translations of Cynic fragments, Hermetic, and Pythagorean texts, as well as the writings of Plato, can be found in:

- Diogenes the Cynic, *Sayings and Anecdotes*. (2012). (Robin Hard, Trans.). Oxford: Oxford University Press.

- *The Way of Hermes: New Translations of The Corpus Hermeticum and The Definitions of Hermes Trismegistus to Asclepius*. (1999). (C. Salaman, D. van Oyen, W.D. Wharton, J.P. Mah, Trans.). London: Duckworth.

- *The Pythagorean Sourcebook*. (1988). (K.S. Guthrie, Trans.). MI: Phanes.

- *Plato: Complete Works*. (1997). (J. M. Cooper, ed.). Cambridge: Hackett. [Contains all the works attributed to Plato, translated by a number of different academics.]

Ancient texts are conventionally referenced differently from modern ones. For example, 'Epictetus *Discourses* (1.1.25)' would mean book one, chapter one, and line number 25 in the original Greek manuscript. For the sake of brevity and readability, I've generally omitted specific line numbers from these references and just pointed the reader to the more general section of a book in question.

You'll find information on suggested further reading for each chapter at the end of this book, along with a more-detailed bibliography section. Where I've referred the reader to one of the ancient sources, I'd recommend using one of the published translations above. In general, the *Loeb Classical Library* series contains reliable English translations of Stoic texts from Epictetus, Marcus Aurelius, and Seneca, although a number of other versions of the most-popular works are now available.

Note on gender

The ancient sources are all written by men and assume that the ideal Sage is masculine. They also tend to refer to Stoics in general in the masculine. I've retained this use of gender in relation to the Sage for the sake of consistency with the source texts but I've deliberately tried to vary the gender assumed when referring to modern (aspiring) Stoics, for the sake of balance often referring to hypothetical students of Stoicism as 'she'. Zeno, the founder of Stoicism, began his training in philosophy by studying for many years with the famous Cynic philosopher Crates of Thebes whose wife Hipparchia of Maroneia was one of the most notable *female* philosophers of antiquity. Zeno and his followers apparently considered men and women to be equals and Stoic schools were known for accepting female students, at a time when this was unusual. We have two surviving lectures from the great Roman Stoic Musonius Rufus, in which he argues that girls have a right to benefit from the same philosophical training as boys because they are capable of possessing the same fundamental virtues of character. They are called: 'That Women Too Should Study Philosophy' and 'Should Daughters Receive the Same Education as Sons?'

The Teach Yourself Breakthrough series has a number of features to help you get the most out of reading this book. *Stoicism and the Art of Happiness* includes the following boxed features:

 'Key idea' boxes that distil the most important ideas and thoughts

 'Remember this' boxes to help you take away what really matters

 'Try it now' boxes to provide you with useful exercises and techniques

 'Focus points' at the end of each chapter to help you hone in on the core message of each chapter.

At the end of the book you will also find a list of resources providing further information and help.

Preface: modern Stoicism

O ye who've learnt the doctrines of the Stoa
And have committed to your books divine
The best of human learning, teaching men
That the mind's virtue is the only good!
She only it is who keeps the lives of men
And cities safer than high gates and walls.
But those who place their happiness in pleasure
Are led by the least worthy of the Muses. (Athenaeus the
Epigrammatist, quoted in Diogenes Laertius, Lives of
Eminent Philosophers)

Well – I'm not the final word on this, Mr. Croker, but what
[the ancient Stoic teacher Epictetus is] saying, it seems to
me, he's saying that the only real possession you'll ever
have is your character and your 'scheme of life,' he calls it.
Zeus has given every person a spark from his own divinity,
and no one can take that away from you, not even Zeus,
and from that spark comes your character. Everything
else is temporary and worthless in the long run, your
body included. You know what he calls your possessions?
'Trifles.' You know what he calls the human body? 'A vessel
of clay containing a quart of blood.' If you understand that,
you won't moan and groan, you won't complain, you won't
blame other people for your troubles, and you won't
go around flattering people. I think that's what he's saying,
Mr. Croker. (Wolfe, 1998, p. 683)

What's this book all about?

This book is about Stoicism, a philosophical tradition founded
in Athens by Zeno of Citium around 301 BC, which endured
as an active philosophical movement for almost 500 years, and
still fascinates people today. However, it's also a 'how to' guide
that will hopefully show you ways in which Stoicism might
provide, or at least contribute towards, a 'philosophy of life' for

the modern world – an art of living with Happiness that aspires to be both *rational* and *healthy*.

If you ask most modern philosophers 'What's the meaning of life?' they'll probably just shrug and say that's an unanswerable question. However, the major schools of ancient philosophy basically each proposed a different answer to that question. In a nutshell, the Stoics said that the goal (*telos*, 'end' or 'purpose') of life is consistently to live in harmony and agreement with the nature of the universe, and to do this by excelling with regard to our own essential nature as rational and social beings. This is also described as 'living according to virtue' or *aretê*, although as you'll see it's best to think of this as meaning *excellence* in a broader sense than the word 'virtue' normally implies – something I'll explain later.

The word 'stoic' (small 's') is still used today to mean being calm or self-controlled in the face of adversity. Curiously, the adjective 'philosophical' is used to mean more or less the same thing, e.g., 'He developed a serious illness but remained *philosophical* about events.' The *Oxford English Dictionary* includes the following, virtually identical, definitions:

> **philosophical.** *adj.* Calm in adversity.

> **stoical.** *adj.* Having or showing great self-control in adversity.

Isn't that striking? It's as though, when it comes to actually *living* philosophically, rather than just talking philosophy, these two words have come to be almost synonymous and interchangeable.

However, to the majority of non-philosophers, the word 'stoical' also means being 'unemotional', or 'having a stiff upper-lip' in the crude sense of *repressing* one's feelings, and that's definitely *not* what it originally meant. In other words, it's not what 'Stoicism' (with a capital 'S') means.

As we'll see, Stoicism, like most ancient Western philosophies, assumed that the goal of life was Happiness (*eudaimonia*), which Stoics believed to coincide both with rational self-love and an attitude of friendship and affection towards others, sometimes described as Stoic 'philanthropy', or love of mankind. For instance, the Stoic Emperor Marcus Aurelius, writing in his journal, repeatedly advises himself to 'love humanity from the bottom of your heart' while rejoicing in doing good to others for its own sake and treating virtue as its own reward (*Meditations*, 7.13).

We might say that a central paradox of Stoicism is therefore its assumption that, far from being heartless, the ideal wise man, called the 'Sage', will both love others and yet be undisturbed by the inevitable losses and misfortunes that life inflicts on him. He has natural emotions and desires but is not overwhelmed by them, and remains guided by reason.

In fact, Stoicism provides a rich armamentarium of strategies and techniques for developing psychological resilience, by changing our feelings *rationally* and *naturally* rather than simply trying to block them out by force. In a sense, ancient Stoicism was the granddaddy of all 'self-help' and its ideas and techniques have inspired many modern approaches to both personal development and psychological therapy. It's generally accepted that the modern psychotherapy that most resembles ancient Stoic 'remedies' for emotional problems is Cognitive Behavioural Therapy (CBT) and its precursor Rational Emotive Behaviour Therapy (REBT). Indeed, the founder of REBT, Albert Ellis, and the founder of cognitive therapy, Aaron T. Beck, both cite Stoicism as the main philosophical inspiration for their respective approaches. In the first major textbook on cognitive therapy, for instance, Beck and his colleagues wrote: 'The philosophical origins of cognitive therapy can be traced back to the Stoic philosophers' (Beck, Rush, Shaw & Emery, 1979, p. 8).

Although CBT is mainly *remedial* in nature, dealing with clinical anxiety and depression, it has also been adapted for use as a *preventative* approach, for generic psychological 'resilience-building'. Ancient Stoic 'therapy' was likewise more of a general resilience-building approach, although it also set out to remedy extreme distress where necessary. CBT also happens to have the strongest evidence base, the strongest scientific support, of any modern form of psychological therapy. So we're looking at an ancient philosophical system, employed for emotional resilience-building, which has inspired a hugely successful modern therapy with a scientifically proven track record.

Stoicism is therefore growing in popularity. However, whenever there's talk of 'modern Stoics', two objections arise. The first is that only someone of exceptional wisdom and moral excellence can be called a *true* 'Stoic' – it's a virtually unattainable ideal. This is illustrated in various comments made by the famous Stoic teacher Epictetus:

> Why did you call yourself a Stoic? [...] Show me a Stoic if you can! Where or how is he to be found? [...] Who then is a Stoic? [...] Show him to me. No, you cannot. Why, then, do you mock yourselves, and trifle with others? Why do you put on a character which is not your own, and walk about like thieves and robbers in these stolen phrases and properties that do not belong to you? (*Discourses*, 2.19)

These are transcripts of lectures and it's most likely that Epictetus was deliberately using hyperbole. Indeed, students of Stoicism were referred to as 'Stoics' throughout antiquity. However, as we'll see, ancient Stoicism has a rich technical vocabulary and the Greek term *prokoptôn* was used to describe a Stoic student or one who is 'making progress' towards the supreme goal of philosophical enlightenment, and becoming a fully fledged Stoic wise man or 'Sage'. We'll tend just to refer to 'students of Stoicism', though, sometimes abbreviating this to 'Stoics', for ease of reading.

Another aspect of Epictetus' position is that students shouldn't normally broadcast the fact they're training in Stoicism but that it would be better to keep it private where possible, to avoid vanity and other obstacles to progress:

> On no occasion call yourself a philosopher, and do not, for the most part, talk among laymen about your philosophical principles, but rather do what follows from your principles. (*Enchiridion*, 46)

However, if we want to make contact with other students of Stoicism and benefit from their example and conversation with them, as his own students did, then we're obviously going to need to disclose the fact that we're studying Stoicism as well. As we'll see, the Internet now provides a way for students of

Stoicism around the world to communicate with each other and form discussion groups, and this has perhaps helped to fuel the resurgence in its popularity. Although the emphasis of Stoicism is very much on diligent practice rather than chit-chat, online resources can help support people in understanding Stoic philosophy and incorporating its practical elements in their daily lives. Maybe we're now entering the era of the *Cyber-Stoic*?

The second objection to modern Stoicism goes beyond terminological quibbles. Some people question how we can study Stoicism today when the original tradition basically died off in late antiquity, along with other 'pagan' philosophical schools, following the rise of Christianity. The Stoic school was an influential philosophical movement, which endured for many centuries in both Greece and Rome, but it gradually came to an end as a living philosophy. The Emperor Marcus Aurelius, who died in 180 AD is the last major Stoic figure we know much about today.

Incidentally, you may have seen the Hollywood film *Gladiator* in which Marcus Aurelius is portrayed by the actor Richard Harris. There's not much reference to Stoicism in that film, although Russell Crowe's character says near the end:

> I knew a man once who said, 'Death smiles at us all. All a man can do is smile back.'

That's not a real quotation from Marcus Aurelius but it's obviously inspired by passages from his personal journal, the *Meditations*, probably the best-known surviving Stoic text today. Many modern readers base their understanding of Stoicism solely on this short book. Despite its popularity, though, the *Meditations* was a private journal of Marcus' Stoic practice and never intended as a comprehensive introduction to Stoicism.

In fact, Zeno's original Stoic school was based on the study of detailed arguments contained in its many founding texts. The early Stoics alone reputedly wrote over a thousand 'books' (although, some of these were probably more like long essays). However, this formal institution was destroyed along with the centres of other major philosophical schools at some point following the sack of Athens by the Roman dictator Sulla in

86 BC. Nevertheless, the Stoic tradition survived for several centuries, during the Roman Imperial period, albeit in a more dispersed and fragmentary form.

By the time of Marcus Aurelius, Stoics typically appear to have met in smaller and more informal groups. They presumably had access to a much more limited handful of Stoic texts, many early Greek writings having already been lost over the intervening centuries. Marcus appears to have drawn mainly on the Stoic teachings of Epictetus as recorded in his *Discourses*, about half of which still survive today. By contrast, he does not make any reference to Seneca, the Stoic author from whom we have the largest volume of surviving writings. Marcus' seemingly impoverished access to the original teachings of Stoicism might be compared to that of a modern student of the subject, although he did also benefit from personal acquaintance with several Stoic tutors and lecturers.

We have to reconstruct a picture of Stoicism from the fragments that remain, over 2,300 years after the school originated. However, unlike Marcus, we now benefit from many volumes of superb modern commentary and analysis (Long, 2002; Hadot, 1998), and examples of people applying Stoicism to modern life (Evans, 2012; Irvine, 2009). In some ways we're therefore no worse off than students of Stoicism in late antiquity and may even have advantages that they lacked, including access to texts they had not read.

Some ancient Stoics were prolific writers and lecturers, who dedicated their lives to educating others. Indeed, early Stoics reputedly taught that all wise men have a natural love of writing the sort of books that can help other people. So perhaps modern students of Stoicism, although far removed from the lofty ideal of the Sage, can nevertheless be expected to enjoy writing self-help books or blogs with the purpose of aiding others and exchanging ideas about the modern relevance of Stoicism. Nobody should dare *claim* to be wise, although everyone should dare to *try* to be so.

The role of a modern author on Stoicism might perhaps be best described as resembling that assumed by Seneca. He says to his aspiring Stoic friends that he is like an invalid in one bed discussing how his therapy is going with the man in the bed beside him. Less than one per cent of the original Stoic literature has survived but, if that were compiled into one publication, it would probably be about seven or eight volumes in length – so not an insignificant amount of material. Unfortunately, we often need the help of modern academic commentators to help us reconstruct the meaning of these early Greek fragments. However, they provide an important resource that can help us understand the underlying philosophical system taken for granted by more widely-read Stoic authors such as Seneca and Marcus Aurelius.

Yet we should be especially cautious that Stoicism does not turn into a deadened and *bookish* subject. One solution to this problem is provided by the first chapter of Marcus Aurelius' *Meditations*, where he shows how an aspiring Stoic may contemplate the virtues of his friends, family, colleagues, and perhaps even some of his enemies, to find traces of inspiration, even though a single example of a *perfectly* wise and good person, or even something approaching this, may be lacking in our lives.

Throughout this book, I'll refer to many specific examples of people, both ancient and modern, whose lives have been changed by Stoicism. My own interest in this area began when I was about 17 years old and a college lecturer suggested I should study philosophy. I began reading the classics, mainly Plato, and went on to do my degree in philosophy at Aberdeen University. I was also a member of the student Buddhist society and regularly practised meditation. I went on various Buddhist retreats because I wanted to find a lifestyle and daily practice that somehow complemented my study of philosophy.

After graduation, I trained in and started to practise counselling and psychotherapy because I felt this gave me a practical vocation that complemented my interest in philosophy. However, I always yearned to bring these three things – therapy, philosophy and meditation – more closely into harmony, and it was only some years later that my eyes were opened to the rich tradition of spiritual exercises in ancient philosophical literature by the writings of the eminent French scholar, Pierre Hadot, such as his *Philosophy as a Way of Life* (1995).

Hadot's marvellous books ignited my interest in Stoicism and inspired me to begin publishing short articles on the subject myself. This led to a longer article on Stoicism for one of the main counselling and psychotherapy journals (2005), and eventually a book on Stoicism and modern psychotherapy called *The Philosophy of Cognitive-Behavioural Therapy: Stoic Philosophy as Rational and Cognitive Psychotherapy* (2010). I've been trying to assimilate Stoicism, in terms of specific practical strategies as well as the overall way I live my life, for over ten years now. I've also had plenty of experience discussing aspects of Stoicism with anxious or depressed clients, in relation to my work as a CBT practitioner. (My previous book in the *Teach Yourself* series, *Build your Resilience* (2012), draws on Stoic philosophy in relation to modern evidence-based approaches to psychological resilience-building.)

I'm interested in Stoicism, therefore, because I agree with what I consider to be its core doctrines, and because I believe its psychological exercises are of practical value in modern living. However, I also find much of the surviving Stoic literature to be both beautiful and profound, and part of its enduring appeal is undoubtedly the literary merit of writings such as the letters and essays of Seneca, and the aphorisms of Marcus Aurelius.

Why focus on Stoic Ethics and psychotherapy?

This book won't give equal weight to all aspects of ancient Stoicism. As we'll see, the Stoics divided their philosophical curriculum into three topics, called 'Ethics', 'Physics' and 'Logic'. (These words aren't very good translations but they're the ones commonly used.) We're mainly going to focus on Stoic Ethics. There are several reasons for doing this:

▶ We know far more about Stoic Ethics than about their Physics or Logic, because the extant writings, particularly those of the 'big three' Roman Stoics – Seneca, Epictetus and Marcus Aurelius – are mainly concerned with this topic, which may have been the central focus of late Roman Stoicism in general.

- There tends to be most interest in Stoic Ethics among modern readers because of its obvious relationship with contemporary self-help and psychological therapies, such as CBT, whereas the remnants of their (theologically-grounded) Physics may be perceived as less relevant today, and ancient Logic can be less accessible to the average reader.

- Some important, albeit unorthodox, Stoics focused *solely* on Ethics. For example, we're told one of Zeno's followers, Aristo of Chios, 'discarded altogether the topic of physics, and of logic, saying that the one was above us, and that the other had nothing to do with us, and that the only branch of philosophy with which we had any real concern was ethics' (*Lives*, 7.160).

- The Stoics generally held their forerunners the Cynics in particularly high esteem and some saw their austere and challenging lifestyle as a 'short-cut to virtue', even though they deliberately eschewed technical philosophical debates about Logic or Physics; this admiration for the Cynic way of life is particularly apparent in the *Discourses* of Epictetus, the only surviving book-length text from an actual Stoic teacher.

- If technical knowledge of Stoic Physics and Logic were absolutely essential to the goal of life, then ancient Stoics would presumably not have revered historical and mythological figures such as Hercules, Socrates and Diogenes the Cynic as exemplary role models. In other words, the role-models ancient Stoics typically sought to emulate, in their daily lives, were not primarily logicians or natural philosophers, but men of great personal virtue and practical wisdom.

- From the outset, all Stoics appear to have agreed that Ethics was ultimately the most important aspect of their philosophy, e.g., Chrysippus, the influential third leader of the school, allegedly said that the only reason for studying Physics was for the sake of Ethics.

Cicero, one of the most important ancient commentators on Stoicism, described the question of what is the supreme 'good' in life, the central topic of Stoic Ethics, as the foundation of their whole philosophy. He says the 'most important' Stoic doctrine was that 'the only good is virtue' and calls this 'the veritable head of the Stoic household' (*De Finibus*, 4.14; 4.44). Epictetus therefore warned his students that excessive concern with Stoic Physics risks becoming a diversion from the central task of living virtuously.

However, as we shall see there is inevitably some overlap between Stoic Logic, Ethics and Physics and so our discussion will bring in some elements of the other topics where it seems necessary or helpful to do so. In particular, we'll be looking at the lived practice of Stoicism in terms of three practical 'disciplines', which scholars have correlated with the three topics of the theoretical curriculum.

Some people feel that modern Stoicism isn't faithful enough to the ancient tradition but hopefully these remarks help to justify the differences. On the other hand, some people feel that *too much* emphasis is placed on what the ancient Stoics said. However, Stoicism (with a capital 'S') is, by definition, an *ancient* philosophy. Even those who adapt it for modern living, generally consider themselves to be united by an interest in the original Greek and Roman tradition, from which they seek inspiration. These texts are still immensely valuable and highly-regarded. In many cases, they're remarkably beautiful. In fact, Seneca (a Stoic) and Cicero (not a Stoic but an important source nevertheless) are renowned as two of the very finest writers of antiquity.

I've therefore quoted the ancient Stoics frequently; partly to provide evidence where some interpretation may be in question, but also because they're frankly much better writers than I could ever hope to be and they deserve to be more widely read. Indeed, these are some of the greatest philosophical minds and most accomplished writers of all time. However, even the ancient Stoics were conscious that a balance needs to be struck between too much and not enough reliance on the original texts of their sect. Writing about three centuries after the Stoic school was founded, Seneca says:

> So am I not following our predecessors? Yes I am, but I allow myself to discover some new thing and to change or abandon others: I am not a slave to them but I agree with them. (*Letters*, 80)

To paraphrase a famous Latin saying: 'Zeno is our friend but truth is an even greater friend.' We now have access to enormous volumes of psychological research, which tell us many things about human nature that the Stoics could not have known so easily. In particular, a large body of research on CBT exists that tells us a great deal about healthy and unhealthy ways of responding to emotional distress. As we shall see, this was a major concern for the Stoics and they were traditionally perceived as the philosophical school with the most explicit 'therapeutic' focus. Readers today are naturally interested in what the Stoics said about therapy, and how it compares to modern research on the subject.

Stoicism was often employed therapeutically, as a remedy for overwhelming distress, as in the many examples of ancient 'consolation' letters, written to help others cope emotionally with traumatic bereavements and other misfortunes in life. However, as noted above, prevention is better than cure, and the main focus of Stoic psychological exercises would be better described as resembling what we now call 'emotional-resilience building'. Hence, Musonius Rufus, one of the pre-eminent Stoic teachers of the Roman Imperial period, reputedly said that 'in order to protect ourselves we must live like doctors and be continually treating ourselves with reason.' He advised his students, the most famous of whom was Epictetus, that we should not use philosophy like a herbal remedy, to be discarded when we're through. Rather, we must allow philosophy to remain with us, continually guarding our judgements throughout life, forming part of our daily regimen, like eating a nutritious diet or taking physical exercise.

This notion of practical philosophy as a foundation for building general emotional resilience seems to appeal to many modern readers and its part of the reason people are drawn to the subject. Just like in ancient times, people who are unsatisfied with life, and in need of emotional healing, are often among those drawn to Stoicism, in search for both peace of mind and a sense of purpose. As we'll see, the Stoic 'therapy of the passions' was an absolutely central component of their ethics, which aimed at nothing less than the transformation of our character, by helping us to flourish, as Nature intended, in accord with wisdom and virtue. Stoic ethics and therapy therefore go hand in hand, lie at the centre of the subject, and are the aspects people tend to find most relevant and intriguing today.

However, there are also aspects of Stoicism which are extremely challenging. Some people will be put off by their fundamentally *uncompromising* stance on ethics. Others will find it refreshing and intriguing, perhaps even quite radical and exciting. The Stoics were undoubtedly regarded as a philosophical force to be reckoned with in the ancient world. Even those who disagreed with them were impressed by the scope and internal consistency of their philosophical vision but they were also criticized for being obscure at times. Cicero wrestled with Stoicism and complained:

> In both its foundations and in the edifice itself Stoicism is a system constructed with great care; incorrectly perhaps, though I do not yet dare pronounce on that point, but certainly elaborately. It is no easy task to come to grips with it. (*De Finibus*, 4.1)

This book focuses on providing a practical introduction to Stoicism and so it doesn't explore the criticisms of their philosophy in much detail. However, Cicero's *De Finibus* provides a classic account of relatively even-handed arguments for and against Stoicism. Plutarch's essay on 'Stoic Contradictions' likewise provides another classical source of criticism. A modern appraisal of Stoicism that tries to provide a detailed technical defence of its doctrines in relation to ethical philosophy can be found in Becker's *A New Stoicism* (1998).

Although a detailed critique of Stoic philosophy is beyond the scope of this book, it's not the intention to portray Stoicism as somehow above philosophical or scientific criticism. On the contrary, readers should take it upon themselves to think through these ideas carefully and question them deeply. Of course, you need to learn what the Stoics actually believed first, before you can do that. So let's plunge right in...

A taste of the Stoic paradoxes

Although Stoicism was a *philosophical* system that prized rational understanding, the original philosophical arguments of Zeno were notoriously terse and remained unconvincing to his philosophical critics. Zeno proclaimed many famous 'paradoxes', which literally meant ideas that go against what the majority believe, flying in the face of popular opinion. They portrayed a radical but impressively coherent world view that attracted many people who wanted to see if it could be defended more rigorously.

The third head of the Stoic School, Chrysippus, one of the very greatest intellectuals of the ancient world, attempted to do this, writing hundreds of volumes of detailed philosophical arguments in defence of Stoic doctrine, particularly engaging with the criticisms made by ancient Skeptics who represented a rival school, the Academy of Plato. He basically transformed Stoicism from the small movement founded by Zeno into one of the philosophical heavyweights of the ancient world.

> For if Chrysippus had not lived and taught,
>
> The Stoic school would surely have been naught. (*Lives*, 7.183)

We're told he was known for making the striking remark to his teacher Cleanthes that he only wanted to be instructed in the core doctrines (*dogmata*) of Stoicism and that he would discover the arguments for and against them for himself. Many modern readers will likewise first be attracted to the attention-grabbing ideas of the Stoics, which promise to turn our prevailing philosophy of life on its head, and then seek to weigh them up rationally in their own terms. Some Stoics even referred to this upheaval in our world-view and system of values, turning away from the conventional view of the majority, as a philosophical 'conversion' (*epistrophê*), literally a 'turning around' or 'U-turn' in life. In this regard, the Stoics were influenced by the Cynics, who we're told would walk against the flow of the crowds leaving a theatre, or walk about backwards in public, to illustrate their desire, paradoxically, to swim against the current in life and go in the opposite direction from the majority of people.

The Stoics therefore recognized that they were saying things many people would struggle to accept at first, although they also believed that their philosophy was ultimately based on common sense assumptions, accessible to everyone on reflection. For example, Cicero defends six notoriously cryptic 'Stoic Paradoxes' in his short book of that title:

1 Virtue, or moral excellence, is the only good (conventional 'goods' such as health, wealth and reputation fundamentally count as *nothing* with regard to living a good life).

2 Virtue is completely sufficient for Happiness and fulfilment, a man who is virtuous lacks no requirement of the good life.

3 All forms of virtue are equal as are all forms of vice (in terms of the benefit or harm they do to the individual himself).

4 Everyone who lacks perfect wisdom is insane (which basically means everyone alive; we're all essentially mad).

5 Only the wise man is really free and everyone else is enslaved (even when the wise man is imprisoned by a tyrant, or sentenced to death like Socrates, he is still freer than everyone else, including his oppressors).

6 Only the wise man is truly rich (even if, like Diogenes the Cynic, he owns nothing that he can't carry in his knapsack).

These puzzles require some explaining, as we'll see. Musonius Rufus apparently used to say that students were expected to be left in stunned silence following his lectures rather than applauding him. They felt that they'd heard something unnerving but powerful and were often unsure what to make of it all at first. I'd say that this is true for modern readers as well. If we don't feel at least slightly unsettled by what the Stoics are saying then we're probably missing something important about their philosophy.

Yet despite the paradoxes, Stoicism was in many respects the most down-to-earth of the Athenian philosophical schools, being grounded in our experience of daily life. We're told Cleanthes, the second head of the Stoa, used to remark: 'Possibly the philosophers say what is contrary to opinion [or 'paradoxical'], but assuredly not what is contrary to reason' (Epictetus, *Discourses*, 4.1).

Case study: The University of Exeter's research project on modern Stoicism

Stoicism has been described as the philosophical inspiration for cognitive behavioural therapy (CBT) because both approaches interpret emotions as being mainly due to our beliefs and patterns of thinking ('cognitions'). They also share the assumption that by altering relevant beliefs we can overcome emotional distress. An impressive body of scientific evidence from clinical trials and other types of research has provided support for the efficacy of CBT, particularly as a treatment for anxiety and depressive disorders.

To some extent, this might be seen as lending *indirect* support to 'Stoic therapy'. However, until recently, there's been no attempt to provide *direct* evidence of Stoicism's psychological benefits.

In November 2012, however, Patrick Ussher, a doctoral student researching Stoicism at the University of Exeter (Ussher, 2012), organized an informal pilot study called 'Stoic Week', under the supervision of Prof. Christopher Gill, a classicist, who has written and contributed to several academic books on Stoicism (Gill, 2006; 2010; 2011).

A multi-disciplinary team of academic philosophers, classicists, psychologists and psychotherapists were involved in the project (myself included). A handbook explaining basic Stoic concepts and practices was made available online for participants to use in their daily lives over a one-week period as an initial feasibility test. (I wrote some sections of the handbook and the book you're reading was partly inspired by this and several of our findings.) It generated a lot of interest and was covered in several articles in *The Independent* and *Guardian* newspapers. There were about 14,000 visits to the project website, called *Stoicism Today*, during the week of the study.

Over eighty people actually participated in the project online, and data were collected from forty-two participants. The philosopher and psychotherapist Tim LeBon, author of *Wise Therapy* (LeBon, 2001), compiled a report that is also available from the website (LeBon, 2012).

So what were the findings? It must be stressed that this was just an initial pilot study and more formal research is underway. The report concluded: 'Extremely promising, interesting results, much scope for further, more focused research.' Data showed a roughly 10 per cent increase across three different self-report measures of psychological wellbeing, after just one week of following the project's Stoic handbook, which is, of course, a very brief period of practice from which to expect much measurable change. There was also a decrease of about 10 per cent in measures of negative emotions, although positive emotions increased by only around 5 per cent. Participants were able to choose from a range of Stoic strategies and reported the three most useful to be the following:

- Stoic mindfulness (*prosochê*)
- The retrospective evening meditation
- The view from above

We'll therefore be exploring these three classic Stoic strategies in more detail, in later chapters. The main finding of the study, though, was that it appeared feasible to construct a handbook of Stoic exercises simple enough for people to download and apply to modern living. Participants enjoyed following the exercises, perceived them as helpful, and were keen to do more. The study wasn't a carefully controlled scientific experiment so we have to be cautious about the findings but the data are suggestive that even practising Stoic exercises for a week may have a positive psychological effect that can be measured using scientifically-validated scales. You can access more information via: http://blogs.exeter.ac.uk/stoicismtoday/. You can also follow @Stoicweek on Twitter to find out about future projects, etc.

Stoicism today in the modern world

What about Stoicism today? Well, there is a growing community of people studying Stoicism around the world, connected via the Internet. If you just type 'Stoicism' into Google, it probably won't take you long to find practising Stoics because there are many who participate in online forums, etc. For example, the International Stoic Forum is an active online discussion group, founded in 1998, with nearly a thousand members.

The International Stoic Forum

http://groups.yahoo.com/group/stoics/

The blogger and philosopher Jules Evans also published a book recently called *Philosophy for Life*, which gives many concrete examples of people who apply ancient philosophy to modern living, particularly Stoicism and related Socratic schools of thought (Evans, 2012). Stoicism has been particularly popular with the modern military. For example, Major Thomas Jarrett, a former Green Beret, has taught a psychological resilience programme to thousands of personnel in the US army, mainly drawing on Stoic philosophy and elements of CBT. Data gathered from questionnaires completed by 900 participants in Major Jarrett's Stoic 'Warrior Resilience Training' programme was suggestive of positive results. For example, the statistics showed his participants felt the training would indeed assist them become more resilient during deployment and on returning home (Jarrett, 2008). A recent book called *Stoic Warriors: The Ancient Philosophy behind the Military Mind* by Prof. Nancy Sherman, former Distinguished Chair in Ethics at the US Naval Academy, has also explored the affinity between Stoic philosophy and contemporary military values (Sherman, 2005).

Many people, on the other hand, will have learned of Stoicism from Tom Wolfe's acclaimed novel, *A Man in Full* (1998). Two of the central characters become 'converts' to Stoicism at pivotal points, and their use of Stoicism becomes central to the climax of the story. The second half of the book contains many references, therefore, to the sayings of Epictetus. One of the characters, Conrad, comes across the writings of the Stoics by accident while imprisoned. When asked if he considers himself a Stoic:

> 'I'm just reading about it', said Conrad, 'but I wish that there was someone around today, somebody you could go to, the way students went to Epictetus. Today people think of Stoics – like, you know, like they're people who grit their teeth and tolerate pain and suffering. But that's not it at all. What they are is, they're serene and confident in the face of anything you can throw at them. If you say to a Stoic, 'Look, you do what I tell you or I'll kill you', he'll look you in the eye and say, 'You do what you have to do, and I'll do what I have to do – and, by the way, when did I ever tell you I was immortal?' (Wolfe, 1998, p. 665)

A good guide to applying Stoicism in the modern world is Keith Seddon's *Stoic Serenity*, which is based on his home-study course in the Stoic art of living (Seddon, 2006). His plain-English explanation of Stoicism is as follows: 'A Stoic can be regarded, perhaps, as someone who continually reminds themselves that their plight is not as bad as it may appear, and that our capacities, to deal with both the petty frustrations of daily life and significant turns of bad fortune, are superior (with philosophy's aid) to how we usually imagine them' (Seddon, 2006, p. 78).

However, the bestselling popular introduction to Stoicism is probably William Irvine's *A Guide to the Good Life: The Ancient Art of Stoic Joy* (Irvine, 2009). Nevertheless, there are a number of key respects in which Irvine's account seems to depart from Stoicism as traditionally understood. He claims that the explicit focus of his book is on the attainment of 'tranquillity' rather than 'virtue' (Irvine, 2009, p. 42).

> The resulting version of Stoicism, although derived from the ancient Stoics, is therefore unlike the Stoicism advocated by any particular Stoic. It is also likely that the version of Stoicism I have developed is in various respects unlike the Stoicism one would have been taught to practise in an ancient Stoic school. (Irvine, 2009, p. 244)

To this, more orthodox Stoics might object that 'tranquillity' (*ataraxia*) is traditionally seen as a positive side-effect of virtue rather than the goal of life itself. To put it crudely, if tranquillity is really your supreme goal in life then you can just take *tranquilizers*. The Stoics argued that the chief good in life must be something that is *both* good itself and 'instrumentally' good, meaning that it brings about good consequences. Tranquillity is typically agreed to be a good thing but it doesn't 'lead anywhere', it doesn't reliably maintain itself or generate other good consequences – it can be misused or abused. A psychopath might experience tranquillity while chopping-up his victims' bodies! However, the pursuit of wisdom and virtue as the chief goal in life leads to something that both maintains itself and brings about other beneficial things, *including* tranquillity.

In this book, therefore, we'll be looking at a modern approach to Stoicism, which *does* resemble, and is deliberately based upon, the characteristic views of the ancient Stoics. We'll be placing Stoicism within its historical context, and examining the philosophical foundations of the school, particularly the core ethical doctrines, widely regarded in antiquity as the essence of Stoicism. In other words, by drawing extensively on the historical tradition, we'll attempt to answer the question: What *makes* someone a Stoic?

The Stoic Hymn to Zeus

Lead me, O Zeus, and thou O Destiny,
The way that I am bid by you to go:
To follow I am ready. If I will not,
Making myself wretched, I still must follow.
The willing are led by fate, the reluctant dragged.

Fragment of a Hymn to Zeus

Cleanthes, the second head of the StoaStoicism and the Art of Happiness

Donald Robertson

1

The way of the Stoic: 'Living in agreement with Nature'

In this chapter you will learn:

▶ *Whom the Stoics were and the essence of their philosophy: that the goal or meaning of life is 'living in agreement with Nature'*

▶ *About the overall structure of Stoicism and the three theoretical 'topics' of the philosophical curriculum: 'Physics', 'Ethics' and 'Logic'*

▶ *How these inform three dimensions of Stoic practice: The Disciplines of 'Desire', 'Action' and 'Judgement'*

▶ *How to contemplate the nature of the 'good' and how to appraise your sphere of control in life*

The duration of a man's life is merely a small point in time; the substance of it ever flowing away, the sense obscure; and the whole composition of the body tending to decay. His soul is a restless vortex, good fortune is uncertain and fame is unreliable; in a word, as a rushing stream so are all things belonging to the body; as a dream, or as vapour, are all those that belong to the soul. Life is warfare and a sojourn in a foreign land. Reputation after life is nothing more than oblivion.

What is it then that will guide man? One thing alone: philosophy, the love of wisdom. And philosophy consists in this: for a man to preserve that inner genius or divine spark which is within him from violence and injuries, and above all from harmful pains or pleasures; never to do anything either without purpose, or falsely, or hypocritically, regardless of the actions or inaction of others; to contentedly embrace all things that happen to him, as coming from the same source from whom he himself also came, and above all things, with humility and calm cheerfulness, to anticipate death, as being nothing else but the dissolution of those elements, of which every living being is composed.

And if the elements themselves suffer nothing by this their perpetual conversion of one into another, that dissolution, and alteration, which is so common to them all, why should it be feared by any man? Is this not according to nature? But nothing that is according to nature can be evil. (Marcus Aurelius, *Meditations*, 2.15)

Self-assessment: Stoic attitudes and core principles

Before reading this chapter, rate how strongly you agree with the following statements, using the five-point (1–5) scale below, and then re-rate your attitudes once you've read and digested the contents.

1. Strongly disagree, 2. Disagree, 3. Neither agree nor disagree, 4. Agree, 5. Strongly agree

1 'The goal of life is to 'live in agreement with Nature' by willingly accepting things outside our control.'

2 'We should also live in harmony with our own human nature by trying to cultivate reason and progress towards perfect wisdom and virtue.'

3 'We should live in harmony with the rest of mankind by seeing ourselves as all fundamentally akin to each other insofar as we possess reason.'

Introduction: What is Stoicism?

What is Stoicism? To recap: it's an important school of ancient philosophy founded in Athens around 301 BC by a Phoenician merchant called Zeno who hailed from the city of Citium in Cyprus. However, as we'll see, Stoicism was also regarded as one of several competing schools inspired by the life and thought of Socrates, the pre-eminent Athenian philosopher, who had been executed a century earlier.

It was originally called 'Zenonism' but came to be known as 'Stoicism' because Zeno and his followers met in the *Stoa Poikilê*, or 'Painted Porch', a famous colonnade decorated with a mixture of mythic and historical battle scenes, situated on the north side of the *agora*, the ancient Athenian marketplace (see Figure 1.1). Sometimes Stoicism, or the Stoic school of philosophy, is therefore just called 'The Stoa' or even the philosophy of 'The Porch'. Like their hero Socrates, but unlike the other formal schools of Athenian philosophy, the Stoics met out in the public marketplace, on this porch, where anyone could apparently listen to them debate. Here Zeno vigorously paced up and down as he lectured, which we're told kept the porch clear of people slouching. The expression 'Stoic philosophy' has therefore been taken to suggest something like a 'philosophy of the street', a philosophy for ordinary people, not locked-up in the proverbial 'ivory towers' of academia. Indeed, until recently, the Stoics were rather neglected by modern philosophy departments. William Irvine, a professor of philosophy, and author of a recent bestselling book on Stoicism, wrote:

Before the twentieth century, those who were exposed to philosophy would likely have read the Stoics. In the twentieth century, though, philosophers not only lost interest in Stoicism but lost interest, more generally, in philosophies of life. It was possible, as my own experience demonstrates, to spend a decade taking philosophy classes without having read the Stoics and without having spent time considering philosophies of life, much less adopting one. (Irvine, 2009, p. 222)

In fact, Stoicism has grown in popularity since the 1970s, partly because of the success of CBT.

However, in the ancient world, as we've seen, Stoicism was, from the outset and for nearly five subsequent centuries, one of the most influential and highly-regarded schools of philosophy. We're told the Athenians greatly admired Zeno, granting him the keys to their city and building a bronze statue of him, in stark contrast to the fate that befell his predecessor, Socrates. They also reputedly voted in favour of an official decree honouring his exemplary 'virtue and self-discipline', with a golden crown and a tomb, built at public expense. This public declaration praised his many years devoted to philosophy in Athens, and described him as a good man in every respect, 'exhorting to virtue and self-discipline those of the youth who come to him to be taught, directing them to what is best, affording to all in his own conduct a pattern for imitation in perfect consistency with his teaching' (*Lives*, 7.10).

The example set by Zeno's conduct was important to the Stoics because they considered emulation of the wise and good to be the best way to learn philosophy. He initially followed the simple and austere way of life adopted by the Cynic philosophers, which exerted an important influence over Stoicism. As a result, his reputation for self-mastery (*enkrateia*) apparently became quite legendary and even proverbial; people could be praised by comparing their self-discipline to that of the example set by Zeno. Cynics were known for enduring physical hardship, and Zeno himself was certainly described as a philosopher toughened by the elements. For instance an unnamed ancient poet wrote of him:

The cold of winter and the ceaseless rain
Come powerless against him: weak the dart
Of the fierce summer sun or racking pain
To bend that iron frame. He stands apart
Unspoiled by public feast and jollity:
Patient, unwearied night and day doth he
Cling to his studies of philosophy. (*Lives*, 7.27)

Where Zeno departed from his initial allegiance to Cynicism, however, was in his greater emphasis on the need to supplement their tough philosophical lifestyle, their 'Ethics', with the study of 'Physics' and 'Logic' as well. As we'll see, the Cynics also viewed all external things as ultimately 'indifferent', whereas the Stoics adopted a more subtle position, allowing themselves to value certain conventional things, while retaining a sense of detachment from them. Nevertheless, the Stoics were particularly concerned with applying philosophy to everyday challenges and especially with the classic Socratic question: How does someone live a good life? They saw themselves as veritable warriors of the mind and would perhaps condemn modern academic philosophy as mere 'sophistry' by comparison.

Key idea: Philosophy as a way of life

It may come as a surprise to realize that ancient philosophy was a fairly practical business. It often emphasized training in psychological exercises or the adoption of a demanding lifestyle, a precursor in some ways of Christian monastic practices. Some philosophers, most notably the Cynics, even turned their nose up at theoretical debate or abstract speculation as a diversion from the true business of cultivating practical wisdom and self-mastery.

The Cynics therefore ridiculed Plato and his followers for their 'Academic' style of philosophy. They believed voluntary poverty and endurance of hardship were better philosophical teachers than books and lectures. Zeno was initially a Cynic, although he studied Logic and Physics as well, and so Stoicism grew out of this tradition. The Stoics' hero, Socrates, also wrote nothing and although he engaged in debates these mainly involved posing difficult questions to other people concerning their beliefs about virtue and the best way of life.

Indeed, ancient philosophers, especially Cynics, were recognizable by their attire and behaviour. Cynics begged for food or ate cheap and simple meals of lupin seeds or lentil soup, and drank only water. They dressed only in a cheap cloak, which they doubled over for warmth in winter, carried everything they owned in a small knapsack, bore an ash staff, perhaps for self-defence, and bedded down on simple straw mats, often sleeping rough in public buildings. Zeno initially adopted a similar lifestyle and some aspects of this may have continued among his followers, although the Stoics were generally less austere than the Cynics. Musonius tells his students that as long as they have the inner virtues of a philosopher: 'You won't need to don an old cloak, go around without a shirt, have long hair, or behave eccentrically', like Cynics (*Lectures*, 16). Elsewhere, however, he advises students to go shirtless and barefoot, which suggests the Stoics saw these Cynic trappings as *optional* to the philosophical way of life.

From the other schools of philosophy, the Stoics drew a broad armamentarium of psychological exercises, including contemplative meditation techniques, which have been explored in detail in several books by the modern scholar Pierre Hadot, such as his *Philosophy as a Way of Life* (Hadot, 1995). Hence, throughout this book we'll be particularly focusing on this *practical* dimension of Stoicism, as an 'art of living', which traditionally held out the promise of attaining *eudaimonia*, supreme Happiness and fulfilment.

Try it now: In at the deep end...

Let's start right now by contemplating the nature of the good. Ponder the following interrelated questions until your head begins to ache:

1 What does it mean, fundamentally, for something to be 'good', as far as humans are concerned?

2 What qualities make a human being a good *person*? (Compare: 'What qualities make a horse a good horse?')

3 What qualities make someone's life a good *life*?

4 Can being a good person *contribute* to having a good life? (The Stoics and most other Graeco-Roman philosophers agreed that it did.)
5 Does being a good person *suffice* for having a good life, even in the face of external 'misfortunes', such as persecution by others? (Was the life of Socrates worse because he was poor and persecuted; would it have been a better life if he'd had good fortune in external matters, if he'd lived an easier and more comfortable life?)

We might call this last point the 'Stoic hard-line'. They were distinguished from other schools of philosophy by their insistence that being a good person, having virtue and honour, is the only true good.

In any case, these are some of the fundamental questions of Stoic Ethics. Indeed, they're some of the cardinal questions of ancient philosophy in general. So don't worry if you don't have a definitive answer yet! People have been arguing over them for nearly 2,500 years. Some people would say that the main thing is to wrestle with the questions, at least, even if the answers sometimes elude us. The Stoics did believe we could arrive at a kind of philosophical certainty in these matters, though not usually without hard study and training.

Case study: The self-mastery of Socrates

We're used to thinking of Socrates as a wise philosopher, but did you realize he was also a decorated military hero and held up as an exemplary model of courage and self-discipline in the ancient world? Zeno was apparently converted to philosophy by reading the Athenian general Xenophon's account of his friend Socrates. According to Xenophon, Socrates was 'the most self-controlled of men' in respect of his physical desires as well as his tolerance of hardship, including extreme heat and cold, having trained himself to have modest needs and to be content with the most basic material possessions. Despite being a pretty tough character himself, Xenophon was clearly impressed by Socrates' strength of character and self-mastery, which closely-resemble the virtues and practices that subsequently became the focus of both Cynicism and Stoicism.

We're told Socrates rigorously trained both his mind and body through his philosophical lifestyle. He argued, paradoxically, that 'it is self-discipline, above all things, that causes pleasure.' By exercising restraint, we learn to only eat when genuinely hungry, drink when thirsty, and so on. Appetite and thirst are the natural 'sauce' of life and the secret to making even coarse bread and plain water seem delicious. Self-control is healthier and actually leads to more enjoyment than self-indulgence, particularly with regard to the most common sources of pleasure in daily life. By contrast, Socrates said that anything that impels us to eat when *not* hungry or drink when *not* thirsty 'ruined stomachs and heads and characters'. Hopefully, this seems more like common sense than self-mortification, although it flies in the face of modern attitudes towards food and drink – we're constantly bombarded with advertising for more convenient and enticing, but often unhealthy, things to consume.

Socrates also taught his students that we should keep the body fit through appropriate physical exercise because it is employed in all human activity, even the act of thinking, as everyone knows that people can't think straight when they have certain illnesses. He apparently favoured dancing alone, at daybreak, as a form of physical exercise, because it involved the whole body rather than just some parts – but this was something that seemed quite eccentric to his associates. Overall, though, we're told that he believed that everyone should care for their health, by learning everything they can about it from experts but also by studying their own constitution, every day, and observing what food, drink or exercise actually do them good. Because everyone is different, he thought that ideally we should become our own physicians, learning from experience what's healthy in our own case. Xenophon likewise believed that just as people who fail to exercise their bodies become physically weak, people who do not train their characters, through self-discipline, become morally weak. The Stoics agreed, and we'll find them placing great emphasis on moral and psychological training in philosophy.

The goal of life: 'living in agreement with Nature'

So what did the Stoics actually believe? Well, that's what this whole book is about. The ultimate goal of life was agreed by all schools of ancient philosophy to be Happiness or *eudaimonia*. We'll explore the Stoic concept of Happiness in more detail in the following chapters. However, Zeno originally wrote

'Happiness is a smoothly flowing life' (*euroia biou*), which was the definition adopted by the other founders of the Stoic school. This obviously raises another question: How did the Stoics believe we might *achieve* a smooth-flowing and Happy life?

Zeno tried to express his philosophy in short 'laconic' statements and notoriously compressed 'syllogistic' arguments, which had to be elaborated by his followers. The *best-known* definition of the Stoic goal of life, which is attributed either to Zeno or to Chrysippus, was simply 'living in agreement with nature', and several variations of this can be found in the Stoic literature. 'Our motto, as everyone knows,' wrote Seneca, 'is to live in conformity with nature' (*Letters*, 5). Indeed, Zeno reputedly wrote a book entitled 'On the life according to nature'. So this became the central slogan and tenet of Stoicism throughout the ages, sometimes abbreviated even further to 'Follow nature'. However, four centuries later, we find the famous Stoic teacher Epictetus explaining to his students that although the chief Stoic doctrines were originally summed up in brief maxims, when we try to explain their meaning it inevitably raises questions, such as 'What is nature in the individual and nature in the universe?', and so the explanation becomes more lengthy.

What, therefore, does it mean to 'live in agreement with nature'? Throughout this book we'll be unravelling that cryptic slogan. However, to begin with, it's worth explaining that the Stoics *also* reputedly said that the goal of life was 'living in accord with virtue', or human excellence. In other words, they believed that we're all born with the responsibility of excelling by bringing our own nature to perfection. This means completing the job left unfinished by Nature herself, by voluntarily making the best use of our highest faculty: reason. Crucially, for the Stoics, adult humans are essentially reasoning creatures and therefore 'to the rational creature the same act is at once according to Nature and according to reason' (*Meditations*, 7.11). So following Nature doesn't mean acting like a 'dumb animal' but rather fulfilling our natural potential as *human* animals. Indeed, Chrysippus reputedly said:

> So, where shall I start from? And what am I to take as the principle of appropriate action and the raw material for

virtue if I give up nature and what is according to nature?
(Quoted in Plutarch, *On Common Conceptions*, 1069e)

The Stoics therefore emphasized the need to contemplate what a perfect human being would be like, someone whose life is both honourable and benefits themselves and others. They envisaged this as someone who has attained complete practical wisdom and 'virtue'. By 'virtue' they actually meant 'excelling' or flourishing in terms of our rational human nature, rather than what we might think of as 'virtuous' behaviour today. As we'll see, the Stoics argued that human nature is essentially rational and social, and so wisdom and justice are the pinnacles of human achievement.

The goal of every human life is for us to voluntarily make progress in that direction. So Stoicism is a philosophy that focuses on teaching us how to excel in life, how to become better human beings, and how to live a good life. It can therefore also seem a little bit like a religion, albeit based primarily on rationality rather than faith, and people have sometimes compared it to Buddhism for that reason. Providing a Western equivalent, in some respects, for the kind of philosophical 'way of life' that's found in many Eastern religions, is part of its appeal for many modern readers.

It follows from the premise that our essential nature is rational that the greatest virtue is wisdom and the greatest vice folly or ignorance. Humans have the gift of conscious knowledge, we're invited by Nature to be spectators and interpreters of the universe, and the Stoics believed our fundamental task in life must be to do that well, by excelling in terms of knowledge and understanding about the most important things in life. This can be summed up as attaining wisdom in the art of living, or 'prudence' for want of a better word. Indeed, the word 'philosophy' literally means 'love of wisdom' in Greek.

The goal of life is therefore the goal of philosophy: to love and attain wisdom, particularly with regard to the way we actually live our lives, which could be described as *moral* or *practical* wisdom. In fact, practical wisdom, knowledge concerning what is good and bad, was thought by the Stoics to be the basis of all other forms of human excellence, which were typically subsumed under the four cardinal virtues of wisdom, justice, courage and self-discipline. As we'll see, the Stoics believed the cardinal virtues are both practical skills and forms of knowledge, involving a firm grasp of what's good and bad in different situations.

Epictetus' school made the central theme of its whole philosophy the doctrine that we must distinguish very carefully between what is 'up to us', or within our power, and what is not. This is because the chief good in life is squarely located within the sphere of our control, in our own actions and judgements, and everything else is classed as fundamentally 'indifferent' with regard to living a good life. This is undoubtedly food for thought, and food that will take some time to chew over and digest properly.

The philosophical conclusion that the chief good, the most important thing in life, must necessarily be 'up to us' and under our direct control is at once the toughest and most appealing aspect of Stoicism. It makes us completely and utterly responsible for the single most important thing in life, depriving us of any excuses for not flourishing and attaining the best possible life, because this is always within our grasp. This fundamental *dichotomy* between what is 'up to us' and what is not has therefore been described as the Stoics' 'sovereign' and most characteristic principle. We'll be coming back to it repeatedly in what follows!

Key idea: 'Living in agreement with Nature'

Stoicism defines the chief goal of life as 'living in agreement with Nature' or following Nature. The word for goal, *telos*, is sometimes translated as 'end' or 'purpose', and arguably comes close to what we call 'the meaning of life'. This didn't mean moving to the countryside or hugging trees, though! Following Chrysippus, the Stoic way of life was interpreted as being in harmony with nature at two levels. On the one hand, Stoics try to live according to their own *human* nature, as inherently rational and social creatures, by excelling in terms of wisdom, justice, and the virtues of self-mastery. The Stoics assumed that Nature is goal-directed and that our ability to reason suggests the possibility of its own completion or perfection, i.e., of attaining wisdom.

On the other hand, following Nature also means accepting our place as part of a whole, the nature of the *universe*, and welcoming our fate, insofar as it is beyond our control to change it. However, these two tasks are complementary because we require virtue to be able to rise above adversity and welcome whatever life sends us. The 'promise' of Stoic philosophy is that by living in agreement with nature, or living virtuously and accepting our fate, we shall attain *eudaimonia*, complete personal fulfilment, wellbeing, and Happiness. We'll return to what this meant in more detail later...

Try it now: Eat like a Stoic

Here's a novel idea... try eating a more healthy diet for the next week. There is an important 'Stoic' twist, though. When you're trying to stick to your plan, rather than motivating yourself by thinking about some desired outcome, such as losing weight or improving your health, etc., focus instead on the *inherent* value of developing self-discipline. Losing weight or improving your health isn't guaranteed with any diet; it's not directly under your control, but partly in the hands of fate. It's also something that's off in the future, a 'hope', a consequence of your actions rather than something happening 'here and now'. By contrast, prudent self-discipline is good and praiseworthy in itself, whatever the long-term result.

You don't need to imitate an ancient Stoic or Cynic diet, just challenge yourself to eat more healthily for a week or so, using your own common sense to guide you. For the record, though, the Stoics followed the advice of Socrates that we should 'eat to live' rather than 'living to eat'. In his lecture on food, Musonius Rufus argued that mastering one's appetite is the very foundation of training in self-control. He says Stoics should drink only water and avoid gourmet meals, preferring vegetarian food that's nourishing but cheap, convenient to obtain, and easy to prepare (for example, milk, cheese, honey and certain fruits and vegetables, etc.). He says Stoics should eat slowly and with mindfulness, exercising moderation and self-control. For some modern readers just having still water for a week, instead of other drinks, might be a good initial challenge.

Remember, the goal is to improve your self-discipline and related 'virtues' or character strengths, rather than to lose weight or gain physical health. If you're exercising self-discipline and perseverance, though, it makes sense to do it in a healthy direction, doesn't it? Stoics refer to physical health and fitness as something 'preferred' but ultimately irrelevant, or 'indifferent', in relation to true Happiness and fulfilment. Cultivating a healthy *character*, is infinitely more important to them than cultivating a healthy *body*. Nevertheless, we develop self-discipline precisely by trying to do healthy and appropriate things in the world, whether or not they turn out as we'd have preferred.

Remember this: Does human nature have a goal?

Some modern readers may struggle to accept the Stoic assumption that mankind has a natural goal. However, we do generally take some goal for granted whenever we talk about being 'harmed'. What sense does it make to complain of being injured unless we assume that there's some more-desirable state to be in? As Seneca puts it, 'What is in keeping with nature is blessed, in life, and it is apparent to our senses what is in keeping with nature, as it is whether something is damaged or not' (*Letters*, 124). However, when speaking of being 'harmed' the majority of us assume the goal that is jeopard ized to be our pleasure, health, long-life, or other external goods. For Stoics, these are 'indifferent', and true 'harm' only relates to our ruling faculty, our mind, which can be injured by descending into vice and nothing else.

The twofold goal of life

Stoic wisdom consists primarily in knowing good from bad, and that means knowing what is under our control and what is not. The inscription 'Know Thyself' from the Delphic Oracle of Apollo, which inspired Socrates, was therefore interpreted by the Stoics as an injunction to continuously monitor and examine their own souls. We truly 'know ourselves' when we separate what is *uniquely* human from what is external to us or shared with other animals. Self-knowledge also means distinguishing what is under our control from what is not. To contemplate and understand our own existence is an ongoing effort, according to the Stoics, requiring a form of 'mindfulness'. Mindfulness is a concept often associated with Buddhist meditation, but which has clear precedents in ancient Graeco-Roman philosophy. As well as being a philosophical contemplation concerning the very nature of human existence itself, mindfulness of this distinction between what is up to us and what is not is one of the main remedies for emotional suffering. This is neatly expressed in the 'Serenity Prayer', a well-known early 20th-century formula, used by Alcoholics Anonymous and many modern therapists (Pietsch, 1990):

> God, give me the Serenity to accept the things I cannot change,
> The Courage to change the things I can,
> And the Wisdom to know the difference.

This is often interpreted simply to mean that we should distinguish between some situations or aspects of the external world that we can change, and others that we cannot. For the Stoics, however, wisdom consists in realizing that the only thing we completely control, by definition, are our own volitions, particularly our *voluntary* judgements and actions.

Chrysippus was apparently the first Stoic to explicitly say that the goal of life should therefore be understood as a *twofold* task: 'taken as living in accordance both with one's own nature and with the Nature of the whole' (*Lives*, 7.88). This subdivision can be seen to run throughout most of the surviving Stoic literature, right down to the *Meditations* of Marcus Aurelius (*Meditations*, 6.58; 12.11):

1 **One's internal nature**: Nobody can prevent you from living according to your own internal nature, as a rational being, i.e., wisely and virtuously.

2 **Nature of the world**: Nothing can befall you externally that is contrary to the universal laws of Nature, which the wise man accepts piously as determined by fate or, in theological language, as the will of Zeus.

In the late Roman Stoicism of Epictetus, this appears to turn into the simple but fundamental distinction mentioned earlier, between what is 'up to us', or under our control, and what is not. However, the Stoics also seem at times to turn this into a threefold division, by further distinguishing between the laws of Nature and the actions of other human beings, among external events. So we can think of 'living in agreement with Nature' as living harmoniously across *three* important dimensions of life:

1 **Self:** Harmony with our own essential nature, with ourselves as rational beings, which requires perfecting reason and virtue and fulfilling our nature.

2 **World:** Harmony with Nature as a whole, which means accepting our fate, insofar as it's beyond our control, as if we'd willed it to happen, rather than complaining and struggling futilely against events.

3 **Mankind:** Social harmony or 'concord' with other people, viewing all rational beings as our kin, and extending our natural affection for others into a heartfelt 'philanthropic' attitude towards the rest of mankind.

It's tempting to see this as connected somehow with the other threefold divisions found in Stoicism, to which we now turn, e.g., linking harmony with our inner self, with the world, and with the rest of mankind to Stoic Logic, Physics and Ethics respectively.

Key idea: Stoicism as a perennial philosophy

The eminent French scholar Pierre Hadot concluded from his detailed scholarly analysis of the *Meditations* of Marcus Aurelius that Stoicism gave clear expression to a 'universal' and 'perennial' philosophical attitude, which crops up in different guises throughout history and around the world (Hadot, 1998, pp. 311–312). Like many other people, he notes similarities between Stoicism and some Oriental philosophies. On this view, the Stoic tradition founded by Zeno and continuing right through to Marcus Aurelius, constitutes just one of a handful of archetypal philosophical attitudes that we find in human history. Hadot sums up four key attitudes at the heart of this generic Stoic-like 'perennial philosophy', which he calls 'eternal Stoicism':

1 The spiritual awareness that humans are not fragmentary, isolated beings but are essentially parts of a bigger whole, both of the totality of all mankind and the totality of the cosmos itself.

2 The basic feeling of serenity, freedom, and invulnerability that comes from accepting that there is no evil but moral evil, and that the only

thing that matters in life is moral integrity or what the Stoics call 'honour' and 'virtue'.

3 Belief in the absolute value of the human person, which Hadot illustrates with Seneca's saying 'man is a sacred thing for man' – a sense of kinship with all mankind which makes the wellbeing of humanity the chief preferred outcome of all moral action.

4 The psychological and philosophical exercise of 'concentration on the present instant', which involves living as if we were seeing the world for the first and last time, while being aware that, for the wise man, each instant intimately connects us to the totality of space and time.

Most people are drawn to Stoic philosophy without having had a chance to wrestle with the complexities of the vast philosophical system and literature associated with it. Rather, they find something in a few fragmentary Stoic quotations that resonates with them because they sense it expresses a more basic underlying set of philosophical attitudes, one of several *perennial* human philosophies.

The three theoretical topics of Stoicism

As mentioned earlier, the whole of Stoic philosophy was divided into three 'topics' (*topoi*), referred to as 'Physics', 'Ethics' and 'Logic'. This division was reputedly introduced by Zeno himself in a book called *Exposition of Doctrine*. As is often the case, it's worth knowing the traditional translations, because you'll come across these in books on Stoicism. However, it needs to be said that they're slightly misleading terms.

1 **Physics** (*phusikê*) is sometimes called 'natural philosophy', but is mainly concerned with what we would call metaphysics and theology as well as ancient natural science; the Stoics were pantheists and determinists, for whom 'Nature' as a whole, 'Fate' and 'Zeus', or 'God', were synonymous. This aspect of Stoicism was influenced by Heraclitus, and perhaps other pre-Socratic philosophers of Nature in what's known as the 'Ionian' tradition.

2 **Ethics** (*êthikê*) is the study of the nature of the good, virtue and the goal of life (and to some extent politics) but also encompasses the study of emotional disturbance (irrational

'passions') and the improvement of human character (*êthos*) in a way that resembles modern self-help and psychological therapy. This part of Stoic philosophy is probably most influenced by the ethical views of Socrates and the Cynics.

3 **Logic** (*logikê*) is the study of definitions and rules, dialectic (philosophical debate) and formal 'syllogistic' logic, an area where the Stoics, particularly Chrysippus excelled; it may also have encompassed rhetoric, although that's not an area the Stoics were usually very concerned with; and in some respects it encompasses aspects of what we would now call psychology or theory of knowledge ('epistemology'). This part of their philosophy was probably influenced by Zeno's time spent studying two ancient schools known as the Megarians and Dialecticians, about which we know little today.

According to an early Stoic metaphor, philosophy is like an orchard or garden. Logic is the orchard wall, that protects everything growing within and makes it secure; Physics corresponds to the fertile soil and trees themselves, the natural source of the fruits that eventually grow and ripen in the orchard, which correspond to Ethics, and probably symbolize human virtue. However, these three topics were somewhat intertwined. Different Stoics disagreed about the correct order for them to be taught in and probably also differed about their relative importance. As we noted earlier, the late Roman Stoics, about whom we know the most, seem to be particularly concerned with Ethics.

Remember this: Stoicism versus eclecticism

Many modern students of Stoicism are probably attracted to some aspects of it more than others and they may even neglect doctrines that Zeno and his followers would have considered essential. However, many ancient philosophers, both Stoics and non-Stoics, were also quite eclectic in their approach so this is nothing new. Cicero provides just one such example of an ancient philosopher who took Stoicism very seriously but didn't agree with all aspects of it, preferring to align himself with the Platonic Academy instead.

In the same way, today's readers will probably be divided into two groups: people who believe in the central ethical principles of Stoicism and are much more committed to it as a whole, and people who more closely resemble Platonists, Aristotelians or even Epicureans, and simply want to assimilate a few selected aspects of Stoic theory and practice. However, there are bound to be elements of Stoicism, particularly parts of Stoic Physics and theology (such as worshipping Zeus!) that might seem quite odd within the context of modern society, and which few people would accept today.

Try it now: Exercise like a Stoic

One of the famous slogans of Epictetus was 'endure and renounce'. You've seen how renouncing unhealthy, or unnecessary, food and drink can be used as a way to practise developing the virtue of self-discipline, or 'moderation' in our diet. Endurance is linked to the virtue of 'courage' and can be developed to some extent simply by learning to tolerate ordinary discomfort or fatigue, of the kind experienced during physical exercise. Musonius says that as we have minds *and* bodies, we should exercise both, although always paying most attention to our mind. 'We will train both mind and body when we accustom ourselves to cold, heat, thirst, hunger, scarcity of food, hardness of bed, abstaining from pleasures, and enduring pains' (*Lectures*, 9).

You don't need to strip naked and hug ice-cold statues in winter to develop endurance, like the Cynics reputedly did. Running, vigorous walking, or yoga stretches are simple forms of exercise, which can challenge us to push our tolerance of physical effort.

For example, Zeno, the founder of Stoicism, was renowned for his physical endurance. Rather than sitting down idly to lecture, as he talked he would pace vigorously up and down the porch where his school gathered. Cleanthes, the second head of the Stoa, was originally a boxer; Chrysippus, the third head, was a long-distance runner. The founders of the Stoa, in other words, were quite keen on physical exercise. However, as we've seen with regard to their views on diet, there's a subtle 'Stoic' twist. Whereas people today often abstain from certain foods because they want to lose weight, or take exercise to improve their health or physical appearance, the Stoics would see these outcomes as 'preferred' but ultimately 'indifferent' things. Their real reason for renouncing certain foods or enduring tough physical exercise would be to strengthen the virtues of 'self-discipline' and 'courage', or endurance.

The three lived disciplines

Epictetus, the most influential Stoic teacher of the Roman Imperial period, also described a threefold distinction between practical areas of Stoic training, which Marcus Aurelius quotes and applies systematically in his *Meditations*. Pierre Hadot has argued, based on a careful scholarly analysis of the texts, that he meant these to be understood as aspects of the three Stoic theoretical topics described above, insofar as they are applied to the art of living (Hadot, 1998, pp. 73-100). These practical disciplines came to describe three ways in which the Stoic aims to live a coherent and unified life, in harmony with himself, mankind, and the whole of Nature.

1 **The Discipline of Desire** (*orexis*) **and Aversion** (*ekklisis*), i.e., of the 'passions', requires us to have desire for and attain the good, to have aversion towards and avoid the bad, and to view indifferent things with indifference. The good is to be defined as being solely in the domain of things under one's control, one's volitions or actions, making wisdom and other virtues the highest good. Hadot provides a detailed argument in support of the surprising conclusion that this is the lived form of Stoic Physics, and deals with the virtue of living in harmony with the Nature of the universe and what is determined by fate. This may be particularly linked with the virtues of *courage* and *self-discipline*, which relate primarily to self-control regarding irrational or unhealthy desire (craving) and aversion (fear), and the alleviation of emotional suffering through the Stoic therapy of the passions.

2 **The Discipline of Action** (*hormê*) requires us to act in accord with our duties or 'appropriate actions' (*kathêkonta*), to do the right thing in terms of our relationships, in the service of mankind, with the addition of the Stoic 'reserve clause', a caveat such as 'fate permitting'. Hadot concludes that this is the applied form of Stoic Ethics, and it relates to living philanthropically and in harmony with the community of mankind. It appears most linked to the virtue of *justice*, which includes fairness and benevolence to others.

3 **The Discipline of Assent** (*sunkatathesis*) requires us to spot initial impressions for what they are and to evaluate them, particularly in terms of the core Stoic doctrines concerning 'good' and 'bad', before giving assent to them if true. Hadot concludes that this is clearly the applied form of Stoic Logic and deals with the virtue of living in accord with our own rational nature. It may be linked to the Stoic virtue of *wisdom*, which is the perfection of reasoning, and this discipline is important because it helps protect the other two.

Put crudely, we might say these deal with our 'feelings', 'actions' and 'thinking' – the three main areas of our conscious experience that we can learn to achieve some voluntarily control over. Epictetus says that of these three, the first, the Discipline of Desire, is the one students should most urgently address because irrational, excessive or unhealthy 'passions' are simply incompatible with the attainment of the good life and prevent us making progress in Ethics or Logic.

We might also describe the first stage of Stoic training, therefore, as the discipline of fear and desire, through practice in self-mastery. As it happens, this is how we're told Zeno began his own philosophical career, becoming a follower of Crates, who taught him to endure hardship and renounce desire for conventional goods, by adopting the Cynic way of life. It was probably only later that he began to study Physics and Logic in any depth by attending the other schools of Athenian philosophy.

Key idea: The three Stoic disciplines of Epictetus

As far as we know, Epictetus was the first Stoic to distinguish between the three disciplines of 'desire and aversion', 'action', and 'assent.' Marcus Aurelius and presumably other followers of Epictetus' school adopted the same tripartite distinction. After a detailed textual and philosophical analysis, the French scholar Pierre Hadot (1998) concluded that these were groups of practical exercises meant to correspond with the Stoic theoretical topics of Physics, Ethics and Logic, respectively.

Other scholars, such as A.A. Long, a leading expert on Epictetus, broadly agree with this interpretation (Long, 2002, p. 117). Hadot also tentatively suggested that they may correspond with the cardinal virtues and with 'living in agreement with Nature' at three different levels. The three 'topics' of Stoicism, and particularly these three disciplines, provide the structure around which the rest of this book is based. Although we'll be focusing more on Stoic Ethics than on their Physics and Logic, we will draw on some elements of those theoretical topics in discussing the corresponding disciplines and psychological exercises found in Stoic literature.

Remember this: Stoicism was not 'unemotional'

It's a common misconception that Stoics were into repressing emotions. That's arguably just due to problems of translation and interpretation. The 'passions' they talk about overcoming were specifically defined as irrational, excessive and unnatural (meaning 'unhealthy') forms of fear and desire, and the consequent feelings of pain (meaning emotional suffering) and pleasure (in the superficial 'hedonistic' sense). Marcus Aurelius' remark about being 'free from passions and yet full of love', or 'natural affection', sums up the Stoic ideal nicely (*Meditations*, 1.9). The early Stoics made it clear that the Ideal was not to be cold-hearted like a stone or statue and their ideal community was founded on mutual love and friendship. 'Love' and 'natural affection', as we'll see, were very highly valued by the Stoics, as were a variety of rational, moderate, 'healthy passions' (*eupatheiai*), comprised mainly of rational joy, feelings of discretion, and well-wishing or affection towards others. The Stoics sought to use reason and training to overcome unhealthy desires and emotions, while making way for healthy ones instead.

Focus Points

The main points to remember from this chapter are:

* ✳ Stoicism has a long history, over 500 years, but its central doctrine remained fairly constant, 'living in agreement with Nature'.
* ✳ Living in agreement with Nature means acting with virtue, insofar as that's under your control, while accepting external events, outside your control, as determined by the whole of Nature.
* ✳ Stoic teaching was divided into three theoretical topics that correspond with three practical disciplines, which we shall be exploring throughout the rest of this book.

Next Step

Traditionally, philosophy held out the promise of a deeper sense of fulfilment and Happiness in life, which motivated students to pursue their studies and the exercises required to progress towards virtue. The next chapter will introduce the promise of philosophy and explore the ultimate goal of Stoicism, the exalted condition of the enlightened Sage called *eudaimonia*, or true Happiness and wellbeing.

2

Stoic Ethics: The nature of the good

In this chapter you will learn:

▶ *The essence of Stoic Ethics: their definition of the supreme good in life as being 'practical wisdom', otherwise known as 'virtue'*

▶ *How the Stoics understood virtue to be both necessary and sufficient not only to be a 'good person' but also to have a 'good life' and attain supreme 'Happiness' and fulfilment* (eudaimonia)

▶ *How Stoics classed certain things as 'indifferent' with regard to Happiness but nevertheless as having some practical value in life*

▶ *How to practise a modern meditation technique, adapted for Stoic contemplation of the highest good*

Begin this very moment to decide the question, 'Where is the nature of good and evil to be found?' (Epictetus, *Discourses*, 2.2)

The principal task in life is this: distinguish matters and weigh them one against another, and say to yourself, 'Externals are not under my control; volition is under my control. Where am I to look for the good and the evil? Within me, in that which is my own.' But in that which is another's never employ the words 'good' or 'evil', or 'help' or 'harm', or anything of the sort. (Epictetus, *Discourses*, 2.5)

For I go around doing nothing but persuading young and old among you not to care for your body or your wealth in preference to or as strongly as for the best possible state of your soul, as I say to you: 'Wealth does not bring about virtue, but virtue makes wealth and everything else good for men, both individually and collectively.' (Socrates in Plato's *Apology*, 30a-b)

Self-assessment: Stoic attitudes towards Ethics

Before reading this chapter, rate how strongly you agree with the following statements, using the five-point (1–5) scale below, and then re-rate your attitudes once you've read and digested the contents.

1. Strongly disagree, 2. Disagree, 3. Neither agree nor disagree, 4. Agree, 5. Strongly agree

1 'Practical wisdom consists in knowing what it means for something to be good, bad or 'indifferent' when it comes to attaining Happiness and fulfilment.'

2 'Whatever is external to my will is 'indifferent' with regard to my ultimate Happiness.'

3 'Although they're ultimately unimportant, it's nevertheless natural and rational to 'prefer' some external things over others'.

What's important about Stoic Ethics?

What is the ultimate source of human Happiness and fulfilment? What do Stoics mean when they say that someone is a good or bad person? What do they mean by saying that external and bodily 'goods' are merely *indifferent* to them? How do they reconcile the need to live in the world, handling property and interacting with other people, with their stringent view that virtue is the only true good? These are the sort of questions addressed in this chapter on ancient Stoic Ethics, which will pave the way for further discussion of Epictetus' three *practical* disciplines.

So what did the Stoics actually mean by 'Ethics'? We'll need to examine the significance of some Greek words to answer that question. First of all, the word 'ethics' (*êthikê*) carried very different connotations for ancient philosophers. It alludes to the development of one's character (*êthos*) and therefore overlaps with modern approaches to self-improvement and psychological therapy. The Stoics saw their Ethics as comparable to athletic or military training and also as resembling a branch of medicine, one treating the mind rather than the body.

In this chapter, we'll focus on the central question: 'What is the nature of the good?' Cicero calls this the 'core' of Stoic philosophy itself. The notion that the essence of the good life is virtue, understood as a kind of practical wisdom, is certainly the characteristic feature of Stoicism. Indeed, when ancient authors compared Stoicism to other philosophical schools they typically focused on their uniquely uncompromising Ethical doctrines, rather than their Physics or Logic.

The essence of Stoic Ethics is the claim that practical wisdom, or 'virtue', by which they basically mean the same thing, is the only true good. The fundamental goal of mankind was therefore defined by the Stoics as 'living in accord with virtue', which was equated with the life according to Nature, and synonymous with living wisely, as a 'philosopher' or *lover of wisdom*. Virtue is both necessary and sufficient for living a good life and attaining *eudaimonia*, regardless of external misfortune or physical hardship. As Cicero wrote:

> The belief of the Stoics on this subject is simple. The supreme good, according to them, is to live according to nature, and in harmony with nature. That, they declare is the wise man's duty; and it is also something that lies within

his own capacity to achieve. From this follows the deduction that the man who has the supreme good within his power also possesses the power to live Happily. Consequently, the wise man's life is Happy. (*Tusculan Disputations*, 5.28)

We might express the Stoic view by saying that being a good *person* is all it takes to have a good *life*, and therefore to be Happy and fulfilled, whatever our external fortune. The life of an enlightened Sage *lacks* nothing of intrinsic importance, even if he is deprived of health, wealth and reputation. The supposedly opulent and hedonistic life of the Great King of Persia is no better, and in fact is much worse, according to the Stoics, than the life of poverty chosen by their hero Diogenes the Cynic, who slept rough and owned nothing but a single cheap garment, and what little food he could fit in his knapsack. Moreover, Diogenes' life would not ultimately have been made any 'better' if fortune had granted him greater wealth and status. Scholars have therefore said that 'the bastion of Stoic ethics is the thesis that virtue and vice respectively are the sole constituents of happiness and unhappiness' (Long & Sedley, 1987, p. 357).

However, these radical opinions are worthless unless they transform our lives. Epictetus, in his typically blunt style, warns his students not to be satisfied with learning about the nature of the good as a set of abstract ideas but that we must vigorously apply them to specific situations and train ourselves systematically in doing so, because we have all had years of practice thinking and doing the opposite. We have to digest these ideas and allow them to permeate our lives, which the Stoics compare to sheep eating grass and using the nutrients to grow their wool. Otherwise we're not true philosophers: we're just commentators on other people's opinions. Any idiot can give a discourse like this, Epictetus says, in the process giving us a convenient summary of Stoic Ethics:

> Of things that are, some are good, and some are bad, and some are indifferent: the good then are virtues, and the things which participate in virtues; and evil things the opposite; and the indifferent things are wealth, health, reputation. (*Discourses*, 2.9)

However, he adds, suppose that in the middle of this lecture on the good, right now, there's a sudden and frightening loud noise or some of the audience begin to laugh and ridicule us. We get upset because our philosophy comes from our lips only, and not from the very core of our being. For that reason, the Stoics stress the need for daily training in philosophy as a way of life, using exercises of the kind described throughout this book.

Case study: Jules Evans and modern Stoicism

Jules, who runs the Well-Being Project at the Centre for the History of the Emotions, Queen Mary University, is co-organizer of the London Philosophy Club, and has been involved with the 'Stoic Week' projects at Exeter University. In a recent article called 'How Ancient Philosophy Saved My Life', published on his blog and in *The Times* newspaper (8 May 2012), he describes the 'breakdown' that led him to seek help from cognitive-behavioural therapy (CBT) and Stoic philosophy. While studying literature at university, Jules experienced worsening panic attacks, depression and anxiety. By attending a CBT-based self-help group, he was able to overcome his panic attacks and to better manage his emotional problems.

Inspired by his success, he travelled to New York, as a trainee journalist, to interview Albert Ellis, the founder of Rational-Emotive Behaviour Therapy (REBT), the main precursor of modern CBT. Jules did the last ever interview with Ellis before he died. Ellis told him about how he'd been directly inspired by ancient Greek philosophy in his pioneering work as a psychotherapist in the 1950s. He'd been particularly inspired by the famous quotation from Epictetus' *Handbook*: 'Men are disturbed not by events but by their opinions about them.' This became the central philosophical inspiration for REBT and most subsequent forms of CBT.

As Jules points out, almost all schools of ancient Graeco-Roman philosophy shared a 'cognitive' approach to the emotions. This interprets emotional distress as being largely due to our individual beliefs and patterns of thinking, which are changeable through philosophical reflection and diligent training in related psychological exercises. Ancient philosophy, in other words, was *inherently* a form of psychological therapy.

Jules concluded that his own emotional problems came, to some extent, from his personal values – putting too much emphasis on winning others' approval, etc. One of the lessons he took from ancient Socratic philosophy was that 'we can take back possession of ourselves, by choosing intrinsic values like wisdom rather than extrinsic ones like status or power.' For the Stoics, the *only* thing of any ultimate importance in life is virtue, particularly wisdom, and 'extrinsic' things are of absolutely secondary value, because they are inherently unimportant when it comes to attaining Happiness and freedom from emotional suffering.

As a blogger and in his book, *Philosophy for Life and Other Dangerous Situations* (Evans, 2012), Jules has written extensively about the relevance of ancient philosophy for modern living, particularly as a means of improving emotional resilience and personal wellbeing. He sums up three of the lessons he derives from Stoicism and other branches of Hellenistic philosophy as follows:

1 Focus on what you can control, and accept what you can't.
2 Choose your role models wisely, a lesson he takes from Plutarch's *Parallel Lives*.
3 Keep track of your thoughts and behaviour by, for example, monitoring them in a personal therapy journal.

He writes: 'Socrates showed us that we all have the power to heal ourselves and change our characters, at any stage of our lives; we might not become perfect sages like him, but I believe we can all become a little wiser and happier.'

Key idea: 'Practical wisdom' and 'virtue'

The Stoics believed that humans are inherently *rational* animals, and uniquely so apart from the god Zeus. So they defined the intrinsic goal of human nature as the perfection of reason, referred to as 'wisdom' (*sophia*), or more specifically *phronêsis*, which means 'prudence', 'moral wisdom' or 'practical wisdom'. The ideal human being, someone both perfectly good and rational, is called the 'Sage' or 'wise man' (*sophos*). Those who aspire to become Sages are therefore called 'philosophers', lovers of wisdom.

Practical wisdom is the essence of all virtue, according to the Stoics. This consists of knowledge, about the nature of the 'good', applied to different aspects of living – so all the virtues are essentially one. As we've noted, the Greek term *aretê* is notoriously tricky to translate. It's usually rendered as 'virtue' but it really refers to excelling in terms of one's natural function or essential character, in a manner that's both healthy and praiseworthy. A strong and fast horse has *aretê*, for example, although we wouldn't call it 'virtuous' in English.

Likewise, the Greek word *kakia*, translated as 'vice', means something more like the 'badness' or 'wretchedness' of a feeble and sickly horse. As humans are naturally rational and social creatures, our two most important virtues are *wisdom* and *justice*, the perfection of reason and of our relationship with others. The remaining cardinal virtues of 'courage' and 'self-discipline' are necessary to overcome the irrational fears and desires ('passions') that would otherwise interfere with living wisely.

Practical wisdom or virtue therefore consists largely in making accurate value judgements. Most importantly, this means judging virtue itself to be 'good', and bodily and external things to be 'indifferent'. Later Stoics also defined prudence as 'reasoning well in the selection and rejection of things in accordance with nature'. This probably alludes to selecting *between* 'indifferent' things on the basis of their natural value, and knowing which ones to 'prefer' over others, a more 'worldly' aspect of wisdom.

By contrast, according to legend, Pyrrho of Elis, the founder of Greek Skepticism, was so 'indifferent' to external things that he had to be steered away from walking off cliffs or into the path of horse-drawn wagons by his followers. This was probably a caricature but it was not a joke made about the Stoics, who were recognized as more pragmatic philosophers, with an interest in the real world and practical affairs. Indeed, the very detachment of the Stoic from 'indifferent' things allows him to make use of them more prudently. According to Seneca, Chrysippus' quipped that the wise man needs nothing and yet he can make good use of anything, whereas the fool 'needs' countless things but can make good use of none of them.

Remember this: External things are not without value

Although the Cynics appear to have believed that external things are completely 'indifferent', the Stoics adopted a position *slightly* closer to the majority of people, and attributed limited 'value' to externals, for the purposes of planning action in the world. External things are completely 'indifferent' or irrelevant with regard to living the good life, or being Happy and fulfilled. However, it's natural for us to seek some in preference to others, as long as we do so with wisdom and virtue. Other people are external to our minds, including our true friends or 'wise and good' people, but wishing for mankind to flourish is the essence of Stoic philanthropy. So virtue consists in wishing others well, with the caveat 'fate permitting', as we shall see in later chapters.

The nature of the good

Musonius says that Nature has set us the goal of flourishing, becoming 'good' men and women, and that 'being good is the same thing as being a philosopher', a lover of wisdom (*Lectures*, 16). Hence, for the Stoics, to be wise and to be good are essentially the same thing. What, then, is the essential nature of the 'good' that the wise man contemplates and that corresponds with his own state of mind? What do we mean when we say something is 'good' or 'bad' or 'indifferent'? We're told Zeno originally gave the following examples, which provide a starting-point for traditional Stoic accounts of Ethics:

► Good things include 'wisdom, temperance, justice, courage, and all that is virtue or participates in virtue'.

► Bad things include 'folly, intemperance, injustice, cowardice, and all that is a vice or participates in vice'.

► Indifferent things include everything else, but most notably: 'life and death, reputation and ill-repute, pleasure and pain, wealth and poverty, health and sickness', etc. (*Anthology*, 2.57-58).

The 'good' and 'bad' are just the traditional cardinal virtues of Socratic philosophy and their opposites, the four cardinal vices. These were all considered to be different forms of practical wisdom (*phronêsis*), the most essentially good thing for man. As we'll see, the word 'indifferent' is slightly misleading as the Stoics, unlike the Cynics, distinguish between some such things as having more 'value' than others, and being 'preferred' in planning the future.

However, this type of value is totally incommensurate with 'the good'. Wisdom and the other virtues are valuable beyond comparison with the bodily and external 'goods' because possession of them perfects human nature and thereby allows us to fulfil the fundamental goal in life, whereas other so-called 'goods' count for *nothing* in this regard. The 'indifferent things' therefore include what the majority of people normally judge as 'good' or 'bad', often summarized as *health, wealth* and *reputation*. The Cynics and Stoics agreed that mankind suffers primarily from a great illusion (*tuphos*, literally a 'mist' or 'smoke'), the assumption that these superficial things are intrinsically good or bad.

These examples were based on several different Stoic definitions of the 'good', in terms of its essential characteristics, which reputedly complement each other and point in the same direction. Perhaps most fundamentally, the Stoics define what is 'good' for us as the fulfilment of our potential, or perfection of our nature. According to Cicero, the Stoic Diogenes of Babylon defined the good as 'what is complete by Nature' and he portrays Cato as saying: 'Those who are wise we all consider to be whole and complete' (*De Finibus*, 4.37).

The early Stoics also defined the good as 'that which is perfectly in accord with Nature for a rational being, *qua* rational' (*Lives*, 7.94). The good for all living things, plants and animals alike, is the perfection of their own nature. As we've seen, the Greek word *aretê*, usually translated as 'virtue', means something more like 'excelling' in terms of one's natural function in life. Humans are inherently both rational and social beings, whose natural goal is therefore to perfect their capacity for wisdom and justice. For Stoics, this is the goal of life handed to us by Nature herself, and the commandment of Zeus, the father of mankind: to bring his unfinished work to perfection.

'Cato' therefore also describes the good for man as 'ripeness' or 'timeliness' (*eukairia*), a surprising but perhaps revealing Stoic technical term. Virtue, like ripeness, does not increase in value over time, because it is found in our nature having achieved its end, and reached perfection. 'That is why, for the Stoics, a happy life is no more desirable or worth seeking if long than if short' (*De Finibus*, 3.46). To have attained *eudaimonia* by excelling in accord with our essential nature, perfecting reason and achieving wisdom, is to flourish and ripen naturally like a fruit.

This is an important Stoic doctrine because it means that prolonging one's life will not necessarily add to virtue, and so death is indifferent with regard to the highest good. In response to those who argue that preserving one's life is good because it allows wisdom to be exercised for a longer period, Cato is portrayed as objecting quite bluntly but somewhat cryptically: 'This argument fails to grasp that while the value of good health is judged by its duration, the value of virtue is judged by its ripeness.' This is another Stoic bombshell; one we'll return to in the chapter on death.

The early Stoics refer to *many* additional qualities possessed by the nature of 'the good', which Diogenes Laertius and Stobaeus both summarized in fairly similar ways. For instance: 'All good things are beneficial and well-used and advantageous and profitable and virtuous and fitting and honourable; there is an affinity to them' (*Anthology*, 2.5d). The Stoics appear to have maintained that these characteristics of the good are preconceptions shared, on reflection, by all mankind, which Nature has created in us free from any contradiction.

> For which of us does not take it that a good thing is advantageous and worthy of being chosen, and something we should seek and pursue in every circumstance? Which of us does not take it that justice is something honourable and fitting? (*Discourses*, 1.22)

We likewise share the basic preconception of 'evil' that it is something 'harmful, to be avoided, something to get rid of in every way' (*Discourses*, 4.1). Epictetus says that conflict arises between us, nevertheless when we try to apply abstract preconceptions to real situations, such as judging whether specific actions are good and just or whether they are not. However, perhaps the two most important qualities of the good are that it is inherently:

- **Beneficial** or helpful (*ôphelimos, from which the name 'Ophelia' derives*), rather than harmful or injurious, 'because [by itself] it is such as to benefit' us in terms of Happiness (*eudaimonia*), being *inherently* good and healthy as a state of mind in its own right – the 'good' is its own reward, the *only* truly beneficial thing for man and its absence, or its opposite, is the only true harm.

- **Honourable** and beautiful (*kalos*), because it is intrinsically praiseworthy, perfectly harmonious and consistent with itself, 'has all the features sought by Nature', and is sufficient in itself to perfect life and bring it to completion.

When the Stoics speak of virtue as honourable, they mean primarily that we naturally and unconditionally praise it in other people and therefore pride ourselves on possessing it also. By saying that it's 'beneficial' they mean that, crucially, virtue is its own reward. It is itself the very perfection of human nature, and the greatest form of wellbeing we can aspire to, although it also tends to bring many other advantages in life, fate permitting.

Being 'honourable' and 'beneficial' are undoubtedly two of the most important characteristics of the good as defined by the Stoics, and they happen to make it clear that Stoic Ethics equates the 'moral' and 'therapeutic' value of practical wisdom and the other virtues. What is 'morally good', or honourable, is identical with what is 'good for us' or healthy. In addition to these qualities above, Epictetus in particular, a former slave himself, refers to wisdom and virtue as 'freedom', in the sense of being a free man but also free from irrational fears and desires, so that badness or vice is described as being a 'slave', in the sense of being enslaved by attachment to external things.

Key idea: The Stoic definition of the chief good

All schools of ancient philosophy agreed that the chief good in life is *eudaimonia*, which I've translated 'Happiness' or 'fulfilment'. This meant living a supremely good life, lacking nothing, and being free from anything bad. However, they disagreed over the precise definition of *eudaimonia* and the best way to attain it. The Stoics were unique in arguing that being a good *person* is completely sufficient to live the good *life*, and attain *eudaimonia*.

Stoics believe that, on reflection, we all share the natural preconception that what is absolutely 'good' in human life must be both 'beneficial' for us or healthy and inherently 'honourable' or praiseworthy. Most ancient philosophers agreed that what is 'good' is 'good for us' or 'beneficial'. This sense of *eudaimonia* as inner 'wellbeing' inevitably meant Stoic Ethics encompassed therapeutic concepts and techniques. Yet the Stoics also defined the good as the 'honourable' or 'beautiful' (*kalos*). Only the good and honourable person is truly beautiful because true beauty resides in our character. The good is also what is genuinely 'praiseworthy', what we admire in ourselves and others.

In addition, the Stoics argue that we all naturally assume our supreme good in life is 'desirable', and are bound to seek it out when we truly grasp its nature. However, the majority of people mistakenly judge external things to be 'good' and therefore experience feelings of desire for things beyond their control, leading to frustration and suffering.

Practical wisdom or virtue, excelling in terms of human nature, is identified as the only truly unconditional 'good' and the key to *eudaimonia* by the Stoics because it meets these criteria of being *intrinsically* beneficial, honourable, beautiful, desirable, praiseworthy, etc. Virtue in this sense is understood to consist of practical skill and moral knowledge, a quality of our conscious mind (*hêgemonikon*), or more specifically of our voluntary thoughts and decisions (*prohairesis*).

Our external actions can also be called 'good' insofar as they embody virtue. Other people, although strictly-speaking only Zeus and the ideal Sage, are also called 'good' insofar as they possess virtue. Only our own virtue is good for us but the wellbeing and virtue of those we love is naturally to be valued. Indeed, the virtue of 'justice' consists in willing others to also flourish and attain good lives, with the caveat: 'fate permitting'. According to the Stoics, 'natural affection' towards others therefore forms an integral part of our own supreme Happiness and fulfilment in life, and our self-interest is synonymous with altruism or a *qualified* interest in the welfare of others, as we'll see.

Remember this: Syllogism showing the good is virtue

Cicero describes a common Stoic syllogism, or 'sorites' argument, derived from Zeno, which heaped one premise upon another to arrive at the conclusion that the good, for man, is essentially synonymous with virtue. It probably functioned as a brief *aide-mémoire*, kept ready-to-hand for challenging situations, which summarized more complex lines of philosophical reasoning:

1 What's good is worth choosing (to have).
2 What's worth choosing is worth seeking (to acquire).
3 What's worth seeking is praiseworthy.
4 What's praiseworthy is honourable and virtuous.
5 Therefore what's good is honour or virtue.

Zeno's argument may contain the seed of what becomes the dominant theme in Epictetus' Stoicism: that only what is 'up to us' is ultimately good, with regard to our Happiness and fulfilment. If what is good is, by definition, what is worth choosing to have and seek out, that might be taken to imply that, rationally speaking, only what is under our control can be considered our 'good' or our duty. As the philosopher Kant would later put it: 'Ought implies can.' This is an important argument both from a philosophical and psychological perspective, as people very often place intrinsic value on things *outside* of their direct control, and doing so undoubtedly contributes to human suffering in many ways.

The virtues and vices

The concepts of 'virtue' (*aretê*) and 'vice' (*kakia*) are absolutely central to the whole edifice of Stoic philosophy. Although *aretê* is usually translated as 'virtue', 'excellence' is perhaps a better translation. It is closer to what we mean by a person's strengths, their positive characteristics, good qualities, what makes them excel, etc. These terms therefore imply both what is honourable versus shameful, and what shows a healthy strength of character versus inner weakness or even sickness.

The Stoics believed that Nature provided humans with an in-built goal, the good life or Happiness, which we attain by progressing towards virtue. Hence, Cleanthes said that all humans incline naturally towards virtue and are like 'half lines of iambic verse', remaining incomplete without it (*Anthology*, 2.5b). Virtue is therefore what 'completes' human nature, and without it something of intrinsic value is always lacking within us, leaving our lives empty and unfulfilled. Virtue can also be understood as harmony or agreement at three levels: with oneself, with reason, with mankind, and with the nature of the universe. By contrast, vice is essentially a state of inconsistency and disharmony, being fundamentally *alienated* from one's true self, from the rest of mankind, and from the universe in which we live.

As human nature is essentially rational, it follows that the highest form of excellence, and the key to living harmoniously, is the perfection of reason or wisdom, and the greatest vice is folly or ignorance. The Sage is therefore essentially the same as the good man, and all bad men are fools.

> [Wisdom] did not itself generate the human race; it took it over, unfinished, from nature. So it ought to watch nature closely and perfect her work as if it were a statue. What is the character of human beings that nature left incomplete? And what is the task and function of wisdom? What is it that it must polish and perfect? If there is nothing to be perfected except a certain operation of the mind, namely reason, then the ultimate good must be to live in accordance with virtue. Virtue, after all, is the perfection of reason. (Cicero, *De Finibus*, 4.34)

The Stoics generally accepted that the different forms of virtue, the ways in which humans excel, can be classified under four broad headings. These are the traditional 'cardinal virtues' of Socratic philosophy, as we've seen, and their opposing vices.

Underneath are the subordinate virtues identified by the early Stoics as these help us to define what they meant.

- **Wisdom** (*sophia*) or **prudence** (*phronêsis*), which opposes the vice of folly or thoughtlessness (*aphrosunê*)

  ▷ Includes excellent deliberation, good calculation, quick-wittedness, good sense, a healthy sense of purpose and resourcefulness

- **Justice, lawfulness, or integrity** (*dikaiosunê*, sometimes 'righteousness'), which opposes wrongdoing or injustice (*adikia*)

  ▷ Includes piety to the gods, good-heartedness or benevolence, public service, and fair dealing

- **Courage or fortitude** (*andreia*, literally 'manliness'), which opposes cowardice (*deilia*)

  ▷ Includes endurance, confidence, great-heartedness, brave-heartedness, and love of work

- **Self-discipline or temperance** (*sôphrosunê*, sometimes 'discretion'), which opposes intemperance or excess (*akolasia*)

  ▷ Includes organization, orderliness, modesty, and self-control

Seneca, for example, describes these as the respective virtues of 'foreseeing what has to be done', 'dispensing what has to be given', 'curbing fears' and 'checking desires' (*Letters*, 120). Epictetus also had a famous slogan, 'endure and renounce' (*anechou kai apechou*, alternatively 'bear and forbear'), which may well correspond with the two closely-related cardinal virtues of courage and self-discipline.

It's possible that some Stoics thought these were the first two aspects of virtue that had to be mastered by novices during their practical training in Ethics, on the way to attaining the loftier virtues of wisdom and justice. However, Zeno accepted the Socratic notion that all virtues are one: 'They say that the virtues follow on each other and that he who has one has them all' (*Lives*, 7.125-126). He reputedly said that the virtues are all forms of knowledge, concerning what is truly good or bad, whereas the vices are forms of moral ignorance. The Stoics therefore also followed Socrates in interpreting vice as essentially a failure to grasp the true nature of the good and to apply the concept appropriately to specific situations.

Try it now: Contemplating the virtues

Strictly speaking, the Stoics believed that only the perfect Sage has attained true virtue. However, we all have reason and therefore the *potential* for wisdom, 'the seed of virtue exists in each one of us' (Musonius, *Lectures*, 2). So we do find Stoics, especially under the Roman Empire, referring to the contemplation of 'virtues' in daily life among those who are making progress towards perfection. Try to consider, therefore, what glimpses of 'virtue' there might be in your own life or the lives of others. Take a few moments to contemplate the questions below:

1 What *potential* virtues or strengths has nature given you and how do they apply to the situations you face, particularly life's challenges?
2 What personal qualities or character strengths do you find most praiseworthy or admirable in other people?
3 How do the virtues compare to each other? Are some more important? Are they all somehow related or not?
4 What do you think would be the most important virtue for the ideal Sage to possess in order to live a complete and fulfilled life?
5 Take a moment to review the previous day, what strengths or glimpses of 'virtue' did you exhibit? What opportunities were there to exhibit others?

Overall, then, which aspects of virtue are you making most progress towards and where might you benefit from developing your character further?

Stoic indifference to 'indifferent' things

If something is neither good nor bad, in the Stoic sense, it is classed as 'indifferent'. By this they mean that fundamentally it can neither help nor harm our flourishing as essentially rational beings, it does not constitute a necessary part of the good life. The Stoics said that something 'indifferent' contributes neither to Happiness (*eudaimonia*) nor unhappiness and whatever can be used well and badly is classed as 'indifferent'. We should learn therefore to be 'indifferent towards indifferent things'

(*Meditations*, 11.16). As mentioned earlier, the classic examples of indifferent things given by Zeno were, among others:

- Life and death
- Good and bad reputation
- Pleasure and pain
- Wealth and poverty
- Health and disease

Health, wealth and reputation, by themselves, cannot help a foolish and unjust man attain the good life. Nor can sickness, poverty or persecution harm the virtuous man's wellbeing. This list includes those things that Stoic developmental theory suggests are naturally valued by human beings from birth. Physical health and survival, in particular, are sought by all animals, above everything else, as ends-in-themselves. However, as Seneca puts it, Stoics come to see that 'Life is neither good nor bad; it is the space for both good and bad', meaning that life can be used wisely or foolishly, virtuously or viciously (*Letters*, 99).

As we've seen, what is good for me is also what I naturally find praiseworthy. However, no matter how many external goods an evil man acquires, this does not render him praiseworthy in our eyes. For example, a notorious tyrant like the Emperor Nero might be the wealthiest and most powerful man in the world but none of that, in itself, helps him come any closer to being a good man and, in fact, his wealth and power simply provide him with more opportunities to engage in vice.

Likewise, a wise and good man like Socrates might be reduced to poverty, imprisoned, and ridiculed, but even if he loses everything the majority refer to as 'good', including his own life, and every so-called 'misfortune' is heaped upon him, that does not make him any less praiseworthy. In fact, *maintaining* his virtues in adversity arguably just makes him more great-souled and admirable. If the externals can neither add nor take away anything from the good or evil of virtue and vice, then they are not intrinsically good things, at least not in the same sense, and they count as nothing with regard to the good life, and our ultimate wellbeing or *eudaimonia*.

To borrow Seneca's analogy, if a horse is weak and ill-tempered then even if it is adorned with the most expensive livery imaginable, we would still not consider it to be a good horse, because these things do not alter its true nature. According to the Stoics, therefore, external 'goods' do not relate to our essential nature as rational and social beings and merely confuse foolish people over the true worth of a man's character.

> So this [virtue] is the only good of a man, and if he has it, even if he is bereft of everything else, he deserves praise; but if he does not have it, despite an abundance of everything else, he is condemned and rejected. (*Letters*, 76)

External 'goods' are not merely of *less* value than virtue but they are totally incommensurate with it: they count for absolutely *nothing* by comparison. The perfectly good and wise man will therefore willingly expose himself to danger, deprivation, or the hostility of others, where necessary, because these things can never *outweigh* virtue. For that reason, the Stoics say the good man will 'at all costs' pursue virtue and avoid vice.

Cicero illustrates this point with the metaphor of a *set of scales*, a kind of 'moral balance', which he attributed to a Peripatetic philosopher Critolaus of Phaselis. Place virtue on one side of the scales. No matter how many external or bodily 'goods' are heaped up on the other side, it will *never* be enough to shift the balance. Epictetus therefore advises his students literally to rehearse saying in response to bodily and external things: 'This is *nothing* to me!' Of course this level of detachment may sound idealistic. It's therefore of great importance to the Stoics to be able to point to countless 'exemplary' individuals who have demonstrated such practical wisdom, virtue, and aloofness from external things. In particular, Diogenes the Cynic provided a common example of a man who prized virtue above any material possession. However, centuries later, among the Romans, Cato was held up as their own Stoic exemplar:

> In his eyes to conquer hunger was a feast, to ward off winter
>
> with a roof was a mighty palace, and to draw across

his limbs the rough toga in the manner of the Roman citizen of old

was a precious robe… (Lucan, *The Civil War*, 2)

The ability to perceive indifferent things *as* indifferent, and being satisfied with what little Nature deems necessary, is itself part of wisdom, the supreme virtue. Hence, Chrysippus reputedly said that to a good man losing his whole estate is merely as though losing one penny, and being sick no more than if he had stumbled (Plutarch, *Stoic Contradictions*).

Key idea: The Stoic concept of the 'indifferent things'

The Aristotelians introduced a hierarchical distinction between three types of things considered intrinsically 'good' in life:

1 Goods of the mind, such as the virtues
2 Goods of the body, primarily physical health
3 External or 'accidental' goods, such as wealth and reputation

Happiness and fulfilment (*eudaimonia*) means living a perfectly good life, complete in itself, and lacking nothing, which the Aristotelians, like many people, decided was a combination of these 'goods'. According to this view, virtue may be important or even essential, but someone cannot be said to have a good life, and to be happy, unless he also has a healthy body and external goods, such as sufficient wealth and good reputation.

Ancient philosophers saw this as close to the attitude adopted by the majority of ordinary people, apart from those who seek pleasure as the most important thing in life. However, whether we have a good and happy life or not is left somewhat in the hands of fate because out of the three categories of 'good', only the first is actually under our direct control. Hence, Aristotle's most influential follower, Theophrastus, apparently wrote: 'Chance, and not wisdom, rules the life of men', which Cicero called 'the most demoralizing utterance that any philosopher has ever made.' By contrast, even Epicurus wrote: 'Over a man who is wise, chance has little power.'

However, following the Cynics, the Stoics adopted the radical stance that falling *outside* of virtue and vice there are only 'indifferent things' (*ta adiaphora*), irrelevant with regard to true fulfilment or *eudaimonia*. For the

Stoic Sage, being a perfectly good person is sufficient to have a perfectly good life. Health, wealth, reputation, etc., literally count for nothing in this regard. Nevertheless, these things do have another sort of value for Stoics. Indeed, some are naturally 'preferred' to others – it's just that this is the wrong type of value by which to assess *eudaimonia*. Health is generally preferable to illness and wealth to poverty, depending on how they're used, but neither is of any value whatsoever when it comes to judging whether someone has lived a good life, according to the Stoics.

Try it now: Stoic meditation on virtue

There's no explicit reference to meditation techniques of this kind in the surviving Stoic literature. However, you may find this a helpful adjunct to traditional Stoic practices. Herbert Benson, a professor of medicine at Harvard Medical School, developed a simplified meditation technique, which has been found effective in a number of research studies as a means of physiological relaxation. This mainly involves repeating a word in your mind each time you exhale. It seems that any word will do, you could just repeat the number 'one'. However, you may wish to repeat a word that relates to your Stoic practice. The Stoics particularly valued contemplation of the nature of the good, so the English word 'good' or perhaps a Greek word like '*aretê*' (virtue) could become your 'centring device', the thing you focus your attention upon, during meditation.

1 Adopt a comfortable position, close your eyes, and take a few minutes to relax, e.g., sit in a chair with both feet flat on the floor and your hands resting on your lap.

2 When you're ready to being, focus your attention on your breathing, breathe naturally, and mentally repeat the word '*good*', or some other word of your choosing, each time you exhale.

3 Repeat this for about 10–20 minutes, or longer if you prefer.

Don't try to block out distractions but simply notice when thoughts or feelings intrude or your mind naturally wanders, and gently return your attention to the exercise as if you're saying 'So what?' Benson's research suggested that this attitude of detached *acceptance* towards distractions was one of the most important factors in meditation. During this exercise, contemplate which aspects of your conscious experience are under your direct control and which are not. Practise accepting, with Stoic 'indifference', any intrusive thoughts or feelings ('impressions') that automatically pop into your mind.

Preferred indifferents and primary value

Although 'indifferent' things are not intrinsically 'good', Zeno suggested that some are nevertheless more 'valuable' than others and 'preferable' to them. The Stoics reputedly quipped that the Sage would prefer to have toiletries to clean himself, when appropriate, than not. Yet such things do not make a virtuous life one *iota* better or more fulfilled. The jargon of Stoicism becomes especially prominent here as ordinary language seems to obscure this distinction. The Stoics say 'indifferent' things have 'selective value' (*axia eklektikê*) if they accord with nature and have 'disvalue' (*apaxia*) if they conflict with nature, although some are neutral even in this regard. Positively-valued things are termed 'preferred' (*proêgmena*) whereas disvalued things are 'dispreferred' (*apoproêgmena*). Basically, the Stoics make a subtle but crucial distinction between two different *types* of value:

1 One sort is the value of truly 'good' things that directly contribute to living the good life: *only* the virtues have this absolute value.

2 However, 'another sort is a certain intermediate potential or usefulness', the value that health, wealth, and reputation have as potentially useful to the wise man, when used wisely (*Lives*, 7.105).

For example, we're told that Zeno classed life and health as examples of 'preferred indifferents'. In other words, health is better than sickness and it's natural to seek it, within reason, but not at the cost of wisdom and virtue. The Stoics reputedly said that although the things naturally valued from birth are 'indifferent' with regard to achieving Happiness (*eudaimonia*), and living consistently in accord with practical wisdom, they are emphatically not 'indifferent' when it comes to our 'appropriate actions' in specific situations, and our survival or natural wellbeing (*Anthology*, 2.7a).

However, pleasure and pain are completely 'indifferent', neither preferred nor rejected, because they are mere side-effects rather than things useful with regard to the art of living wisely. Epictetus warns his students against ever using the words 'good' and 'bad', or even 'helpful' and 'harmful' to refer to 'indifferent' events. However, Chrysippus allegedly conceded that, when speaking loosely, it might be permissible for someone to call 'preferred and dispreferred' things 'good and bad' as long as we remain mindful of the things we're talking about, and do not wander into confusion about their true nature, while accommodating ourselves to the customary language used by the majority of people. The underlying insight, that practical wisdom is incomparably superior in value to external things, is more important than whatever words we happen to use to express ourselves.

The concept of 'preferred indifferents' is also linked to what Zeno called the *kathêkonta*, a Stoic's 'appropriate actions' or 'duties', or what it would be *reasonable* to do in any given situation. It's not enough to say that, in general, we should act virtuously, with wisdom, justice, courage, or self-discipline. How do we orient ourselves and know exactly what to do in a concrete situation? For example, Epictetus appears to enumerate some of the most popular areas of 'appropriate action' discussed by Stoics as follows (*Discourses*, 3.21):

1 To eat and drink appropriately for a human being.

2 To dress appropriately for a human being.

3 To get married and have children.

4 To lead the life of a citizen in a society.

5 To wisely and virtuously endure insults and foolish behaviour from other human beings, though they may be unwise and vicious.

The Stoic teachers considered it their duty to provide guidance on specific cases. In his *Discourses*, therefore, we can see Epictetus providing suggestions to people attending his lectures with regard to concrete problems they're facing. However, giving specific advice requires complex judgements of probability, which introduce uncertainty, whereas the core ethical doctrine that virtue is the only good can be grasped with absolute certainty. The Stoics therefore varied considerably in the details of their practical ethical guidance. For example, Cicero tells us the Stoic scholarchs Antipater and Diogenes disagreed as to whether or not it is morally 'appropriate' for a man who sells his house to volunteer explanations of all its defects to every potential buyer.

As we'll see when we come to discuss the Stoic 'discipline of action' in more detail, the appropriate actions of a Stoic can be understood as those which are undertaken in accord with the natural 'value' something is judged to have for my own wellbeing and that of others, whom I care about. However, any idiot can do the right thing for the wrong reasons. We make progress towards the 'perfect actions' (*katorthômata*) of the Sage only insofar as we begin to select things more consistently in accord with practical wisdom and virtue.

According to Marcus Aurelius, as we'll see, this requires training ourselves to undertake all of our actions, not only in accord with their natural value, but also accepting the outcome with equanimity, whether things go as we'd have 'preferred' or not, as this is the basis of virtue. Indeed, 'selective value' only applies to our *future*, where there is still opportunity to change things. Once events have already overtaken us, this distinction no longer applies. We have no choice but to accept what it's too late to change; there's no point saying you'd 'prefer' not to have become ill because you can't change the past. The Stoics seek to eliminate this sort of meaningless rumination because they class our past as unchangeable and therefore *completely* 'indifferent'. Hence, the Sage generally prefers to experience health rather than illness but once he has become ill he willingly accepts the fact it's happened. As Chrysippus reputedly said, if our feet could attain wisdom they would wish to be thrust into the mud, as this is both their natural function in life and their inevitable fate.

Try it now: Write a philosophical consolation letter

People often console others who have suffered some apparent misfortune by telling them 'It's not the end of the world' – but *why* is it not? What philosophical *arguments* might be rallied to persuade our friends of this? Read some of the ancient consolation letters such as those of Seneca to *Polybius*, *Marcia*, and his mother *Helvia*. Some of his letters to Lucilius are also of this kind (*Letters*, 63; 93; 99). Try to make a brief list of the main arguments he employs to reassure, encourage, and console. What do you make of his reasoning and the persuasive force of his remarks?

If possible, try to write a brief letter of consolation yourself, addressed to an imaginary friend. Make it of a similarly 'philosophical' nature by drawing on the material in this chapter and anything else you've read or learned about Stoicism. It might be useful for you to review this letter once you've finished working through the whole book, to see if you would change anything about it. For now, though, just focus on the Stoic argument that the good life comes from virtue alone, and that one's external fortunes are irrelevant ('indifferent') with regard to living a complete and fulfilled existence. How would you persuade someone of that who has seemingly experienced a great misfortune, such as bereavement, persecution, destitution or betrayal? If you find this difficult, just try to imagine how you would *paraphrase* parts of the consolation letters of Seneca, perhaps adapting them to similar situations in modern life.

Remember this: Stoics disagreed on this subject...

The doctrine of 'preferred indifferent' things is one area where Stoics disagreed among themselves, some arguing that certain things are intrinsically preferred, others claiming the value of external things varies depending on circumstances. Some Stoics, such as Aristo of Chios, apparently leaned more towards Cynicism, which viewed all things as totally 'indifferent'. Others, such as Panaetius and Posidonius, leaned more towards the Aristotelian view that some bodily or external 'goods' are important for *eudaimonia*.

All Stoics firmly rejected Epicureanism, though, viewing bodily pleasure and the avoidance of pain as totally 'indifferent' with regard to the good life. Most traditional Stoics agreed that virtue was the only true good and sufficient by itself for the good life, regardless of our health, wealth, or reputation. They would normally accept that it is both natural and rational to 'prefer' whatever serves our own physical welfare and that of our friends and loved ones, as long as seeking this is in accord with wisdom and virtue. Philosophers who departed too much from the conventional Stoic view seem to have broken away, occasionally, sometimes becoming followers of another school.

Focus Points

The main points to remember from this chapter are:

* The goal of philosophy is Happiness (*eudaimonia*) but this is achieved primarily through practical wisdom, or virtue, which brings about harmony within oneself, with others, and with Nature as a whole.

* Philosophy is essentially the 'love of wisdom', or knowledge of what is good, bad, and 'indifferent' with regard to living a Happy life.

* The chief good for man is this practical wisdom, or virtue, which is good in the sense of being both 'honourable' and 'beneficial'.

* Some indifferent things are 'preferable' to others but none of them count for anything in terms of attaining Happiness or the good life, according to the Stoics.

Next Step

Having examined the nature of the 'good' and 'indifferent' things, we should explore more closely what was meant by *eudaimonia* or 'Happiness' and the next step is traditionally to explore the Stoic theory of the 'passions', because Happiness was thought to be impossible while experiencing emotional distress. This leads us into the domain of Stoic psychotherapy, or the 'therapy of the passions', which was an integral part of ancient Ethics, and the overall 'promise of philosophy', the motivation Stoic students had for persevering in their long and challenging pursuit of wisdom.

3

The promise of philosophy ('therapy of the passions')

In this chapter you will learn:

▶ *About the ancient Stoic concept of perfect 'Happiness' or* eudaimonia, *the promise of philosophy*

▶ *That Stoics sought to replace unhealthy 'passions', or pathological fears and cravings, with opposing 'healthy passions', such as rational joy and benevolent, affectionate feelings towards others*

▶ *How unhealthy 'passions' are ultimately based on voluntary judgements and actions, which follow the initial automatic reactions Stoics call 'proto-passions'*

'It looks as if the most unquestionable good was happiness, Socrates.'

'Provided that it isn't composed of questionable goods, Euthydemus.'

'Why, what constituent of happiness could be questionable?'

'None; unless we include in it beauty or strength or wealth or fame or something else of that kind.' (Xenophon, *Memorabilia*, 4.2)

'What is it, Passion, that you want? Tell me this.'

'What I want, Reason? To do everything I want.'

'A royal wish; but tell me it again.'

'Whatever I desire I want to happen.' (Cleanthes, quoted in Galen, *On Hippocrates' and Plato's Doctrines*, 5.6)

Self-assessment: Stoic attitudes to Happiness (*eudaimonia*)

Before reading this chapter, rate how strongly you agree with the following statements, using the five-point (1-5) scale below, and then re-rate your attitudes once you've read and digested the contents.

1. Strongly disagree, 2. Disagree, 3. Neither agree nor disagree, 4. Agree, 5. Strongly agree

1   'Happiness, or the best life, consists in living in accord with virtue.'

2   'Emotional disturbance comes from placing too much value on things outside our direct control.'

3   'Although our initial emotional reactions may be automatic, we can choose whether to continue going along with them or not.'

What is the ancient 'promise of philosophy'?

What does Stoic philosophy demand from us? What promise does it hold out in return? What are the causes of the irrational desires and emotional disturbances for which people seek a remedy in philosophy? What about positive feelings like joy, tranquillity and love?

Before getting further into theory and practice, it's traditional to explore what motivates people to become students of Stoic philosophy in the first place. Stoicism is a hard road to follow but we're told its benefits should, in a manner of speaking, be common sense – with a bit of help, we should be able at least to *glimpse* them from the outset. Although only the perfect Sage enjoys *eudaimonia*, Seneca claims that unless we embrace philosophy, the *love* of wisdom, life is not even bearable, because emotional disturbances are allowed free rein. Indeed, the initial motive for most people to study Stoic philosophy was simply the alleviation of their own suffering, although the ultimate goal is to excel as a human being.

So the promise of philosophy consists of both the supreme Happiness and fulfilment (*eudaimonia*) of the Sage and the aspiring Stoic's gradual progress towards overcoming disturbing desires and emotions (*apatheia*), sometimes called the Stoic 'therapy of the passions'. As far as the ancient Stoics were concerned: 'The philosopher's school is a doctor's clinic' (*Discourses*, 3.23).

Curiously, the Stoics appear to attribute the exhortation to philosophy to Zeus himself, who promises us relief from suffering. Musonius Rufus taught that Zeus 'orders and encourages' us to study philosophy. According to him, in a nutshell, the law of Zeus orders humans to be good, which means being philosophers, loving wisdom, being virtuous and magnanimous, rising above pain and pleasure, and being free from animosity towards others.

Epictetus follows his teacher, and frequently places similar words in the mouth of Zeus, starting with the first of his compiled lectures. He actually breaks away from his conversation with students to describe an imaginary dialogue between himself and Zeus, who is portrayed as saying he has given us a small portion of himself, our 'ruling faculty', which gives us the power to make choices and decisions in life. It is our duty to take care of this divine faculty above all else, as it is our only true possession, and we are granted complete freedom in employing it. If we can learn to prize wisdom above all other things, 'Zeus' assures us we will never be obstructed, never become upset or complain, and never become angry with or subservient to any other person.

The point Epictetus was making is that the basic principles of Stoicism are learnable from reflection on human nature. They're fundamentally common sense, as Zeus has planted the seed of virtue deep within all of us and so the goal of life is in our very nature. Elsewhere, he asks his students whether Zeus or Nature has not already given them their orders, clearly enough, from the day they were born. Nature has given us what is ours, our judgement and volition, to use freely, in accord with virtue. She has placed everything else beyond our direct control, subject to obstacles and interference. 'Guard by every means that which is your own, but do not grasp at that which is another's.'

Although the words vary, most of the time Epictetus portrays Zeus as thundering the same basic Stoic message: 'If you wish any good thing, get it from yourself' (*Discourses*, 1.29). Nature itself teaches us that if we want true Happiness, and the good life, we must seek it within ourselves rather than in external things. If we can only do this consistently, Epictetus says, we will achieve perfect freedom, and liberate ourselves from emotional suffering.

Happiness or fulfilment, *eudaimonia*, was known in ancient times as 'the promise of philosophy'. As we've seen, all schools of philosophy basically agreed that this was what they were aiming for, but they disagreed about precisely what it meant. In fact, their different definitions of *eudaimonia* distinguished one school from another. Zeno described it very concisely as a 'smoothly flowing' or serene life, a life of freedom from being thwarted or obstructed in what we seek to achieve. He made it clear that this is achieved by living in harmonious agreement with Nature, and in accord with virtue. However, 'life is warfare', and the Stoic achieves serenity by arming himself to face whatever may be inflicted on him by the vicissitudes of events, the turning 'Wheel of Fortune'. The promise of philosophy was therefore the promise of both Happiness and the emotional resilience to retain it in the face of setbacks.

For what does the promise amount to? This: that, heaven willing, philosophy will ensure that the man who has obeyed its laws shall never fail to be armed against all the hazards of fortune: that he shall possess and control, within his own self, every possible guarantee for a satisfactory and Happy life. In other words, that he shall always be a Happy man. (Cicero, *Tusculan Disputations*, 5.7)

Elsewhere Cicero portrays Happiness in terms of the 'inner citadel' of Stoicism: 'We want the Happy man to be safe, impregnable, fenced and fortified, so that he is not just largely unafraid, but completely' (*Tusculan Disputations*, 5.41). One of the most important philosophical arguments of the Stoics was that it is impossible to imagine someone who is on the one hand a wise and good man, having attained perfect *eudaimonia*, and, on the other hand, still plagued by emotional disturbance or pathological desires. The Stoics famously refer to these as the 'passions' (*pathê*); they believed them to be the root cause of all human suffering, and essentially toxic to *eudaimonia*.

The ability to overcome unhealthy fears and desires is termed *apatheia*, being 'passionless' or rather without passions of the problematic sort. It's where our word 'apathy' comes from, but that's not what it means. As Keith Seddon, a modern Stoic author, puts it, 'The Stoic will be *apathês*, without passion (not apathetic, but dispassionate), but not wholly without feeling' (Seddon, 2006, p. 140). The Stoics also refer to the Sage as having attained 'tranquillity' (*ataraxia*) and 'freedom' (*eleutheria*) from 'enslavement' by the passions.

However, these endeavours to overcome the 'passions' have caused much confusion and led to the widespread misconception that the Stoics are somehow 'unemotional' or seek to repress their feelings. This is largely based on a *misunderstanding* caused by problems of modern translation and interpretation – it's simply *not* what they meant. This misinterpretation was *repeatedly* addressed by the ancient Stoics themselves, though. So let's pause to reflect on what they actually said...

> They [the founders of Stoicism] say the wise man is also
> passionless [*apathê*, whence our word 'apathy'], because
> he is not vulnerable to them. But the bad man is called
> 'passionless' in a different sense, which means the same as
> 'hard-hearted' and 'insensitive'. (*Lives*, 7.117)

Zeno meant that the wise man was not enslaved by his feelings
of fear or desire, but we're explicitly told here that's not the
same as being 'hard-hearted' and 'insensitive', which is the false
impression many people have today of Stoicism. The Roman
Stoic Laelius was portrayed, centuries later in a dialogue by
Cicero, as saying that it would actually be the greatest possible
mistake to try to eliminate natural and healthy feelings such as
those of friendship, because even animals experience affection
for their offspring, which Stoics viewed as the foundation of
human love and friendship (*Laelius*, On Friendship, 13).

We would not only be *dehumanizing* ourselves by eliminating
such natural feelings, he says, but reducing ourselves below
animal nature to something more like a mere tree trunk or
a stone. We should therefore turn a deaf ear to anyone who
foolishly suggests that the good life entails having 'the hardness
of iron' in terms of our emotions. Epictetus subsequently taught
his students that we ought not to be free from passions (*apathê*)
in the sense of being unfeeling 'like a statue', because Stoics
do care about their family and fellow citizens, for whom they
continue to have 'natural affection' and a sense of kinship or
'affinity'. Finally, Seneca, likewise, says:

> There are misfortunes which strike the sage – without
> incapacitating him, of course – such as physical pain,
> infirmity, the loss of friends or children, or the catastrophes
> of his country when it is devastated by war. I grant that he
> is sensitive to these things, for we do not impute to him the
> hardness of a rock or of iron. There is no virtue in putting
> up with that which one does not feel. (*On the Constancy of
> the Sage*, 10.4)

There's a strange problem, as Seneca points out here, with the
notion that the Stoic Sage is completely devoid of emotion.
It recalls a story about Diogenes the Cynic, who was asked

by a Spartan if he was feeling cold, when training himself by stripping naked and embracing a bronze statue in winter. Diogenes said he was not, and the Spartan replied: 'What's so *impressive* about what you're doing then?'.

As Seneca implies, the Stoic virtues of 'courage' and 'self-discipline' appear to presuppose that the Sage actually *experiences* something akin to fear and desire – otherwise he has no feelings to overcome. A brave man isn't someone who doesn't experience any trace of fear whatsoever but someone who acts courageously *despite* feeling anxiety. A man who has great self-discipline or restraint isn't someone who feels no inkling of desire but someone who overcomes his cravings, by abstaining from acting upon them.

The Sage conquers his passions by becoming stronger than them not by eliminating all traces of emotion from his life. The Stoic ideal is therefore not to be 'passionless' in the sense of being 'apathetic', 'hard-hearted', 'insensitive' or 'like a statue' of stone or iron. Rather, it is to experience natural affection for ourselves, our loved ones, and other human beings, and to value our lives in accord with nature, which arguably opens us up to experiencing certain natural emotional reactions to loss or frustration.

The Stoics call these 'proto passions' and as we'll see later, the Sage does feel these emerging emotions but does not go along with them, or dwell on them, as people ordinarily do. Hence, Seneca elsewhere explains that whereas the Epicureans mean 'a mind immune to feeling' when they speak of *apatheia*, this 'unfeelingness' is actually the opposite of what the Stoics mean. 'This is the difference between us Stoics and the Epicureans; our wise man overcomes every discomfort but feels it, theirs does not even feel it' (*Letters*, 9). The virtue of the Sage consists in his ability to endure painful feelings and rise above them, while continuing to maintain his relationships and interaction with the world, to *care* sufficiently about ourselves and others but not enough to anxiously *worry*.

In fact, the earliest Stoic writings defined the 'passions' they sought to overcome as consisting of irrational, excessive and unhealthy forms of fear and desire. They are said to be 'unnatural' in the sense of *harming* our natural pursuit of fulfilment in life. It's somewhat less well-known that these were contrasted with a range of 'healthy passions' (*eupatheiai*), which although not pursued directly by the Stoics were thought to 'supervene' as a kind of additional reward following virtuous living.

As several of the leading academic scholars of Stoicism have emphasized: 'The inclusion of 'good feelings' in the Stoics' mental repertoire shows that their philosophy did not countenance extirpation of all emotions' (Long, 2002, p. 245). Indeed, healthy feelings such as love and 'natural affection' towards others play an important but often overlooked role in Stoicism. When Marcus Aurelius described the Stoic ideal as being 'free from passions and yet full of love', he clearly meant that the 'passions' in question are bad or unhealthy feelings, to be distinguished from what Stoics call 'natural affection' or rational love for others.

The problem of the passions inevitably meant that a kind of ancient psychological therapy was integral to Stoicism as a way of life. Indeed, the topic of *eudaimonia* naturally links Stoic Ethics to psychological therapy. Most ancient philosophies equated the 'good' in life with what is 'good for us', 'beneficial' or 'helpful' (*ôphelimos*), in the sense of contributing to our fundamental health and wellbeing, not physically but mentally and morally, in terms of our character. You could therefore say that 'self-help' was an integral aspect of Stoic Ethics, and this not only resembles *modern* therapy but was quite explicitly presented as a form of medicine or therapy for the mind by ancient authors.

The Stoics therefore, more than any other school, focused on philosophy as a way of life, and specific ways of training themselves to overcome their unhealthy passions and progress towards the lofty ideal of virtue. Some people have argued that Stoicism is purely a philosophy, with an ethical emphasis, and should not be confused with a psychological therapy. However, these two things were seen as equivalent by Zeno and his followers. Stoicism therefore neatly combines ethics, self-improvement and *psychological therapy*.

Case study: 'The Choice of Hercules'

Zeno, the founder of Stoicism, was reputedly inspired to study philosophy after reading the second book of Xenophon's *Memorablia* of Socrates. This begins with a chapter in which Socrates recounts Prodicus' famous allegory known as 'The Choice of Hercules'. Like their forerunners the Cynics, the Stoics viewed Hercules, the greatest of Zeus' sons, as an exemplary role model, demonstrating the self-discipline and endurance required to be a true philosopher. Zeno himself was perhaps compared to Hercules and we know that his successor Cleanthes was dubbed 'a second Hercules', on account of his self-mastery. The story symbolizes the great challenge of deciding who we actually want to be in life, what type of life we want to live, the promise of philosophy, and the temptation of vice.

We're told Hercules, when a young man, found himself at an isolated fork in the road, where he sat to contemplate his future. Uncertain which path to take in life he found himself confronted by two goddesses. One, a very beautiful and alluring woman, was called *Kakia*, although she claimed that her friends called her 'Happiness' (*Eudaimonia*). She charged in front to ensure she spoke first, promising Hercules that her path was 'easiest and pleasantest', and that it provided a short-cut to Happiness. She claimed he would avoid hardship and enjoy luxury beyond most men's wildest dreams, living like a king by the labour of others.

Hercules was then approached by the second goddess, called *Aretê*, a plain-dressed and humble woman, though naturally beautiful. To his surprise, she told him that her path would require hard work from him and it would be 'long and difficult'. Hercules would face danger, he would be tested by many hardships, perhaps more than any man who had lived before, and have to endure great loss and suffering along the way. 'Nothing that is really good and admirable', said *Aretê*, 'is granted by the gods to men without some effort and application.'

However, Hercules would have the opportunity to face each adversity with courage and self-discipline, and to show wisdom and justice despite great danger. He would earn true Happiness by fulfilling his natural potential as a hero and reflecting on the knowledge of his own praiseworthy and honourable deeds.

Hercules, of course, chose the path of *Aretê* or 'Virtue' and was not seduced by *Kakia* or 'Vice'. He faced continual persecution, from the goddess Hera, and was forced to undertake the legendary Twelve Labours, including slaying the Hydra and ultimately entering Hades, the Underworld itself, to capture the monster Cerberus with his bare hands. He died in extreme agony, poisoned by clothing soaked in the Hydra's blood.

However, Zeus was so impressed by his greatness of soul that he elevated him to the status of a God in his own right. Whether or not reading this particular story inspired Zeno's conversion to the life of a philosopher, it certainly influenced later generations of Stoics. They treated it as a *metaphor* for the good life: that it's better to face hardships, rise above them, and thereby excel, than to embrace easy living and idleness, and allow your soul to shrink and deteriorate as a result.

Try it now: Praiseworthy versus desired

This is a simple 'values clarification' exercise to help you begin reflecting on your own philosophy of life. Assume there's no inherently right or wrong answer; these questions are just meant to help you look at things from a different perspective.

1 Take a piece of paper and draw a table with two columns.
2 At the top of the first column write the word 'praiseworthy'. Underneath make a list of things you find most praiseworthy in other people, what you *genuinely* admire about them. Consider your heroes, real or fictional, living or dead, your family, friends, colleagues, etc.
3 Once you've finished, write the word 'desired' at the top of the second column. Underneath list all the things you most desire in life. Consider the things you take most pleasure in, and those you most fear losing, as well as the things you spend most time and energy pursuing.
4 Finally, ask yourself to what extent these two columns differ from each other. Are the things you most desire and seek out in life the same as the things you find most praiseworthy in others? Why are they not the same?

How might it affect your perception of yourself if you desire, and achieve, things that you do not find praiseworthy in general? If you find that the things you currently desire in life are not those you genuinely admire in others, you might want to consider what would happen if you were to desire for yourself those things you find most truly praiseworthy.

The Stoic concept of Happiness (*Eudaimonia*)

Eudaimonia is therefore the ancient promise of philosophy. The word *eudaimonia* is usually translated as 'Happiness', although that doesn't capture the philosophical meaning very well. It refers more to the overall quality of someone's life rather than their mood. Alternative modern translations therefore include 'good fortune', 'prosperity', 'blessedness', 'wellbeing' or 'flourishing', etc. An ancient dictionary of philosophical terms attributed to Plato but probably written by his immediate followers defined it as follows:

- The good composed of all goods;
- An ability which suffices for living well;
- Perfection in respect of virtue;
- Sufficient beneficial things for a living creature. (*Definitions, Eudaimonia*)

However, it basically refers to the blessed or exalted condition of someone who is living a good life. Whereas for other philosophical schools that might imply someone enjoying external good fortune, for the Stoics being a good person and having a good life are synonymous. Bodily and external things are therefore completely irrelevant ('indifferent') with regard to *eudaimonia*. Happiness and unhappiness consist in how we respond to events, and the use we make of them.

Taken literally, the word *eudaimonia* actually means 'having a good *daimon*', the divine spark or spirit within – we still speak today of 'being in good spirits'. In theological terms, Chrysippus therefore interpreted *eudaimonia* as the smoothly flowing life that comes from bringing our *daimon*, our innermost spirit, into complete harmony with the Will of Zeus, by bringing our judgements completely into agreement with our fate. Centuries later, Marcus Aurelius interpreted the word in a similar manner, referring to the perfection of the divine spark within or ruling faculty, in accord with nature.

Philosophical *eudaimonia* is a condition in which a person of excellent character is living optimally well, flourishing, doing admirably, and steadily enjoying the best mindset that is available to human beings. The Stoics in particular took the complete attainment of such a condition to be well-nigh impossible, yet so worth striving for that no human being who grasped its attractions would wish to settle for less. (Long, 2002, p. 193)

In fact, they said the perfect Sage, who had attained *eudaimonia*, must be as rare as the Ethiopian phoenix – which is undoubtedly very rare indeed! On the other hand, as Pierre Hadot said, the ancient Stoics would gladly have called the world 'a machine for making sages' (Hadot, 1998, p. 161). The Stoics believed that Nature *wants* us to flourish and to perfect ourselves, we have been handed life in order to bring ourselves to a state of completion, by excelling in accord with virtue. Nature planted within each of us the capacity to dream, as it were, and envisage an ideal human being, called the 'Sage' or 'wise man' by Stoics, and thereby to navigate towards that distant goal.

So what difference is there, if any, between *eudaimonia* and virtue in Stoic philosophy? Well, the Stoics certainly make virtue both necessary and sufficient for *eudaimonia*. However, Chrysippus reputedly said that even if someone acts with wisdom and virtue his life is not yet Happy but Happiness 'supervenes' on him when these actions become secure and fixed, through firmly-grasped knowledge (*Anthology*, 5.907).

As we shall see, the Stoics also refer to certain 'healthy passions', which automatically 'supervene' upon virtue. Zeno reputedly said that good things include the various virtues but also, in some accounts 'healthy passions' (*eupatheiai*) such as 'joy and good spirits and confidence and well-wishing'. Centuries later, Musonius Rufus taught that when we act virtuously and according to our own nature: 'A cheerful disposition and secure joy automatically accompany these attributes' (*Lectures*, 17). It comes as a surprise to some people to learn that Stoicism was intended as a fundamentally joyful or cheerful philosophy of life!

Key idea: Stoicism as the art of Happiness or *Eudaimonia*

This book is about Stoicism as the philosophical 'art of living', or art of attaining Happiness. 'Happiness' isn't a word people tend to associate with Stoicism, so it may come as a surprise that it was the promise of philosophy, the overarching goal of their entire philosophical system. As we've seen, *eudaimonia* is particularly difficult to translate, although most ancient philosophers agreed on it being the goal of life. *Eudaimonia* is the supreme Happiness or fulfilment attainable by human beings, a lofty or even godlike state. We're using a capital letter because 'happiness' isn't a perfect synonym and this word is notoriously tricky to translate. We'll sometimes leave it untranslated, therefore, a bit like the Sanskrit word *nirvana* in books on Buddhism. '*Nirvana*' is actually a good analogy because '*eudaimonia*' carries the same sense of a uniquely exalted human condition, it's the supreme achievement in life and the goal of all philosophy.

It's more than just a feeling, though, and Stoicism could hardly be called a 'feel-good' philosophy. It was traditionally defined as the sum of all good things, the things required for the 'good life' or 'living well'. However, the Stoics insisted that once we go through a kind of philosophical 'conversion' (*epistrophê*) we will see through the smokescreen (*tuphos*) of conventional values and learn to equate *eudaimonia* completely with the life according to virtue, rising above both external fortune and misfortune alike. We've seen that Zeno also referred to this as the 'smoothly flowing' life, the life of perfect serenity and freedom attained by the ideal Sage. For the Stoics, being a wise and good person is both necessary and sufficient to enjoy a supremely good life, or *eudaimonia*, whatever fortune befalls us. We might say *true Happiness comes from within* or as Epictetus put it: 'If you want anything good, get it from yourself.'

Try it now: Two-column control appraisal

Let's try a simple experiment, which we might call 'control appraisal'. Remember that the Stoics were specifically concerned with the aspects of life that are under our *direct* control, those *always* under our control, where our decisions can never be thwarted.

1 Pick a specific situation or problem that's bothering you.
2 Draw two columns headed 'control' and 'not control'.

3 Now try to list all the aspects of the situation that are under your
   direct control in the column headed 'control'.
4 List all the aspects that are outside of your direct control in the other
   column ('not control').
5 Think about this carefully. Go back and review it if necessary. The
   Stoics would say that only things truly under our direct control ('up to
   us') are our voluntary thoughts and intentions to act. Everything else
   can potentially turn out against our wishes.

Imagine that you're metaphorically drawing a circle around your sphere of
control, defining the boundaries of your will – this is where your freedom
and power exist in any situation. How much time do you spend worrying
about the aspects that are not under your direct control and how much
focusing on the aspects that are completely up to you? What would
happen if you focused more on the aspects under your direct control,
doing what you can to the best of your ability? What if you accepted that
those outside your direct control may or may not turn out as you hope?
Try to apply this exercise repeatedly to different situations. What general
lessons can you draw from the experience?

The Stoic theory of the 'passions'

The Stoics had quite a specific psychological theory so this is an
area where Greek jargon is unavoidable. In particular, the word
'passion' is used in a special sense. Cicero's 'Cato', struggling
to translate Greek Stoicism into Latin, says that the 'passions'
make the lives of most people a misery and that he was tempted
simply to translate this term as 'illness' but thinks 'emotional
disturbance' or perturbation makes more sense as a general
term (*De Finibus*, 3.35). In fact, our modern word 'pathology',
the study of suffering, comes from the same Greek root as
'passion', a word which still denotes suffering in phrases such as
'The Passion of Christ'.

When Stoics talk about the ordinary 'passions' experienced
by the majority of people, they mean that these are typically
disturbing desires and emotions of an irrational, unhealthy, and
excessive sort. They're contrasted with the 'healthy passions'
experienced by the Sage. However, especially among the Roman
Stoics, it appears to have been accepted that those making

progress, aspiring Stoics, may experience glimpses of these healthy desires and emotions, though lacking perfect wisdom.

Nevertheless, the majority of ordinary people are dubbed 'sick' or 'insane' by the Stoics because our lives are blighted by toxic fears and desires. Just as there are ailments in the body, physical illnesses, so too there are ailments of the mind, which Stoics claim are based on faulty value judgements. For example, the Stoics hold that mistakenly judging superficial things to be intrinsically 'good', 'helpful' or desirable is the basis of excessive craving for pleasure, wealth, reputation, etc.

We may also suffer from irrational judgements about what is 'bad', 'harmful' or aversive, such as fear or hatred for things that are actually 'indifferent' with regard to our ultimate wellbeing, including pain, hardship, poverty, or ridicule, etc. In other words, the majority of ordinary people lack fulfilment and peace of mind because their values are confused and internally conflicted. We waste our lives chasing after an illusion of Happiness, based on a mixture of hedonism, materialism and egotism – crazy, self-defeating values absorbed from the foolish world around us.

These 'passions' are therefore intimately connected, possibly even identical, with our judgements and behavioural inclinations. For example, we're told that the passion of avarice, an excessive feeling of craving towards wealth, is the judgement that money is intrinsically 'good', combined with the intention to obtain it. The early Stoics described three closely related aspects of these disturbing 'passions':

1 Irrational judgements about what's good or bad.

2 Unnatural (or unhealthy) mental activity.

3 Excessive impulses to action, or intentions to obtain what's 'good' and avoid what's 'bad'.

People try to excuse all sorts of morbid or blameworthy behaviour by saying 'it's natural' to feel and act that way. By contrast, the Stoics describe the 'passions' as fundamentally 'against' our essential nature as rational beings and therefore in conflict with the supreme Stoic goal of living in 'accord' with nature.

In his book *On Passions*, Zeno apparently classified them into four categories: *pain, fear, craving* and *pleasure*. Stoic passages compiled by the ancient commentators, Diogenes Laertius and Stobaeus, add further subdivisions, which are included below to help clarify what's meant.

1 'Pain' (*lupê*), sometimes translated as 'suffering', or 'grief': An 'irrational contraction' of the soul, over the failure to avoid something judged 'bad' or to obtain something judged 'good'.

   Irrational 'pain' takes the form of unhealthy feelings of pity, envy, resentment, sorrow, anguish, etc.

2 'Fear' (*phobos*): The (irrational) 'expectation of something bad' or harmful. Irrational 'fear' takes the form of feeling dread, nervousness, worry, shame, shock, panic, etc.

3 'Craving' (*epithumia*), meaning 'hunger' or 'lust': An 'irrational striving' for something falsely judged to be good or beneficial. Irrational 'craving' takes the form of futile yearning, hatred, anger, sexual lust; as well as love of pleasure, love of wealth, love of reputation, etc.

4 'Pleasure' (*hêdonê*), as in 'hedonism': An 'irrational elation over what seems to be worth choosing', i.e., what is falsely judged to be good or beneficial. Irrational (unhealthy) 'pleasure' takes the form of self-indulgence, decadence, being verbally-enchanted (or seduced by flattery), sadistic joy in someone else's misfortune, etc.

'Fear' and 'craving' are apparently more *fundamental* because 'pain' results when we fail to obtain (or lose) what we crave and when we fail to avoid what we fear; whereas 'pleasure' results when we do obtain what we crave or avoid what we fear (the pleasure of 'relief').

When the Stoics talk about the passion called 'pain' they clearly have in mind *emotional* pain, 'suffering' or 'grief', rather than the physical sensation of pain. Cicero explains that for Stoics the Greek term *hêdonê* ('pleasure') can refer either to pleasurable feelings in the mind or pleasant sensations in the body. The irrational passion of 'pleasure' is really the 'sensuous delight of the exultant mind', as he puts it, which is 'bad' or 'harmful' because it's based on an over-valuation of bodily or external things.

By contrast, mere bodily sensations of pleasure and pain are classed as ultimately harmless and 'indifferent' by the Stoics. Notice also that the examples of 'pleasure' the Stoics list are obviously *unhealthy* feelings rather than what we might call a healthy 'pleasure'. These include the egotistical pleasure that comes from being seduced by flatterers, sadistic or malicious pleasure in the misfortune of others, or self-indulgent pleasures, which corrupt and weaken our minds. Seneca refers to these as 'empty' pleasures and we might even call them 'toxic' or 'pathological'.

Finally, note that the irrational desires, or cravings, include feelings of sexual lust but also *angry* or *hateful* feelings, which the Stoics interpret as desire for another to suffer harm. In fact, anger often seems to be the passion that the Stoics were most concerned about. We actually have a whole book by Seneca, entitled *On Anger*, about the Stoic approach to prevention and therapy of this specific passion.

Key idea: 'Good' and 'bad' passions

The Stoics sought to overcome 'passions' (*patheiai*), desires and emotions, they considered irrational, excessive and 'unnatural' (or unhealthy). These passions fundamentally go *against* our essential nature as rational beings because they're based on ignorance about the true nature of the good. Cicero's 'Cato' translates the Stoic term 'passion' as 'emotional disturbance' or 'illness' – so we're basically talking about 'pathological' fears and cravings. Zeno placed them in four categories often translated as 'fear', 'desire', 'pain' and 'pleasure'. The majority of people are enslaved by these 'passions' insofar as they fear or desire external things, beyond their direct control.

However, Stoics seek to replace them with 'good' or 'healthy' passions (*eupatheiai*). These are mindful 'caution' rather than irrational fear, enlightened 'joy' rather than unhealthy and indulgent pleasures, and 'willing' what is truly good rather than craving things that are ultimately 'indifferent'. According to the Stoics, there's no rational alternative to the fourth 'passion', voluntary emotional suffering. Although the majority of people either crave or fear countless things in life, the Sage only desires *one* thing. He feels rational desire in the form of a 'wish' for virtue, all virtues being essentially forms of practical wisdom. He likewise experiences rational aversion in the form of 'caution' or mindfulness not to slip into folly and vice.

 Try it now: Percentage control appraisal

This is a quicker version of the 'control appraisal' exercise above, which you may find it easier to do in response to situations in your daily life.

1 Again, pick a specific situation or problem that's bothering you.
2 Rate how much control you have over the whole situation, from 0–100 per cent.
3 If you didn't rate it 100 per cent, then why not? What aspects are not under your control?
4 If you didn't rate it 0 per cent, then why not? What aspects are under your control?
5 What would happen if you focused more on doing your best with the aspects under your control while accepting that the other aspects may not go as you wish?

What else can you learn from this exercise? Try to apply it to a variety of situations in daily life and thereby train yourself to be more aware of the boundaries of your freedom and volition. In every situation, the answer may be fairly similar because arguably only your own voluntary thoughts and actions are yours to control without any possibly hindrance.

Automatic emotional reactions

The Stoics acknowledged that passions begin with an initial 'involuntary movement' of the soul, an emotional 'reflex' reaction we cannot really control. Seneca actually explains that nothing which rouses the mind spontaneously, without its voluntary assent, can be called a 'passion' in the Stoic sense. Flushing, tears, changes in breathing, etc., are merely reflex-like emotional reactions to some impression rather than full-blown passions, and so Stoics called them '*proto passions*'. Once they've happened, the Stoic has no choice but to accept them as outside of her direct control, but she can choose not to perpetuate them further. In his consolation to Polybius, who was grieving the loss of his brother, for example, Seneca wrote:

> Nature requires from us some sorrow, while more than this is the result of vanity. But never will I demand of you that you should not grieve at all. (*Polybius*, 18.4-5)

Reason guides us towards a balanced response, which is the mark of natural affection rather than an unbalanced mind, allowing our *automatic* emotional reactions to run their course, without choosing to morbidly ruminate over events. He adds: 'let your tears flow, but let them also cease, let deepest sighs be drawn from your breast, but let them also find an end' (*Polybius*, 18.6).

Another good example of an automatic emotional reaction is blushing. Seneca says a young philosopher, prone to it, will probably continue to blush even if he attains perfect wisdom and becomes an enlightened Sage. 'For no amount of wisdom enables one to do away with physical or mental weaknesses that arise from natural causes; anything inborn or ingrained in one can by dint of practice be allayed, but not overcome' (*Letters*, 11). Philosophy does not have absolute dominion over our physical nature and even a Sage may initially blush or stammer under certain circumstances, although he will regain his composure later. Wisdom offers no remedy for this because it is not a voluntary action to begin with.

One of the clearest discussions of the role of proto-passions is found in Seneca's *On Anger*, where he appears to describe the stages of passion as follows:

1 The proto-passion, or 'first movement' of the mind, arises involuntarily as a 'preparation for emotion', an automatic reaction triggered by external impressions or bodily sensations, such as shock in response to a sudden, startling noise; we can no more avoid this than we can avoid reflexes such as blinking when a finger is poked towards our eye, although Seneca thinks that constant training might perhaps weaken some of these reactions eventually.

2 In the 'second movement', we give 'assent' to the initial disturbing impression fusing it with the value judgement that it concerns something absolutely 'good' or 'bad', 'helpful' or 'harmful', from which further judgements follow about what it is appropriate to do ('it is appropriate for me to be avenged since I am injured') – ordinarily this voluntary 'assent' happens so habitually that we barely notice it occurring, but it can be counteracted by suspending judgement or focusing on an opposing judgement, such as the idea of what a Sage would do in the same situation.

3 In the 'third movement', we lose control, 'passion' arises, which overthrows reason, by allowing us to be 'carried away' into excessive, irrational, and unhealthy desires and emotions, which seek to have their way at all costs, even at the expense of wisdom and virtue.

An ancient writer called Aulus Gellius tells a related story in his *Attic Nights*, written in the second century AD. During a stormy trip at sea, an unnamed Stoic philosopher was seen to become pale and nervous. Once ashore, Gellius asked how a Stoic, who is 'supposed to have no emotions', grew so pale in the storm. The Stoic explained himself by taking out a copy of Epictetus' *Discourses*, and reading a passage from the lost fifth book. According to Gellius, Epictetus says that when a terrifying sound surprises us, such as thunder or a falling building, or when we're suddenly confronted by news of some impending danger, even the Sage's mind is necessarily disturbed, because the initial impression forces itself on our mind, and he may grow pale and shrink back automatically for a moment. This isn't due to the judgement that something intrinsically 'bad' is about to happen but because of very rapid, involuntary, bodily reactions.

However, the Sage will not give his 'assent' to these terrifying impressions, by making corresponding value judgements. He rejects them completely, judging there to be no reason to continue being afraid. We might imagine him saying to himself: 'Even though I feel myself growing pale, I know it's just my body reacting to the choppy waves, and there is no real danger for me to fear.' This is the key difference between the Sage and ordinary people. The foolish person assents to his initial impressions of danger or impending harm, 'confirming them with his judgement', and concludes that he is right to cower in fear. The Sage, by contrast, is affected only superficially and momentarily, but he remains consistent in his philosophical judgement that things that appear terrifying are actually 'indifferent' and don't deserve to be feared. They are 'empty terrors' like someone wearing a frightening mask that might startle us at first until we realise that it's just a mask and nothing genuinely terrifying.

Key idea: The Stoic 'therapy of the passions'

The Stoics argued that it is impossible to imagine the ideal Sage suffering from emotional disturbance, due to irrational fears or unhealthy cravings. He must therefore have attained *apatheia* or freedom from irrational 'passions', although he may still experience brief *automatic* emotional reactions without going along with them. For that reason, a kind of psychological 'therapy of the passions', which Epictetus calls the 'discipline of desire and aversion', is essential to the practice of Stoicism. This has confused some people who mistakenly assume that psychological therapy is a completely modern concept. In fact, the practice of philosophy as a 'medicine' or therapy for the mind, was common to most ancient schools of philosophy, and particularly associated with the Stoics.

A good example is provided by the ancient genre of writing known as the 'consolation letter'. These were carefully structured rhetorical and philosophical essays intended to help the recipient cope emotionally with a serious 'misfortune', most often bereavement. They offer reassurance and encouragement, but also philosophical-therapeutic strategies, contemplative exercises, and persuasive arguments, designed to moderate emotional distress. Although philosophers of different schools composed these letters, they're particularly associated with Stoicism and we still have several examples of Seneca's today. However, Stoic psychological therapy was also applied in other contexts:

✳ Seneca wrote many *Letters* to a (possibly fictitious) student of Stoicism called Lucilius, for whom he acts as a kind of personal philosophical mentor, a bit like the relationship between a modern coach or therapist and their client.

* Epictetus delivered *Discourses* to groups of students, which were transcribed, and show him offering practical advice on specific problems of living to them, in a way that could be (loosely) compared to a modern self-help or therapy workshop.
* Marcus Aurelius wrote a personal *journal* recording his use of Stoic psychological exercises, such as systematically contemplating the virtues of others or his own mortality, which is known as the *Meditations*.

These happen to be the three main surviving bodies of Stoic writings, all coming from the late or 'Roman Imperial' period of the Stoic school, and demonstrating the different forms Stoic therapy could take.

Remember this: Our initial emotional reactions may be automatic ('proto-passions')

Although the ideal Stoic Sage must be free from unhealthy 'passions', he may occasionally experience disturbing feelings *automatically*, such as being shocked by a sudden loud noise. The unhealthy 'passions' are based on value judgements that are under *voluntary* control, they're feelings that we've allowed ourselves to go along with by 'assenting' to our initial impressions.

By contrast, the Stoics refer to certain initial automatic feelings as 'proto-passions' (*propatheiai*), the involuntary emotional reactions preceding full-blown pathological fears and desires. Stoics accept these feelings as reflex-like reactions, beyond their direct control, and neither morally 'good' nor 'bad' in themselves. Examples include involuntarily crying, trembling, stammering, blinking, sweating, blushing, yawning or being suddenly startled. These are more due to external stimuli or bodily processes than to our voluntary assent to value judgements.

However, we potentially *do* control what happens next, our *voluntary* response to these initial *automatic* emotional reactions, whether we 'assent' and go along with them or step back from them instead. The Sage may receive a sudden shock but does not continue to worry about it, whereas the majority of people allow themselves to be 'carried away' by their anxious impressions. The Stoics observed that the distress of other animals naturally runs its course. After being startled, animals gradually relax; after a loss their distress eventually fades. Our automatic reactions will often likewise fade naturally over time, once the initial impressions are no longer 'fresh' in our minds, as long as we don't perpetuate our feelings by going along with them and giving our assent to faulty value judgements.

Remember this: Folly needs countless things

The majority of people desire and fear countless external things in life. However, the Sage desires only one thing, virtue, and he is cautious about only one thing, vice. He is the same in every circumstance because what is most important lies within him, and not with external events, which are constantly changing. For example, the Earl of Shaftesbury, an early modern follower of Stoicism, describes unhealthy feelings of 'pleasure' or 'elation', which are impulsive and agitated, insatiable and lead to subsequent remorse and even disgust, and to which 'a thousand things are necessary', because they depend on countless external causes. He contrasts these with the rational joy of the Sage, which is serene and gentle, pure and simple, incapable of excess, leading to contentment and self-sufficiency, and to which 'there is nothing necessary but what depends upon ourselves', because it comes from confidence in the fact that one is a good person, acting with virtue (Shaftesbury, 2005, p. 151).

What about the 'good' or 'healthy' passions?

It's important to emphasize the role of joyful and affectionate feelings in Stoicism, because this helps to rectify the misconception that Stoicism is about being *emotionless*. In fact, the ancient Stoics aspired to replace the bad or unhealthy passions, as defined above, with 'good' or 'healthy' ones, naturally associated with wisdom and virtue. Diogenes Laertius says that good passions such as 'joy' and 'cheerfulness' are not themselves virtues but temporarily 'supervene' as consequences of them. Although, strictly-speaking, only the perfect Sage possesses these 'good passions', the Stoics tend to speak of those making progress as experiencing glimpses of them. They only fall into *three* categories, because there is no voluntary, rational and healthy form of emotional pain or grief:

1 **'Joy' or 'delight'** (*chara*) is a feeling of rational 'elation' (positive emotion) over virtue, as the truly good, which is the alternative to irrational pleasure; healthy 'joy' can take the form of delight, good cheer or peace of mind (tranquillity).

2 **'Caution' or 'discretion'** (*eulabeia*) is a feeling of rational aversion towards vice as truly bad and harmful, which is the alternative to irrational fear; healthy 'caution' can take the form of a sense of dignity and self-respect or a sense of purity and sanctity.

3 **'Wishing' or 'willing'** (*boulêsis*) is feeling of rational desire for virtue as genuinely good and beneficial, which is the alternative to irrational craving; healthy 'wishing' can take the form of affection, kind-heartedness, and benevolence, presumably the wish for oneself and others to flourish in accord with virtue

Seneca explains that Stoic joy comes from reflecting on our own virtuous actions, something we are all capable of experiencing albeit in glimpses compared to the secure joy that takes root within the perfect Sage (*Letters*, 76). However, he emphasizes that, unlike the Epicureans who make feelings of pleasure (and the absence of pain) the chief good in life, feelings of 'joy' are *not* the Stoic's motive for acting in a virtuous way. She is not *guaranteed* to experience it in every circumstance, especially when acting quickly without opportunity for reflection, and similar feelings can arise from other (non-virtuous) causes. Indeed, even robbed of this feeling, she will not hesitate to face adversity with honour, viewing these appropriate actions as her duty and their own reward.

Indeed, the Stoics were clear that virtue somehow must be absolutely its own reward, otherwise cracks appear in the edifice of morality that make it vulnerable to collapse under pressure. The good feelings or 'healthy passions' are a sort of 'added bonus' but they cannot be the primary motive for action because they're not entirely under our control. Stoics have to be willing to act with courage and integrity *despite* their feelings rather than *because* of them, and even when fears and desires are calling them in the opposite direction.

In other words, when the call to arms resounds, the Stoic hero cannot be left waiting for a 'warm glow' of positive emotion to descend before rushing forward into battle. Although a special sense of joy often follows in its wake, virtue is its own reward and the only thing worth desiring for its own sake.

Remember this: Stoic joy and tranquillity

The Stoics therefore assume that tranquillity must be part of *eudaimonia* but it's really a consequence of attaining wisdom and the other virtues rather than the primary goal itself. By contrast, Irvine makes attaining rational joy and tranquillity the chief goal of his modern version of Stoicism because he believes it will appeal to modern readers, claiming that it is 'unusual, after all, for modern individuals to have an interest in becoming more virtuous, in the ancient sense of the word' (Irvine, 2009, p. 42).

However, the ancient Stoics defined virtue as practical wisdom, something that's arguably still as relevant today as it was 2,300 years ago. Philosophy means the 'love of wisdom' not the 'love of joy and tranquillity', after all. Joy and tranquillity 'automatically accompany' the wisdom and virtue of the Sage, as Musonius Rufus put it. The risk, in part, is that people who prize pleasant feelings above virtue will try to achieve them by lazy methods, and thereby fall back into vice.

To put it crudely, feelings like joy and tranquillity are *only* truly good and healthy insofar as they are the consequences of practical wisdom and virtue and not if they result from other causes. It's not really consistent with Stoicism to pursue them for their own sake, at all costs or at the expense of wisdom and virtue. What if you could somehow gain perfect, lifelong tranquillity, for example, by stuffing your face with tranquillisers every day or having a lobotomy? You probably wouldn't praise that as the 'good' life if someone else did it.

Tranquillity is also something of a 'dead end' as a goal because it doesn't lead on to other good things or maintain itself in the way that practical wisdom does. Wisdom is the ability to know how to use everything beneficially, and it can even reflect on and evaluate itself. Nevertheless, if living in agreement with nature, and in accord with virtue, is the goal of life, it must entail some form of prevention or therapy for pathological fears and desires. Stoicism therefore contains a psychological therapy, a precursor of modern CBT, although the real goal is virtue, and tranquillity is a kind of added bonus.

Focus Points

The main points to remember from this chapter are:

* The promise of philosophy, according to the Stoics, is that by living in accord with wisdom and virtue, following Nature, we may attain perfect Happiness and fulfilment (*eudaimonia*).
* Although *eudaimonia* includes certain feelings, such as joy and tranquillity, these are not the central goal of Stoic practice but merely positive *side-effects* of virtue.
* The Stoic Sage experiences 'healthy passions' that are rooted in his practical wisdom, such as joy, caution, well-wishing and affection.
* The ancient Stoics conceded that automatic emotional reactions ('proto-passions'), such as stammering or blushing, have to be accepted, as beyond our control, but believed we can change what happens next, by withholding our 'assent' to the initial impressions that upset us.

Next Step

Having learned about Stoic Ethics and the theory of the passions, it's time to begin looking in more detail at the armamentarium of Stoic psychological exercises, beginning with the 'discipline of desire and aversion', the aspect of Stoic practice most closely related to the study of Physics, which is central to the therapy of the passions.

4

The discipline of desire (Stoic acceptance)

In this chapter you will learn:

▶ *That the 'discipline of desire' was a form of therapy for the passions, based on psychological exercises drawn from Stoic Physics*

▶ *How to contemplate the present moment, and that Stoicism is essentially a 'here and now' philosophy*

▶ *How to practise the attitude of acceptance called* amor fati *or 'love of one's fate', in accord with the Stoic theory of causal determinism*

I care only for what is my own, what is not subject to hindrance, what is by nature free. This, which is the true nature of the good, I have; but let everything else be as God has granted, it makes no difference to me. (Epictetus, *Discourses*, 4.13)

All that is in accord with you is in accord with me, O World! Nothing which occurs at the right time for you comes too soon or too late for me. All that your seasons produce, O Nature, is fruit for me. It is from you that all things come; all things are within you, and all things move towards you. (Marcus Aurelius, *Meditations*, 4.23)

Self-assessment: Stoic attitudes and the discipline of desire

Before reading this chapter, rate how strongly you agree with the following statements, using the five-point (1-5) scale below, and then re-rate your attitudes once you've read and digested the contents.

1. Strongly disagree, 2. Disagree, 3. Neither agree nor disagree, 4. Agree, 5. Strongly agree

1 'All things are determined by strict causal necessity, including my own actions.'

2 'When we ground our attention in the 'here and now', and take things one step at a time, hardships often becomes easier to endure.'

3 'Rather than seeking for events beyond our control to happen as we wish, we should wish them to happen as they do.'

What is the discipline of desire?

Why should we 'accept' whatever befalls us in life and what did the Stoics mean by this? What's the difference between this and just 'giving up' and resigning ourselves passively to bad things? These questions are addressed by the first of Epictetus' three Stoic disciplines, the discipline of desire (*orexis*) and aversion (*ekklisis*). It might also be described as the discipline or therapy of the 'passions' because it involves the prevention or remedy of unhealthy desires and irrational fears. We'll often refer to it therefore as the 'discipline of desire' or 'therapy of the passions'.

According to Epictetus, the goal of this discipline is not to be frustrated in our desires nor to fall into what we would avoid, our aversions, and this is achieved by learning to embrace our fate with equanimity. This philosophical attitude towards events is encapsulated in one of the Stoic *Handbook's* most striking and important maxims:

> Seek not for events to happen as you wish but rather wish for events to happen as they do and your life will go smoothly. (*Enchiridion*, 8)

This passage seems to be alluding to the serenely 'smooth flowing' life that Zeno originally defined as the goal of Stoicism, which is one sense of 'living in agreement with Nature'. The discipline of desire is therefore particularly associated with the achievement of serenity, which means overcoming emotional suffering (*apatheia*).

Hadot likewise describes the discipline of desire as consisting in a refusal to desire anything other than what is willed by the Nature of the universe, our fate (Hadot, 1998, p. 129). He interprets it as the virtue of living in harmony with the whole of Nature, through Stoic acceptance. Marcus says that the discipline has to do with Epictetus' advice to abstain completely from desires and fear none of the things that are not 'up to us', or within our control. It seems sure to be related therefore to Epictetus' famous slogan 'endure and renounce'. He meant that novice Stoics should begin by training themselves each day:

1 To *endure* what they irrationally fear, or find aversive, with courage and perseverance.

2 To *renounce*, or abstain from, what they irrationally crave, through discretion and self-discipline.

The majority of people crave sensory pleasure, health, wealth, reputation, and other 'indifferent' things, which they naively judge to be intrinsically 'good' and necessary for Happiness, and they fear and avoid their opposites: physical pain and discomfort, sickness, poverty and ridicule. The desire for *wealth* and fear of *death* are sometimes portrayed as the most important passions to overcome. Seneca puts this in striking language when he says the promise of philosophy is that the glitter of gold shall no more dazzle our eyes than the flash of a sword, and that we may thereby 'trample with great courage on what all men desire and fear' (*Letters*, 48).

As we've seen, the Cynics adopted a very austere lifestyle, voluntarily embracing complete poverty, and extreme physical hardship. Although, the Stoics thought this was admirable, perhaps even a 'short-cut to virtue', they felt it wasn't necessary or appropriate for most people. They were also concerned that some Cynic practices become problematic when done for 'show', and so Epictetus counsels his students to conceal certain aspects of their training, where possible, from others. Also, from the Stoic perspective we don't need to actually renounce all 'indifferent' things completely, just as long as we remain emotionally detached from them.

Epictetus doesn't mean that we should torture ourselves. It's more that if we want to live wisely, we need to strengthen our self-control, by training ourselves, in a reasonable manner, to endure hardship and renounce pleasures that are unhealthy or to which we're overly-attached. However, some Stoics, such as Seneca, do recommend that we periodically practise living as simply as possible and enduring a tougher lifestyle, sleeping on a camping mat, drinking only water, and eating only the most basic food, to build our endurance and self-control. He advises his Stoic student to spend three to four days or more a month living as if impoverished, reducing things to 'a real straw mattress and soldier's blanket and hard rough bread' (*Letters*, 18). In the ancient world, of course, many people lived like that normally, and soldiers on campaign may have endured similar conditions. If that still sounds self-punitive, consider that for modern Stoics, simply engaging in physical exercise, sticking to a healthy diet, or going camping for a week in a tent, might provide fairly 'normal' and 'healthy' ways of developing endurance and abstinence.

Epictetus also stresses that this first discipline is the most important for new students of Stoicism because it deals with the passions, which cause turmoil when we perceive ourselves to have suffered a misfortune because our desires or aversions conflict with our fate. We can't think clearly when in the grip of violent desires or emotions so, of course, practical philosophy has to begin with a kind of therapy of the passions, to clear the ground for Ethics and subsequently Logic.

Students in Epictetus' school were therefore advised to set aside discussion of the other two disciplines until they'd made progress with the discipline of desire. As noted earlier, this echoes the philosophical career of Zeno who began as a Cynic, focused almost exclusively on gaining self-mastery. The fact we're troubled and life doesn't go smoothly, because of our upsetting desires and emotions, is a warning sign that we haven't completely digested the basic doctrine of Stoic Ethics: that virtue is the only true good and what is not 'up to us' is ultimately indifferent. As long as I have the sense that things are going against me, that I'm failing to get what I desire or getting things I'm averse to, that shows that I'm enslaved to my passions and still barely a novice. The Sage, by contrast, has perfect freedom because he only desires what is within his control, and so he's never thwarted, and his life goes smoothly.

Hadot called the goal of this preliminary discipline '*amor fati*', meaning loving acceptance of your fate – a phrase he borrows from the 19th-century German philosopher Friedrich Nietzsche. Nietzsche wrote the famous maxim: 'From the military school of life – what does not kill me can only make me stronger', which also sounds like a description of the Stoic discipline of desire. To live in harmony with one's fate in this way is to cease being alienated from Nature as a whole, and to become a true 'Citizen of the Cosmos'.

Someone who follows the discipline of desire, therefore, and accepts the role life has assigned him is 'no longer a stranger in his homeland' but rather 'a man worthy of the world which has created him' (*Meditations*, 12.1). Whether we realize it or not, we are all living out the lives fated for us, either willingly or reluctantly. Zeno illustrated this with a striking metaphor: the wise man is like a dog tethered to a cart, running alongside and smoothly keeping pace with it, whereas a foolish man is like a dog that struggles against the leash but finds himself dragged alongside the cart anyway. Seneca likewise said that Zeus is like a general and mankind his army, we must follow his lead whether we like it or not, but 'it is a bad soldier who follows his commander grumbling and groaning' (*Letters*, 108).

Another metaphor attributed to Chrysippus was that human life is like the foot of someone walking through mud, presumably barefoot or in open sandals. If the foot had a mind of its own and understood its function in life then it would willingly accept its fate, voluntarily plunging itself again and again towards the muddy ground, smoothly and without hesitation. Finally, the famous *Hymn to Zeus* written by Cleanthes said: 'The willing are led by fate, the reluctant dragged'. Epictetus encouraged his students to contemplate the words of this prayer regularly. However, as the journalist and author Oliver Burkeman notes in his discussion of Stoicism's relevance for modern life, this philosophical acceptance does *not* mean passive resignation, and a Stoic who finds herself in an abusive relationship would not be expected to put up with it, but perhaps to take action to leave it.

We'll learn more about the Stoic discipline of *action* later but, in a nutshell, Stoics would naturally 'prefer' to leave abusive situations, and take appropriate action to protect themselves, because their future is uncertain. However, once abuse has happened, wisdom would consist in accepting the facts, the reality of the situation, without morbidly wishing things could be different, because we can't change the past.

As we'll see, the 'discipline of desire', or 'therapy of the passions', is intimately related to Stoic Physics. At first, this might seem odd, but there are many examples of contemplative exercises in the Stoic literature, which are apparently based on natural philosophy and theology and yet play an important role in shaping our desires and aversions. In Hadot's account the discipline of desire therefore encompasses several important psychological exercises, related to Stoic Physics:

1 Focusing attention on the 'here and now' as the locus of our control and therefore of the chief good.

2 'Physical definition' of external events and the 'method of division' or analysis into elements.

3 Accepting events as determined by causal necessity or fate, or alternatively greeting them with rational joy as being the Will of God.

4 'The view from above' and related cosmological meditations.

5 Contemplation of the homogeneity ('sameness') and impermanence of all external things.

6 Perhaps also contemplation of the 'eternal recurrence' of all things, as found in Nietzsche.

We'll return to some of these exercises later, because they related to more complex cosmological exercises. However, in this chapter, we'll focus the key Stoic practices of contemplating the 'here and now' and practising *amor fati* by willingly accepting one's fate as determined by causal necessity.

Case study: Zeno's Shipwreck

Zeno, the founder of Stoicism, was a Phoenician merchant from the port of Citium in Cypress. When he was aged thirty, so the story goes, he was travelling from Phoenicia to the Greek port of Piraeus with a cargo of highly-valuable purple dye (*porphura*), made from the *murex* sea snail, when he was shipwrecked, and lost all of his wealth. He wound up in Athens where he became a follower of the famous Cynic Crates and spent the next twenty years studying under some of the leading philosophers of the period. Rather than seeing his loss as a catastrophe, therefore, we're told he said 'It is well done of thee, Fortune, thus to drive me to philosophy' and even joked: 'I have had a good voyage this time, now that I have been shipwrecked'(Lives, 7.4-5). For the Stoics, moral wisdom of the kind sought by Socrates and Zeno is priceless, and incomparably more valuable than even the greatest fortune.

Some ancient authors disputed this story, but whether it's historically accurate or not what matters is perhaps the example it provides of an absolute 'love of wisdom' and the corresponding attitude of philosophical indifference to loss or external 'misfortune'. The Cynics lived somewhat like beggars so it's possible that having lost a fortune at sea, Zeno found it natural to adopt their simple life, devoid of any possessions except a staff, a cloak, and a knapsack for food. As the Cynics used to say, poverty may be a better teacher of philosophy than books or lectures.

Henceforth, the metaphor of a ship on troubled seas was commonly employed in Stoic literature to symbolize the challenge of facing adversity in life. For example, alluding to a seemingly ruinous shipwreck like the one suffered by Zeno, Epictetus says to his students that they should train themselves to respond to impressions such as, 'Your ship is lost' by simply stating the facts 'Your ship is lost' without adding any value judgement or complaining. Even if the metaphorical 'waves' of fortune can sweep away our body and all our possessions, they can never overcome and shipwreck the ruling faculty of our mind, the seat of wisdom and virtue, unless we allow them to do so.

Key idea: Freewill and determinism (compatibilism)

Cicero says the Stoics did not mean anything remotely superstitious by the term 'fate' but rather a concept in philosophy of Nature or 'Physics'. Stoic 'fate' is basically the sequence or chain of causation, which produces everything in the universe: 'nothing has happened which was not going to be, and likewise nothing is going to be of which Nature does not contain causes working to bring that very thing about' (*On Divination*, 1.125-6). In fact, the Stoics were technically philosophical 'compatibilists' who believed that all events in life are rigidly determined by a 'string of causes', going back to the start of the universe, but that this is not mutually exclusive with the facts of human freedom.

This might seem puzzling to many people but it's still an influential philosophical position today because it's argued that the popular assumption that freewill and determinism are incompatible is based on a verbal misunderstanding. When we speak about someone having 'freedom' in daily life we normally just mean that nothing obstructs them from acting in accord with their own desires. There's no logical inconsistency between that everyday notion of 'freedom' and the notion that our character and desires are themselves the product of prior causes, based on the assumption that all things in life are determined by strict causal necessity.

It's only when we go further and try to claim that we should be not only 'free *to*' act but 'free *from*' prior causes that we introduce the problematic and arguably incoherent notion of *metaphysical* freewill, which is something the Stoics would reject. The type of 'freedom' the Stoics were concerned with is the type that comes from practical discipline, or developing sufficient endurance and restraint to overcome domination by our irrational passions.

Try it now: Dwelling in the 'here and now'

We'll be looking at other exercises later that work with 'mindfulness' and attention to the 'here and now' in more depth. However, for now, just begin experimenting with greater attention to the present moment in the following ways:

✳ Throughout the day, practise bringing your attention back to the present moment, rather than allowing it to wander off into daydreams, rumination about the past, or worry about the future.

✳ If you have to think about something else, that's okay, but try to keep one eye on the present moment, by noticing how you're using your body and mind try to be aware of each second that passes.

✳ If it helps, imagine that you're seeing the world for the first time, or that this is your last day of life, and concentrate your attention on how you actually think and act, from moment to moment.

✳ Remind yourself that the past and future are 'indifferent' to you, and that the supreme good, and *eudaimonia*, can only exist within you, right now, in the present moment.

Start by making the effort to spend more of your day being aware of the 'here and now', particularly your own thoughts and actions. Evaluate this process, though. What are the 'pros and cons' of doing this? How could you make more of the advantages and deal with or prevent any perceived disadvantages?

Remember this: The 'Lazy Argument'

The majority of people respond to the Stoic theory of determinism – the idea that absolutely everything in life *necessarily* happens as it does – by saying 'What's the point doing anything then, if everything is determined?' Chrysippus dismissed this as a crude logical fallacy called 'The Lazy Argument' (*argos logos*) because it both justifies being lazy and, arguably, involves lazy thinking itself. Events are not determined to happen in a particular way, *regardless* of what you do, but rather *along with* what you do. Your own thoughts and actions are necessitated as part of the whole 'string of causes' that forms the universe. The outcome of events still often depends on your actions, though.

Things are only 'fated' as a consequence of the causes that precede them, in the way a match would be bound to ignite when you strike it, if nothing prevents that happening. The Stoics mean that fate works 'through' us, so that even if there are things in life that seem to require great effort on our part to achieve, whether or not we make the effort is fated along with the outcome. You're reading these words, according to the Stoics, because causal necessity has brought you to this specific point.

What happens next will depend, in part, on what you choose to do next because you are a tiny but essential cog in the vast machinery of the universe. However, your choices themselves are the consequences of a massive string of causation, set in motion countless billions of years before you were even born, at the beginning of the universe.

Contemplating the 'here and now'

In his scholarly analysis of the *Meditations*, Hadot refers to a scene in the well-known film *The Dead Poets Society* (1989) where Robin Williams' character, a teacher of English literature, makes his students closely observe an old photograph showing a group of the school's former pupils, now long deceased (Hadot, 1998, p. 171). He asks one of them to read aloud the poem 'To the Virgins, to Make Much of Time' (1648) by Robert Herrick, which was inspired by the philosophical themes of transience and mortality in ancient Roman poetry:

> Gather ye rosebuds while ye may,
> Old Time is still a-flying;
> And this same flower that smiles today,
> Tomorrow will be dying.

He compares this to the saying *Carpe diem* ('Seize the day!'), a quote from the Roman poet Horace, who drew upon both Stoicism and Epicureanism. The contemplation of deceased generations and the transience of one's own life was a psychological strategy commonly employed by Hellenistic philosophers and poets to encourage us to value the present moment or 'here and now'.

This emphasis on the 'here and now' was an important psychological exercise in Stoicism, particularly in Marcus'

Meditations. It relates to all three Stoic disciplines as only our *current* judgements, desires, and actions, are truly 'up to us' at any given moment.

> Everything other than its own activity is indifferent to the faculty of thought. Everything that is its own activity, however, is within its power. Moreover, even among these latter activities the faculty of thought concerns itself only about the present; for even its past or future activities are now indifferent to it. (*Meditations*, 6.32)

However, the concept of the 'here and now' seems to be especially linked to Stoic Physics and our relationship with Nature. Hadot particularly notes two benefits that follow from the Stoic focus on the present moment:

1 Hardships become more bearable, being reduced to a succession of fleeting moments, making it easier to accept our fate.

2 Greater mindfulness is brought to the (virtuous or vicious) quality of our own current actions (Hadot, 1998, p. 132).

Marcus explicitly describes this *first* method, saying: 'remind yourself that it is not the future nor the past, which weighs upon you, but always the present and this present will seem smaller to you if you circumscribe it by defining and isolating it' (*Meditations*, 8.36). That's a bit like saying: 'I just need to get through this one moment at a time.' By focusing on what's present to us rather than worrying about the future, we can take things step by step, and overcome obstacles that might otherwise seem overwhelming.

The Stoic strategy of seeing the present moment in isolation, in this way, appears to be closely related to another technique, which Hadot called 'physical definition'. This involves cultivating the calm detachment of a natural philosopher or scientist. We are to practise describing an object or event purely in terms of its objective qualities, stripped of any emotive rhetoric or value judgements, to arrive at an 'objective representation' (*phantasia kataléptiké*). (We discuss this elsewhere in relation to the 'discipline of judgement'.) However, especially in the writings of Marcus Aurelius, this may also involve a kind of 'method of division', in which the event becomes broken down through analysis, calmly dissected into its individual components or aspects.

This is one fundamental respect in which Stoic Physics, or 'natural philosophy', evolved into a psychological or therapeutic exercise. For example, Marcus notes that if we dissect a seductive dance or piece of music into its individual components, in this spirit of objective analysis, it loses its power to charm our minds. When we find ourselves overwhelmed by worry or rumination, we should likewise, face individual aspects of events one at a time, viewing them more objectively. Indeed, we should head immediately for the parts of any process, except virtue and other goods, and divide them up until we get to the point where we can look down on things in a detached manner.

The *second* benefit of grounding one's attention in the present moment is that it intensifies the experience of self-awareness. Otherwise, we tend to become carried away by our thoughts about the past or future, and lose touch with the present moment. Seneca describes this in an extraordinary passage, in which he astutely observes that most human suffering relates to rumination about the past or worry about the future, and that nobody confines his concern to the present moment.

> Wild beasts run away from dangers when they see them. Once they have escaped, they are free of anxiety. But we are tormented by both the future and the past. (*Letters*, 5)

However, for Stoics, the good can only exist in the 'here and now' because that's where our voluntary actions originate. Yet everything in life conspires to make our thoughts wander from their own source. The more this happens the less mindful and more *mindless* we become. The majority of people try to seek Happiness in a roundabout way, by means of external things they hope to obtain in the future. By contrast, Stoics try to focus attention on becoming good right now, in the present moment, because that is the direct and only route to *eudaimonia*. By grounding our attention in the 'here and now', undistracted by the past or future, we can properly confront the challenge of accepting 'indifferent' things with equanimity, while cultivating wisdom and justice in our actions. Stoic therapy of the passions therefore requires continual and intense attention to our moment-by-moment experience.

Key idea: The 'here and now'

Ancient Stoicism was very explicitly a 'here and now' philosophy, although many people today associate this notion more with Oriental philosophies, particularly Buddhism. In fact, the modern English expression 'here and now' actually comes from a common figure of speech in Latin: *hic et nunc*. The exercise of living centred in the present moment is emphasized throughout Marcus Aurelius' *Meditations*. For Stoics, the past and future are 'indifferent' because they're not under our control, 'good' and 'evil' can only truly reside in the present moment. Humans surpass other animals in their ability, through language and reason, to recall the past or plan for the future. However, doing so leads us to neglect the seat of our volition in the present moment, where virtue potentially originates.

Stoics therefore train themselves to focus attention on the present moment, often by reminding themselves that they could potentially die the following day and should therefore 'seize the day' and seek to flourish and attain Happiness in the 'here and now'. In other words, the most important thing in the universe is situated within you, right here in the present moment.

Try it now: Divide and conquer

Try using this exercise with several different situations to see if you can alter your emotional response by dissecting things into their component parts, splitting your experience up, and viewing it in a more detached way.

1 Close your eyes and spend a few minutes picturing a recent situation in which you felt strong desires or emotions, which you judge it would be rational and healthy to change.
2 Take time to describe events to yourself verbally, without any value judgements, inferences or emotive language; instead, imagine you're like a scientist making notes on what you can observe about the situation, from a detached and impartial perspective.

3 Divide the situation into its component parts and try to think of them one by one, separately from each other, breaking things down into their individual elements; for example, the smell of some food, the different ingredients on the plate, the colours, etc.

4 Consider each of these elements in turn, apart from the others, and ask yourself in response to each one: 'Does *this* really justify *those* feelings?'

5 Focus on accepting each element as 'indifferent', completely irrelevant with regard to *eudaimonia*.

If the individual components of a situation taken one at a time, independently of one another, are bearable, then why should you be overwhelmed by them taken together? Continue to practise analysing things in this way, breaking them down further if necessary, until it becomes more familiar and habitual to do so.

Remember this: The stoic concept of freedom

It was a famous Stoic 'paradox' that the Sage is believed to be absolutely free, even when imprisoned or exiled by a powerful tyrant. This was often put to the test because ancient philosophers were quite frequently imprisoned, exiled or even executed! The freedom of the truly wise man consists in following his own rational nature, by doing what is within his control in accord with wisdom and virtue. His mind is like a blazing fire, which consumes anything cast into it. Every obstacle to his actions just becomes an opportunity for him to exhibit magnanimity and the other virtues. He only wants to live wisely, adapting to events in a manner harmonious with reason, and nothing can prevent him from doing this. What stands in the way *becomes* the way. Just another opportunity to exercise virtue, which is all he really wants to do in life.

According to the Stoics therefore a man is free if his desires are not thwarted. However, if we only desire what is within our control, then we can never be frustrated, and our freedom is guaranteed regardless of circumstances. By contrast, if we desire things which are potentially outside our control, then we become slaves to fortune and to our passions. Perhaps worse, if someone else controls what we desire, then we effectively become enslaved to that person. The Stoics liked to discuss examples of wise men defying tyrants. The majority of people can be controlled by tyrants who may be able to threaten their lives or seize their property, the things they desire to keep. However, the perfect Sage views these as 'indifferent', and so the tyrant can lay his hands on nothing that the Sage desires, nor expose him to anything he fears.

Loving your fate and joyful acceptance

Epictetus actually describes a three-stage process to his students, which relates to the discipline of desire. He begins by emphasizing the need for Stoics to train themselves rigorously to adhere to their principles, having certain phrases constantly ready-to-hand day and night. These should be written down, read over, analysed and discussed, until they have been memorized and understood. We should then rehearse all the possible catastrophes that can befall us in life, things the majority of people fear, and prepare for them in advance.

> Then, if one of those things happens which are called 'undesirable', immediately the thought that it was not unexpected will be the first thing to lighten the burden. For in every case it is a great help to be able to say, 'I knew the son whom I had begotten was mortal.' [A famous saying, attributed to various wise men.] For that is what you will say, and likewise, 'I knew that I was mortal', 'I knew that I was vulnerable to exile', 'I knew that I might be sent off to prison.' (*Discourses*, 3.24)

We discuss the importance Stoics place on anticipating these things at length in the chapter on 'premeditation of adversity' but for now let's consider what Epictetus tells his students they should do when the anticipated event actually happens. There are three steps he recommends:

1 Tell yourself that you have already anticipated that this particular misfortune might happen to you, e.g. 'I knew that my son was mortal.'

2 Remind yourself that what is not up to you is therefore 'indifferent' with regard to *eudaimonia, e.g.,* 'This is external therefore it does not truly harm me.'

3 Epictetus says the third step is the 'most decisive': Tell yourself that it was therefore sent to you as fated by Nature or the Will of God and determined by the string of causes that constitutes the whole, e.g, 'If this is the will of Nature then so be it.'

The discipline of desire culminates in our willing acceptance of events, whether the majority judge them 'good' or 'bad', as being determined by the whole of Nature.

The Stoics undoubtedly emphasize the goal of cultivating 'indifference to indifferent things' and yet they also talk about greeting all external events with piety or even joy – which seems like a puzzling contradiction. Hadot explains this as follows:

> Since such an [external] event does not depend upon me, in itself it is indifferent, and we might therefore expect the Stoic to greet it with indifference. Indifference, however, does not mean coldness. On the contrary: since such an event is the expression of the love which the Whole has for itself, and since it is useful for and willed by the Whole, we too must want and love it. In this way, my will shall identify itself with the divine Will which has willed this event to happen. To be indifferent to indifferent things – that is, to things which do not depend on me – in fact means to make no difference between them: it means to love them equally, just as Nature or the Whole produces them with equal love. (Hadot, 1998, p. 142)

Marcus speaks of the need to 'find satisfaction' in the external events that befall us, that we should 'greet them joyfully', 'accept them with pleasure', 'love' them and 'will' them to happen as determined by our fate. Hadot compares this to Nietzsche's concept of *amor fati*, meaning 'love of fate'.

> My formula for what is great in mankind is *amor fati*: not to wish for anything other than that which is; whether behind, ahead, or for all eternity. Not just to put up with the inevitable – much less to hide it from oneself, for all idealism is lying to oneself in the face of the necessary – but to *love* it. (Nietzsche, *Ecce Homo*, 10)

Nietzsche describes this attitude as closely-related to something resembling another exercise based upon Stoic Physics, the contemplation of the All or the 'view from above':

> Everything that is necessary, when seen from above and from the perspective of the vast economy of the whole, is in itself equally useful. We must not only put up with it, but *love* it. [...] *Amor fati*: that is my innermost nature. (*Nietzsche contra Wagner*, Epilogue)

Elsewhere Nietzsche said that by making ourselves completely satisfied with anything at all, even one instant, we thereby say 'Yes' to the whole of existence and to ourselves, we accept and affirm the whole of eternity in a single timeless action. This perhaps resembles a cryptic remark attributed to Chrysippus: 'If one has wisdom for one instant, he will be no less happy than he who possesses it for all eternity' (in Plutarch, *On Common Conceptions*, 8.1062a).

Key idea: Nietzsche's *amor fati*

Pierre Hadot borrows the Latin term *amor fati*, meaning love of one's fate, from the 19th-century German philosopher Friedrich Nietzsche. Nietzsche was a professor of classical philology, the study of language, and he probably coined this expression himself. Although, the Stoics don't appear to have used the phrase, Hadot felt it captured their philosophical attitude towards life extremely well.

Of course, Nietzsche's philosophy is not the same as Stoicism, although we'll mention a few other similarities in due course. The concept of *amor fati* encapsulates the Stoic attitude of acceptance fundamental to the discipline of desire. The Sage has a sense of natural 'piety' or reverence towards the universe as a whole and, although he does what he judges appropriate in any given situation, sometimes requiring great courage or self-discipline, he nevertheless accepts the outcome with complete equanimity. It seems absurd to say that the Sage would joyfully accept even the death of his child. However, it would probably be more accurate to say that he experiences a kind of joyful acceptance of life as a whole, even if it includes individual events that the majority of people would judge to be 'bad' or even 'catastrophic'.

Try it now: Stoic acceptance exercises

Take a few minutes to try to practise radical acceptance by willing things to be as they actually are, rather than as you might wish them to be. It may well be rational and healthy to prefer things to be a certain way in the *future*, fate permitting. However, you can't change the distant past or even what's just happened. You can only try to influence the future, to an uncertain degree, by changing your *current* thoughts and actions. So focus on accepting that the past cannot be changed anymore and that the future may not be as you'd have preferred. Try the following thought-experiments:

1 Imagine that the universe has been designed to present you with challenges, from time to time, perhaps as if they are a form of therapy prescribed by Zeus, so that you can progress towards Happiness by accepting them and responding appropriately, in accord with virtue.

2 Similarly, imagine that you unconsciously chose and created your own fate, in its entirety, to help yourself learn and grow as an individual.

3 Contemplate the idea that events, and your response to them, could not have been otherwise, but were strictly *determined* by the laws of Nature to be exactly as they were; as the Stoics put it, we don't pity infants' inability to speak because we see it as natural, and there's likewise no more point being upset about misfortune, necessitated by fate, than being depressed because you don't have wings like a bird.

4 Tell yourself that nothing in life matters, ultimately, except your current voluntary response to events, which by definition you can choose at any time; accept everything else, everything bodily or external, as being 'indifferent', absolutely trivial, compared to your ability to rise above them 'magnanimously', which begins with this very attitude of acceptance itself.

Try to find other ways in which you can help yourself rehearse an attitude of philosophical acceptance and practise this regularly throughout the day.

Remember this: Acceptance is not resignation

The majority of people confuse acceptance with resignation. The ancient Stoics were not at all 'doormats', though. Their mythical role-model was Hercules, who overcame the 'Twelve Labours' with legendary courage and endurance. Zeno's follower King Antigonus of Macedonia was one of the most powerful military leaders of the period, and Zeno's favourite student, Persaeus, gave his life defending his rule. Cato became a Roman hero, particularly to the late Stoics, after he marched the shattered remains of the Republican army through the deserts of Africa to make their last stand at Utica against the tyrant Julius Caesar's advancing legions. The Emperor Marcus Aurelius was arguably the most powerful military and political leader of his lifetime and led his armies repeatedly into battle to protect Rome against barbarian incursions. Stoic literature is packed with references to other heroic men of action. In fact, Stoics are committed to taking 'appropriate action' in the world, as we'll see when we come to discuss the 'discipline of action'.

Focus Points

The main points to remember from this chapter are:

✻ The discipline of desire and aversion is particularly related to the Stoic therapy of the passions, and the acceptance of things outside of our control as our fate and part of Nature as a whole.

✻ Contemplation of the 'here and now' is an integral part of Stoic practice, particularly in relation to the discipline of desire.

✻ *Amor fati*, or willing and even joyful acceptance of your fate is also a fundamental element in Stoic practice.

Next Step

Having discussed the irrational 'passions', in the next chapter we'll look in more detail at Stoic attitudes towards healthy feelings of love and friendship. The social dimension of Stoicism was said by Epictetus to explain why Stoics are not simply hard-hearted or insensitive like stone or iron, presumably because it's based on the fundamental concept of 'natural affection', the basis of Stoic philanthropy.

Love, friendship, and the ideal Sage

In this chapter you will learn:

▶ *That the Stoic way of life is not* unemotional *and how the Stoics sought to cultivate 'natural affection' and friendship towards the rest of mankind*

▶ *That Stoics define true beauty as residing in our character rather than our external appearance*

▶ *How Stoics contemplate the hypothetical ideal Sage, and the 'virtues' of exemplary figures, in order to emulate their attitudes and conduct*

No school has more goodness and gentleness; none has more love for human beings, nor more attention to the common good. The goal which it assigns to us is to be useful, to help others, and to take care, not only of ourselves, but of everyone in general and of each one in particular. (Seneca, *On Clemency*, 3.3)

And if you come across a man who is never alarmed by dangers, never affected by cravings, happy in adversity, calm in the midst of storm, viewing mankind from a higher level, and the gods from their own, is it not likely that a feeling will find its way into you of veneration for him? (Seneca, *Letters*, 41)

Self-assessment: Stoic attitudes towards others

Before reading this chapter, rate how strongly you agree with the following statements, using the five-point (1-5) scale below, and then re-rate your attitudes once you've read and digested the contents.

1. Strongly disagree, 2. Disagree, 3. Neither agree nor disagree, 4. Agree, 5. Strongly agree

1 'What makes a person truly beautiful is their character rather than their physical appearance.'

2 'To truly love someone you have to fully accept that you may lose them one day.'

3 ''It's important to contemplate what a perfectly wise person would do and believe when facing different problems in life.'

Stoicism and the philosophy of love

The popular idea of ancient Stoics is that they aspired to be coldly rational, like a robot, or 'Mr Spock' in Star Trek. However, what if this turned out to be a *misconception*? What if overcoming our irrational and unhealthy 'passions' entailed cultivating rational and healthy emotions in their stead? Stoic Ethics was based on the natural experience of 'familial affection' that humans and other animals feel for their own offspring. We can even approach it from that perspective, as providing in some respects a *philosophy of love, natural affection and friendship*.

As we've seen, the word 'philosophy' (*philosophia*) means '*love* of wisdom' and the Stoics took this expression literally. *Philia* can be translated as 'love', 'affection' or 'friendship' – that's what this chapter's about. As humans mature we naturally develop greater affinity for our own *rational* nature. We seek to preserve our character, not just our lives, and to flourish mentally as well as physically. This process is left *incomplete* by Nature and so the goal of life is to finish the job voluntarily, progressing towards the perfect wisdom and virtue of the ideal Stoic Sage.

Stoics refer to this excellence and flourishing as that which is truly beautiful and *lovable*. Zeno reputedly said in his *Republic* that only those who have wisdom and the other virtues can be considered true citizens, friends, relatives and free men and that those who lack wisdom are doomed to be 'hostile and enemies and slaves and alien to each other, parents to children, and brothers to brothers and relatives to relatives' (Laertius, *Lives*, 7.32-33). However, aspiring Stoics, despite their folly and imperfection, clearly aspire to love virtue, as the supreme good in life. Moreover, when we encounter *other people* who possess virtue, as Cicero puts it, our 'natural affection' is aroused by the 'shining light of goodness and excellence' in their character. Even if we've never met them in person but only heard about them in stories, we are drawn to the wise and good, and make moral progress by emulating their example.

For Stoics, the only perfectly virtuous beings are Zeus and the ideal Sage. However, although the majority of people do not, strictly-speaking, meet the exacting Stoic criteria for virtue, they may offer *glimpses* of it. The Stoics, particularly those of the Roman Imperial period, clearly believed that we can learn from contemplating examples of 'virtue' among ordinary people, even our enemies or philosophers of opposing schools. Natural affection therefore extends to all mankind, even the foolish and vicious, because we possess reason in common and the 'seeds of virtue'. Stoics therefore wish all humans would flourish, become enlightened, and live harmoniously, fate permitting.

For example, as we've seen, Marcus Aurelius tells himself repeatedly to 'love mankind' and praises his Stoic tutor Sextus of Chaeronea for being 'free from passion and yet full of love' or 'natural affection' for others (*Meditations*, 1.9).

Epictetus told his students that the common *misconception* that Stoics aim to be emotionless, to have hearts of iron or stone, is undermined by the 'discipline of action', particularly the way Stoics engage with their familial and social relationships. The rival school of Epicurus, who denied any intrinsic fellowship among mankind, traditionally sought tranquillity and freedom from emotional distress (*apatheia*) by avoidance of social responsibility, and confining themselves to a close-knit circle of friends instead.

The Stoics, by contrast, believed that we are essentially social creatures, with a 'natural affection' and 'affinity' for *all* people. This forms the basis of Stoic 'philanthropy', the rational love of our brothers and fellow citizens in the universe, or 'cosmic city' – the true meaning of 'cosmopolitanism'. A good person 'displays love for his fellow human beings, as well as goodness, justice, kindness and concern for his neighbour', and for the welfare of his home city (Musonius, *Lectures*, 14).

Of course, other people are 'external' to me and so *their* virtue is not *my* good, it's not 'up to me', and cannot contribute directly to my Happiness or *eudaimonia* – it's ultimately their business not mine. However, among external things, which are classed as 'indifferent', the virtue of others apparently constitutes a *special case*. Stoics were typically willing to call other people 'good', albeit in a sense different from that in which something is 'good' or 'helpful' for me, and they never tire of giving examples of 'good' men.

Goodness in other people naturally arouses our affection and friendship, not because it's of some material advantage to us, but because it's the mirror image of our own potential for virtue, and so loved for its own sake. For instance, the Roman statesman Laelius the Wise, renowned for his own exemplary friendship with Scipio Africanus the Younger, had studied Stoic philosophy under the scholarchs Diogenes of Babylon and Panaetius. In a dialogue entitled *On Friendship*, Cicero portrays him saying that 'nothing else in the whole world is so completely *in harmony with Nature*' as true friendship, a profound agreement in the feelings and values of two people, supported by mutual goodwill and affection.

Next to achieving wisdom and goodness ourselves, says 'Laelius', having wise and good friends is the most precious thing in the whole world, the most valuable of all 'external' things. Seneca likewise wrote that even the Stoic Sage 'wants to have a friend and a neighbour and a housemate', although he is nevertheless contented and self-sufficient without them (*Letters*, 9). He is able to go without a friend but he prefers *not* to go without one. Indeed, the Sage prefers to have as many friends as possible because of his natural affection for mankind, although he does not *need* them for his own Happiness.

As social beings, it is in our relationships that we have most opportunity to flourish. Indeed, the Stoics argued that our own self-interest, as rational beings, happens to coincide with the wellbeing of others. We flourish as individuals by attaining the virtues of wisdom and justice, but these bring us into greater harmony with the rest of mankind. Animals naturally fight over external things such as food, when they are scarce. By contrast, nobody can take wisdom and virtue from us, and they are not depleted when shared with others. Stoics view the things the majority of people fight over with detachment and indifference and they can afford to love even those who are foolish and vicious.

Stoic philanthropy therefore isn't just superficial but we should 'love mankind' from the bottom of our hearts, and take joy in doing good to others for its own sake, viewing virtue as its own reward. We benefit other people the most by helping them to live in harmony, without conflict, and bringing our society a tiny step closer to Zeno's dream of an ideal Stoic Republic, a perfect community of enlightened friends. Ranking virtue as the chief good in life allows the Stoic to wish even her enemies well, because if they were wise and just they'd no longer be enemies. Indeed, although our affection should naturally be reserved for the beauty of virtue, Stoics nevertheless extend it to people who lack wisdom, and may even act like enemies, as all of us have the faculty of reason, and therefore the *seeds* of virtue.

It is a man's especial privilege to love even those who stumble. And this love follows as soon as you reflect that they are akin to you and that they do wrong involuntarily and through ignorance, and that within a little while both they and you will be dead; and this above all, that the man has done you no harm; for he has not made your 'ruling faculty' worse than it was before. (*Meditations*, 7.22)

In a sense, Stoics view foolish and vicious people as if they were small children throwing a tantrum. They don't really understand what they're doing and it makes no sense for us to be angry with them.

What is it to have Natural Affection? Not that which is only towards relations, but towards all mankind; to be truly *philanthrôpos* [philanthropic, a lover of mankind], neither to scoff, nor hate, nor be impatient with them, nor abominate them, nor overlook them; and to pity in a manner and love those that are the greatest miscreants, those that are most furious against thyself in particular, and at the time when they are most furious? (Shaftesbury, 2005, p. 1)

Shaftesbury compared Stoic philanthropy to the loving attitude of a mother or nurse to sickly children in her care. Indeed, for the ancient Stoics, the 'natural affection' (*philostorgia*) of parents for their offspring is of profound importance. For example, Musonius said that through studying Stoicism, rather than becoming somehow unemotional, mothers may acquire a deeper and more philosophical love for their own children: 'Who, more than she, would love her children more than life?' (*Lectures*, 3).

In a sense, to become a Stoic is to learn what it means to have natural affection for our friends and family, in accord with wisdom and virtue. However, as we've seen, Stoics also expand it into the more pervasive attitude called 'philanthropy' or love of all mankind. This notion, that Stoicism teaches a more profound, expansive sense of parental love and affection, definitely clashes with the popular misconception of Stoics as emotionless robots, though, doesn't it?

Key idea: 'Natural affection' and 'affinity' or 'appropriation'

In Stoicism, love and friendship are important concepts, particularly the kind called *philostorgia*, experienced between close family members and sometimes translated as 'natural affection' or 'family affection'. Stoics sought to emulate Zeus, the father of mankind, who has perfect wisdom, justice and natural affection towards us, his children, and was to them a 'god of friendship' and 'protector of families'. As their affinity with perfect reason grows, the natural affection of philosophers therefore expands into 'philanthropy' or love of mankind. *Oikeiôsis* is a related Stoic technical term, for which there's no easy English translation. It literally means bringing something or someone into your household. It can therefore be translated as 'appropriation', meaning taking ownership for something. However, it is also translated as 'affinity', meaning the affectionate bond that we're predisposed to have with our own offspring and other blood relatives. We can arguably think of it as a natural process of psychological *identification* with those for whom we have affection.

We're born with an instinctive affinity for our own bodies and, if we reproduce, our own offspring. However, as we acquire reason, we become capable of progressively greater affinity or identification both with our own faculty of reason and with mankind as a whole. However, the majority of people remain alienated or in conflict with their own true nature and with the rest of humanity. Stoics aspire to develop a sense of kinship with the rest of mankind, insofar as we all possess reason and the seed of virtue. Chrysippus therefore wrote that the wise and good man, who lives in perfect harmony with reason and Nature, is *alienated from nothing* whereas the foolish and morally bad man has affinity with nothing.

The more this sense of affinity and natural affection expands to include all mankind, and ultimately Nature as a whole, the more rational and healthy it becomes. The ideal Stoic Sage therefore lives in harmony and affinity with his own true nature, with the rest of mankind, and with Nature as a whole. Marcus Aurelius therefore repeatedly says that the purpose of human life is fellowship and we should show genuine natural affection to others we encounter in life, even those who oppose us.

Case study: The Last Days of Socrates

The most important Stoic example of a near-Sage is undoubtedly Socrates. Xenophon, whose account inspired Zeno to study philosophy, called Socrates 'the perfect example of goodness and happiness' (*Memorabilia*, 4.8). His execution is covered in the chapter on contemplating death but it's also worth considering his conduct in court. In 399 BC, aged about 70, Socrates was put on trial in Athens on two charges: corrupting the morals of the youth and teaching impiety, perhaps atheism – all of which he denied.

The charges, which seemed utterly absurd to Socrates' friends, may have been a façade. Put bluntly, perhaps he simply asked too many questions, rocked the boat, and became a nuisance to the rich and powerful of his day. The jury convicted Socrates, apparently by a small majority. Athenian law allowed the accused and his prosecutor to propose alternative punishments, which the jury then chose between. Socrates, after joking that he should be 'sentenced' to free meals, finally offered to pay thirty pieces of silver, a substantial amount of money. Most of the sum was put up by his friends and supporters, as he was not wealthy himself and did not charge a fee for teaching philosophy.

What impressed the Stoics was the example Socrates provided of a man meeting his fate with perfect equanimity and unwavering commitment to his principles. His defence in court, reported in Plato's *Apology*, was remarkably *unapologetic*. Rather than defending his life, he used the opportunity to defend the philosophical *way* of life. He spoke freely and lectured the jury on wisdom and virtue rather than, as men normally did, parading his tearful wife and children before them, and begging for mercy. Perhaps irritated by this, the jury voted in favour of the death penalty nominated by his accusers, and sentenced him to commit forced suicide by drinking a hemlock-based poison. It may be that he was expected to flee into exile instead but he remained and drank the poison, despite the protestations of his followers. He immediately became a kind of philosophical martyr whose death sent shockwaves through the ancient world. Socrates provided a timeless example of someone who loved wisdom more than wealth, reputation, and even his own life, and thereby secured the future of rational philosophy in Western society, for millennia to come..

Remember this: Stoicism as a philosophy of 'love' and altruism

If ancient Stoicism seems stern or cold-hearted, it can be useful to remember the central role that *love* plays in their philosophical system. In particular, the love and affection people naturally tend to have towards their own children and close family (*philostorgia*) is taken as the basis for the philanthropic attitude Stoics aspire to cultivate towards all mankind.

We might even approach Stoicism from this perspective, and see it as fundamentally a 'philosophy of love', an attempt to understand how our natural self-love and familial affection is transformed by reason into the Stoic love of wisdom and mankind: *philosophy* and *philanthropy*. Stoics assume that my intention to help others, whether in terms of external things or virtue, inherently benefits me because it *constitutes* a form of virtue and flourishing. In this sense, there is no difference between self-interest and altruism. What is healthy and 'beneficial' for me is synonymous with what is 'honourable' and praiseworthy, including justice, benevolence, and natural affection towards others.

Stoic philanthropy and 'affinity' for others

Epictetus said that 'when a child is born it is no longer in our power *not* to love it or care for it'; it's natural for parents to care, for instance, if their child is hurt (*Discourses*, 1.11; 1.23). Our natural affection for those close to us is not *eliminated* by Stoicism but rather expanded, and transformed in accord with wisdom and virtue. As Seneca puts it, Stoics view all mankind as part of the whole of Nature, akin to each other and to God, as if members of a single body, and sharing an affinity, which forms the basis for mutual love and friendship.

Marcus likewise says that if we think of ourselves as separate parts of mankind rather than limbs of a single organism, we cannot yet love others wholeheartedly nor delight in the wellbeing of mankind as something good in itself. This natural affection for the rest of mankind, just because we share reason and the potential for virtue, is referred to as 'brotherly love' (*philadelphia*, like the city) or 'love of mankind' (*philanthrôpia* = philanthropy). According to Hadot, the Stoic discipline of action, particularly in Marcus' writings, culminates in love towards all mankind and an almost mystical sense of unity with others.

> It cannot, then, be said that 'loving one's neighbour as oneself' is a specifically Christian invention. Rather, it could be maintained that the motivation of Stoic love is the same as that of Christian love. [...] Even the love of one's enemies is not lacking in Stoicism. (Hadot, 1998, p. 231)

The Stoic ideal of love might also be compared to the concept of *karunā* or compassion for all other 'sentient' beings, in Buddhism, although Stoicism, like Christianity, is mainly concerned with other *rational* beings, a love of all mankind.

Nevertheless, our primitive affection for others only becomes *good* when associated with wisdom and virtue. When love participates in vice, and the false impression that bodily pleasure or external gain are intrinsically 'good', it's apparently degraded into animalistic 'lust' or 'craving' (*epithumia*), one of the irrational passions incompatible with our ultimate Happiness and wellbeing.

> The Stoics actually both say that the wise man will experience love, and they define love itself as the effort to make a friendship from the semblance of beauty. Which love, if there is any in the world without disquietude, without longing, without anxiety, without sighing, then so be it! For it is free from all lust. (*Tusculan Disputations*, 4.72)

Love entails a benevolent wish for others to flourish naturally, like a ripening fruit, and to attain Happiness in accord with virtue. Perhaps this was the motivation of Zeno and his successors, who lectured and wrote many books concerning philosophy for the benefit of others. However, the progress of others towards virtue is an external event, beyond my direct control, which Stoics qualify with the 'reserve clause'. For example: 'I wish you to flourish and attain Happiness, *fate permitting*.'

How do we help others? Zeno taught them about virtue, which is considered the greatest benefit, although the Stoics recognize that not everyone is receptive to learning. For example, Cicero's 'Cato' explains that once we grasp our essential kinship with the rest of mankind, we're driven by a rational wish to benefit as many people as possible, especially by educating them about practical wisdom, what is good and bad in life.

For Stoics, nevertheless, leading by example, as Zeno did, and improving ourselves in order to help others by providing a role model, is presumably more important than lecturing them. However, Stoics also recognized that when dealing with the majority of people, we must sometimes act or talk 'as if' we agreed with conventional values, treating 'indifferent' things as intrinsically good or bad. When we see someone weeping with sorrow, according to Epictetus, we should outwardly show sympathy, while guarding against inwardly agreeing with their faulty value judgements (*Enchiridion*, 16). A Sage might view the same 'catastrophe' with supreme indifference. It's nevertheless reasonable to 'prefer' bodily and external 'goods' for ourselves and other people, as long as we don't confuse them with Happiness.

The cardinal virtue that most obviously deals with the social sphere, with our relationships, is 'justice' (*dikaiosunê*). The Stoics use this word to encompass both dealing fairly with others and acting with benevolence towards them, wishing for them to flourish in accord with virtue, 'fate permitting', while distributing external things among them fairly. Seneca therefore says living with justice shall require a Stoic to 'count his friend as dear as himself, to think that an enemy can be turned into a friend, to rouse love in the former and temper hatred in the latter' (*Letters*, 95). When we act with wisdom and justice towards others, and really *believe* in what we're doing, we naturally feel goodwill towards them.

However, the 'healthy emotions' require consistency and that's only possible if our underlying attitude of benevolence is, in a sense, unconditional, and does not waver just because others change their behaviour, even if they act badly or like enemies. Crucially, although loving others is within our control, being loved in return is not, which means the Stoic should love others whether or not she is loved by them.

> Come on, let us see now if thou canst love disinterestedly. 'Thanks my good kinsman (brother, sister, friend), for giving me so generous a part, *that I can love though not beloved.*' (Shaftesbury, 2005, p. 108)

Epictetus therefore says that people can only truly be friends, and love one another, if they place their self-interest primarily in the wellbeing of their own character or volition, through the cultivation of wisdom, justice and the other virtues. Nevertheless, when we desire, first and foremost, to become just, fair and benevolent ourselves, in all of our relationships, we implicitly also wish others to flourish.

Key idea: Friendship and beauty in Stoicism

Zeno's ideal Stoic Republic was composed of Sages who lived in friendship and harmony with one another. The words used for 'friendship' also mean 'love' or 'affection' between friends, and intimate friendship appears to have been the purpose even of sexual love in Stoicism. Zeno also said that only perfect Sages are capable of true friendship and non-Sages are bound to be enemies. However, it's not clear if he meant this to be taken literally, as Stoics typically considered friendship, albeit of an imperfect sort, to be within our grasp and worth cultivating. Neither Zeno nor his successors claimed to be Sages, but they clearly didn't think of themselves as the enemies of their students! Anyway, Stoics certainly believed that it was important to emulate the ideal Sage, who exhibits love and friendship towards others.

The majority of people pursue friendship for mutual advantage, in terms of 'indifferent' things such as wealth or reputation but this is *not* the true friendship of the wise. Having friends around you is a 'preferred indifferent', naturally valued for its own sake but beyond our direct control. However, friendship in the truest sense means being yourself a friend *towards* other people because they *deserve* your friendship rather than for some 'external' advantage. Seneca actually says the Sage wants to have friends, although content and self-sufficient without one, mainly so he can exercise the virtues of friendship himself, in the relationship. However, gaining friends who reciprocate your affection, is described by

Cicero's 'Laelius' as second in importance only to *being* wise and good, suggesting he views it as the most valuable of all 'preferred indifferents'. Stoics therefore seek to acquire wise and good friends (and mentors) for themselves, presumably with the caveat 'fate permitting'.

According to the early Stoics, 'the good' (*agathos*) is also (*kalos*), which can mean either 'beautiful' or 'honourable' in Greek. For Stoics, these are virtually synonymous anyway because they consider the essence of human beauty to be virtue, rather than one's external appearance. Likewise, Xenophon said that Socrates frequently joked about the mutual love between himself and his close circle of friends but that 'anyone could see that what attracted him was the state of being gifted not with physical beauty but with excellence of mind and character' (*Memorabilia*, 4.1).

We consider each thing to be 'beautiful' in a way that's most appropriate to its nature: what makes a horse beautiful is different from what makes a necklace beautiful. When humans excel in terms of their essential nature, as rational animals, we make ourselves beautiful in the *true* sense, whereas folly and vice make us 'ugly' characters. Epictetus therefore says we should aim to 'beautify that which is our true nature – the reason, its judgements, its activities' (*Discourses*, 4.11).

Try it now: The 'circles' of Hierocles

The Stoic philosopher Hierocles, a contemporary of Marcus Aurelius, described psychological practices for expanding *oikeiôsis*, our sense of 'affinity' for others. He says our relationships can be represented as a series of concentric circles, radiating out from ourselves and our closest kin (see Figure 5.1). Stoics should attempt to 'draw the circles somehow towards the centre', voluntarily reducing psychological distance in their relationships. He even suggests verbal techniques, analogous to calling acquaintances 'friend' or calling close friends 'brother'. Hierocles elsewhere recommends treating our brothers as if they were parts of our own body, like our hands and feet. Zeno's saying that a friend is 'another self', perhaps likewise encourages us to take others deeper into the circle of our affinity and natural affection. Hierocles' comments about *oikeiôsis* might therefore be turned into a contemplative exercise:

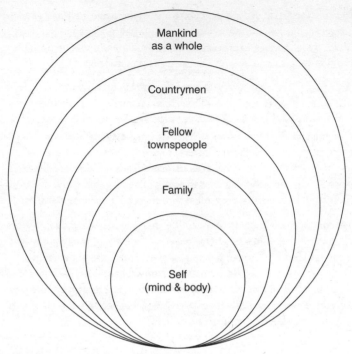

Figure 5.1 Simplified circles of Hierocles

1 Close your eyes and take a few moments to relax and focus your attention on your imagination.
2 Picture a circle of light surrounding your body and take a few moments to imagine that it symbolizes a growing sense of affection towards yourself as a rational animal, capable of wisdom and virtue, the chief good in life.
3 Now imagine that circle is expanding to encompass members of your family, or others who are very close to you, whom you now project natural affection towards, as if they were somehow parts of your own body.
4 Next, imagine that circle expanding to encompass people you encounter in daily life, perhaps colleagues you work alongside, and project feelings of natural affection towards them, as if they were members of your own family.

5 Again, let the circle expand further to include everyone in the country where you live, imagining that your feelings of affection are spreading to them also, insofar as they are rational animals akin to you, and capable of virtue.

6 Imagine the circle now growing to envelop the entire world and the whole human race as one, allowing your feelings of rational affection to spread out to every other member of the human race, developing a sense of kinship with them insofar as they possess reason and therefore the capacity for progressing towards wisdom.

Try to continue this attitude throughout your daily activity. Seneca argued that expanding natural affection into a philanthropic attitude that encompasses the rest of mankind teaches us to love more philosophically, without over-attachment to any specific individual. He goes so far as to say: 'he who has not been able to love more than one, did not even love that one much' (*Letters*, 63). The Sage is not infatuated with anyone. He loves everyone as much as he is able, while accepting that they are changeable and that one day they will die.

How does a Stoic love?

Epictetus asked his Stoic students, quite bluntly, 'How, then, shall I become loving and affectionate?' (*Discourses*, 3.24). His answer was that we should become affectionate in a manner consistent with the fundamental rules and doctrines of Stoic philosophy. If what we're calling 'love' or 'affection' makes us enslaved to our passions and miserable, then it's not 'good' for us, and that's a sign something is wrong.

> The Stoic loves other people in a very free, giving way. His love is not at all conditional upon its being reciprocated by the person loved. The Stoic does not compromise his own moral integrity or mental serenity in his love for others, nor is his love impaired by his knowledge of the mortality of his loved ones. Rather, the Stoic's love and natural affection are tempered by reason. His love and affection serve only to enrich his humanity, never to subject him to psychic torment. (Stephens, 1996)

First and foremost we should remind ourselves that some things are under our control, whereas others are not, and that only what is 'up to us' can truly be good, or part of our *eudaimonia*. One of the keys to grasping this is to love someone 'as a mortal', who may leave us at any time. We should also look to the example of wise and good men, such as Socrates, who loved his notoriously troublesome wife and children.

According to Epictetus, wise men remember that their families are merely parts of the whole of Nature (aka Zeus), which they love above all. The Stoic Sage therefore loves others in accord with the 'discipline of desire', accepting that the relationship is ultimately beyond his direct control, and that change or loss may be our fate. Love is thereby turned from an irrational 'passion', a kind of 'lust' or 'craving' characterized by over-attachment or dependence, into a more 'philosophical' or detached form of affection. This brings us into harmony with Nature by placing our relationships with others within the broader context of our relationship with the whole of existence.

By contrast, when we love without wisdom, we become overly attached to individual things or people, forgetting that external events are outside of our control. This causes us to revert to irrational 'craving', and to vacillate between love and hate depending on external circumstances: 'in short you grieve, fear, envy, are disturbed, you are changed' (*Discourses*, 2.22). Epictetus actually says all the enmity between people is down to a single judgement of this kind, they 'put themselves and what belongs to themselves in the category of things which lie outside the sphere of volition' (*Discourses*, 2.22). We see dogs playfully fawning on each other and might say that they 'love' one another as 'friends' but if we throw a piece of meat between them then a fight breaks out and they are quickly pitted against each other. Throw some land or money between father and son, he says, and we will see how fragile the bond is between them, as long as external things are confused with our ultimate good (*Discourses*, 3.24).

The Sage, by contrast, who has a firm grasp of the true nature of the good, will be unperturbed within himself, straightforward in his dealings with other wise men, and patient and tolerant towards the unwise, as though towards someone who is simply making a mistake with regard to things of great importance.

Try it now: Socrates' love charm (empathize like a Stoic)

Stoics believed that it is more important to love than to *be* loved. We're naturally *social* animals and so the goal of 'living in agreement with Nature' involves living harmoniously with the rest of mankind, even vicious people who treat us as their enemies. However, being loved by friends and family is highly preferable to being surrounded by enemies, fate permitting. Ironically, philosophers claim making yourself genuinely lovable is the best way to win genuine friends, by having a beautiful character and cultivating rational friendship towards others.

Seneca likewise joked that the Stoic philosopher Hecato of Rhodes had discovered a powerful love potion: 'if you wish to be loved, love' (*Letters*, 9). This notion that virtue is a powerful 'love charm' or 'magic spell' for winning friends and being loved, is attributed to Socrates in Xenophon's far older *Memorabilia* and *Symposium*. Nevertheless, although we may prefer others to reciprocate our affection, it's fundamentally 'indifferent' whether or not they actually do so.

How do we love people who don't reciprocate friendship and affection, though? Stoics carefully trained themselves to deal with difficult people, and particularly to avoid responding with anger. Following Socrates, they advise us to put ourselves in other people's shoes, and understand they have a reason for what they do, at some level (mistakenly) assuming their actions are appropriate and in their own interests. For example, try the following advice:

> Whenever you meet someone, say to yourself from the outset, 'What are his assumptions concerning what is fundamentally good and bad in life?' When someone acts like your enemy, insults or opposes you, remember that he was only doing what seemed to him the right thing, he didn't know any better, and tell yourself: 'It seemed so to him'. (*Enchiridion*, 42)

Do not be surprised when people act as they do. If they assume pleasure is the most important thing in life, or that wealth *or status* are intrinsically good, they are bound to act accordingly. Try to view them as foolish or misguided, like children, rather than malicious. Remember that they act like enemies because they fail to recognise it's in their own interest to be wise and just, and remain enslaved by attachment to the illusion of external 'goods'.

Remember this: Stoics do not have hearts of stone or iron

The early Stoics, probably Zeno and Chrysippus, and later Epictetus, Seneca and Marcus Aurelius, all challenged the misconception that Stoicism means being hard-hearted or unemotional. They say that being 'free from passions' does not mean being like a statue, or a man made of stone or iron. Although bodily and external things are beyond their direct control, Stoics nevertheless try to take 'appropriate action' to protect themselves and others, fate permitting. The fact they care about mankind perhaps opens them up to experiencing automatic emotional reactions, the 'proto-passions' which even the Sage experiences. However, the Sage, employing the virtues of courage and self-discipline, is not 'carried away' by his feelings, and does not allow them to develop into full-blown irrational 'passions'. He is therefore not *unfeeling* but rises above his initial emotional reactions, while exhibiting both reason and natural affection in his actions.

Why is the Sage important to Stoicism?

Stoics love virtue and those who embody virtue, which ultimately means the ideal Sage whose character is supremely 'beautiful' in Stoic terms. This concept of someone perfectly wise and good gives the aspiring Stoic direction, structure, and consistency in her practice.

> Since the dawn of Greek thought, the sage has functioned as a living, concrete model. Aristotle testifies to this in a passage from his *Protrepticus*: 'What more accurate standard or measure of good things do we have than the Sage?' (Hadot, 1995, p. 147)

The practice of emulating the ideal Stoic Sage is comparable in some ways to the imitation of Christ, Mohammed, Buddha and other founders of religions. However, the Sage was explicitly a fiction. Stoics were doubtful he ever existed in the flesh and if he did, they say he must be as rare as the Ethiopian phoenix. They used the concept as a *hypothetical* ideal to contemplate and compare themselves against. However, they also studied numerous examples of *relatively* 'wise and good' men, which played a very important role in their training. For example, Marcus reminded himself: 'to have constantly in mind one of the ancients who lived virtuously' (*Meditations*, 11.26).

At the start of his philosophical career, Zeno consulted the Oracle of Delphi and was advised to take on 'the complexion of the dead', which he took to mean he should adopt the lifestyle of an ancient philosopher. We're told that after reading Xenophon's *Memorabilia*, he immediately asked a nearby bookseller: 'Where are men like this Socrates to be found?' It appears the 'dead man' Zeno sought to study and emulate, first and foremost, was Socrates, who had been executed several generations earlier.

In the absence of a living Socrates, the Stoics trained themselves to contemplate his life so that, unlike his own wayward followers, they could continue to benefit from his example even long after his death. Although Zeno provided a living role model to his students, Stoics were not *dependent* on the presence of their beloved teacher, having learned to construct their own inner guide. Epictetus' students, rather impudently perhaps, asked him whether he was a Sage himself. He replied, 'By the gods, I wish and pray to be, but I am not yet!' 'I can, however, show you one', he continues, 'so that you no longer have to search for an example', and he refers them first to Diogenes and then Socrates (*Discourses*, 4.1). Epictetus mentions Diogenes the Cynic more than twice as often as Zeno, and Socrates *four* times as often. These were certainly the two main exemplars studied in his school, and this may possibly have been true also of Zeno's Stoicism.

Epictetus therefore frequently reminds his students that the life of Socrates is always available to them, ready to hand, as a model of excellence in various areas of life, and that we should contemplate his example if we seek freedom and *eudaimonia*. He goes so far as to state that now that Socrates is dead, the memory of him is of no less benefit to mankind, and perhaps even of greater benefit than when he was alive. He even dubs aspiring Stoics 'emulators of Socrates'.

> Socrates fulfilled himself by attending to nothing except reason in everything that he encountered. And you,

although you are not yet a Socrates, should live as someone who at least wants to be a Socrates. (*Enchiridion*, 51)

However, ancient Stoics contemplated and discussed a very wide range of individuals whose conduct was considered worth emulating. This might extend to traces of virtue in one's friends and family, and even one's opponents, or philosophers of rival schools, such as Epicurus or Plato.

Although there has perhaps never been a *perfect* mortal Sage, the Stoics believed that there was always at least *one* perfect *immortal* being: the god Zeus. The Stoic Zeus has perfect reason and virtue, like the Sage, and so the Stoics often refer to contemplating his perspective on human affairs because 'in everything one says and does one must act as an imitator of God' (*Discourses*, 2.14). Whether or not we believe in God, though, we might view their comments the basis of a kind of psychological exercise. Hercules, the favoured son of Zeus, was also revered by the Cynics and Stoics as a mythic hero and role-model. The ideal Sage is therefore godlike, a mortal having progressed so far that his wisdom and *eudaimonia* equal that of Zeus. The aspiring Stoic tries to make progress towards perfect wisdom by regularly contemplating the Sage and emulating his thoughts and actions.

Key idea: The nature of the Sage

The Stoic Sage is the hypothetical ideal of a perfect 'wise man' (*sophos* or *phronimos* in Greek; *homo sapiens* in Latin!). The word is often capitalized because it indicates something abstract rather than a real person. The Sage is supremely virtuous, a perfect human being, and the closest mortal approximation to Zeus. He is a completely good person, who lives a completely good and 'smoothly flowing' life of total serenity, he has attained perfect Happiness and fulfilment (*eudaimonia*). He lives in total harmony with himself, the rest of mankind, and Nature as a whole, because he follows reason and accepts his fate graciously, insofar as it is beyond his control. He has risen above irrational desires and emotions, to achieve peace of mind. Though he prefers to live as long as it is appropriate, and enjoys the 'festival' of life, he is completely unafraid of his own death.

He possesses supreme practical wisdom, justice and benevolence, courage and self-discipline. His character is absolutely praiseworthy, honourable and beautiful. Stoics therefore contemplate the hypothetical ideal of the Sage in order to grasp the perfection of human nature in general. Philosophers, 'lovers of wisdom', naturally love and admire him as the ideal embodiment of wisdom. This concept of perfection is something that Stoics can navigate by as they make progress towards virtue themselves. However, the Stoic Sage is notoriously paradoxical. He is the sort of person whom we can call truly rich even when he owns nothing, he is the only truly free man even when imprisoned by a tyrant, he is the only true friend even when persecuted as an enemy, he remains Happy and lives a blessed life even if subjected to the sum total of all external misfortunes.

How to contemplate the Sage

The exercise of contemplating the ideal Sage serves a number of closely-related functions in Stoic practice:

► A way of envisaging the goal of life, the perfection of human nature, in concrete form

► A guide to the correct (virtuous) attitude and appropriate course of action.

► An imaginary observer and commentator on our own actions, in the absence of a living Stoic teacher.

► A way of gaining 'cognitive distance' and preventing ourselves being 'carried away' by irrational or unhealthy impressions.

After having contemplated his qualities, Stoics would simply ask themselves 'What would the Sage do?' when confronted with difficult situations. Marcus Aurelius likewise reminds himself to 'Look into their minds, at what the wise do and what they don't' (*Meditations*, 4.38). In the same way, therefore, that a Christian might ask 'What would Jesus do?' Stoics asked themselves what the Sage, or exemplary individuals like Socrates, Diogenes, Zeno or Cato, would do.

Epictetus also says that we can prevent ourselves being 'carried away' by troubling impressions if we have the image of the Sage ready-to-hand and set that up as a contrast and comparison. One of the most widely-cited passages from Epictetus' *Handbook*, which reminds us that we are not upset by things themselves but by our judgements about them, is immediately followed by the example of Socrates, who saw death itself as neither good nor bad.

> Death, for instance, is nothing catastrophic, or else it would have appeared so to Socrates too. But the catastrophe lies in our own judgements about death, that death is catastrophic. (*Enchiridion*, 5)

Imagining someone plausibly judging the situation to be 'indifferent', gives us greater psychological flexibility and 'cognitive distance' from our automatic impression that it is awful. It gives us the space to consider whether our initial impression may be false.

Although he doesn't control their actions, and even Socrates had wayward students, the wise man does help others by his presence and the example he sets for them to emulate. Hence, Musonius says that 'to eat, drink, and sleep while being observed by a good man is very beneficial' (*Lectures*, 11). The followers of Epicurus therefore placed importance on possessing portraits or rings bearing his likeness, which may perhaps have helped them imagine his salutary presence accompanying them in life. The British Museum actually possess an ornate gem from the Roman imperial period depicting Zeno, the founder of Stoicism, which possibly served a similar purpose. Seneca likewise says that Stoics should keep likenesses of great men and even celebrate their birthdays. He lists his favourite philosophical role models as:

▶ Socrates

▶ Plato – perhaps *surprisingly* for a Stoic!

▶ Zeno, the founder of Stoicism

▶ Cleanthes, the second head of the Stoa

▶ Laelius the Wise, one of the first famous Roman Stoics

▶ Cato of Utica, the great Roman Stoic political hero

Elsewhere, he gives a beautiful account of this practice, drawing on Epicurean teachings:

> 'We need to set our affections on some good man and keep him constantly before our eyes, so that we may live as if he were watching us and do everything as if he saw what we were doing.' This, my dear Lucilius, is Epicurus' advice, and in giving it he has given us a guardian and a moral tutor – and not without reason, either: misdeeds are greatly diminished if a witness is always standing near intending doers. The personality should be provided with someone it can revere, someone whose influence can make even its private, inner life more pure. Happy the man who improves other people not merely when he is in their presence but even when he is in their thoughts! And happy, too, is the person who can so revere another as to adjust and shape his own personality in the light of recollections, even, of that other. (*Letters*, 11)

The image of this exemplary person should therefore be recalled frequently 'either as your guardian or as your model', as someone observing us, and perhaps offering guidance, or as an ideal to emulate. Seneca puts it nicely when he says that we need the concept of a genuinely 'wise and good' person as a standard against which to measure ourselves because 'Without a ruler to do it against you won't make the crooked straight.'

Try it now: What would the Sage do?

Begin by patiently contemplating what character the ideal Stoic Sage, someone with supreme wisdom and virtue, would have, until you're reasonably clear about this concept.

1 Before, during, and after, certain situations or tasks, ask yourself 'What would the ideal Stoic Sage do in this situation?'
2 You may find it helps to begin by contemplating historical or mythological characters, such as Hercules, Socrates or Cato, or possibly Stoic authors who you may know quite well, such as Seneca, Epictetus or Marcus Aurelius. How would one of these individuals deal with the events you face?

3 Alternatively, think of role models closer to home, such as friends, colleagues or family members whom you admire. What would they do that's worth emulating?

4 Most importantly, ask yourself what a true Sage, with *perfect* practical wisdom, would do. Go through the other virtues, particularly justice, courage, and self-discipline.

5 This should lead you to consider what you would do yourself, if you possessed greater wisdom and virtue.

Try to prepare for events using the example of a wise and good person as your guide, or to refer back to this afterwards and learn from the experience by considering how you could handle things differently in the future if following their example. Alternatively, imagine you're being *observed* by a perfectly wise and good Sage, who invisibly accompanies you, monitoring your thoughts, actions, and feelings. How might you respond differently to things, for example, if Socrates or Cato were watching you? What words of advice might they offer? Ask yourself both 'What would the *Sage* do?' and 'What would the Sage tell *me* to do?'

The seeds of wisdom in everyone

For Stoics, strictly-speaking, everyone except the Sage is equally foolish and devoid of virtue. However, some people have made more *progress* towards true wisdom and virtue than others. The later Stoics, in particular, frequently talk more loosely about the 'virtues' of ordinary people. They clearly thought we can learn by contemplating these traces or glimpses of 'virtues' in others, even if they are not perfect Sages. Indeed, contemplating the virtues of those around us, our friends, family and colleagues – perhaps even our 'enemies' or those who create difficulty in our lives – may have the additional benefit of improving our relationships with them. Hence, Seneca says 'we should equip our lives with distinguished models, and not always resort to the old ones', such as Socrates presumably (*Letters*, 83).

> For after all, those are the people we are obliged to take our models from; perfect wisdom, of course, they have not attained, though we are entitled to select those who

approach that ideal most closely. (Cicero, *Laelius: On Friendship*, 11)

Marcus Aurelius reminds himself to continually have before his mind's eye the virtues of his friends and associates, such as their modesty and generosity, because nothing brings such a healthy sense of rational joy as this simple contemplation. He carries out this psychological exercise throughout the whole first chapter of the *Meditations* by reviewing the virtues of the most significant individuals in his life, often condensed into a few words. The longest, and penultimate, section concerns his adoptive father, the Emperor Antoninus Pius.

> From my father [I might learn] gentleness, and an unwavering adherence to decisions reached deliberately; and indifference to so-called honours; and a love of work and thoroughness; and readiness to hear suggestions for the common good; and a dogged determination to give every man his due. (*Meditations*, 1.16)

He continues for several pages, finally concluding with the words:

> One might say of him what we're told [by Xenophon] of Socrates, that he could abstain from or enjoy those things that many people are not strong enough to refrain from and too much inclined to enjoy. But to have the strength to persist in the one case and to abstain in the other is typical of a man with a perfect and indomitable mind.

From his own Stoic teacher, Sextus of Chaeronea, Marcus says he learned 'the conception of a life in accordance with Nature' but also 'dignity without affectation, an intuitive consideration of friends, and tolerance of the unlearned and unreasoning'. Even if some among his friends, family and teachers were not very wise he could nevertheless identify their strengths and learn to imitate them. The first step to doing so, however, is putting them into words. By naming and describing the 'virtues' of others, Marcus helps himself to memorize and rehearse them throughout the rest of the exercises in the *Meditations*.

Remember this: Was anyone really a Sage?

Although the Stoics used many examples of 'wise and good' men from history, they tended to think of perfect wisdom as something unattained by any living person, even Zeno and the other founders of Stoicism. The Sage is therefore usually referred to as an abstract *hypothetical* ideal. However, some exemplary individuals had progressed closer to the ideal. Socrates was the Stoics' favourite example of a *near*-sage, and second to him came Diogenes the Cynic. Sometimes Zeno, Pythagoras, Heraclitus and others are held up as exemplary wise men. The late Roman Stoics also revered the famously austere Cato of Utica as symbolic of their ideal, and perhaps also the gentler figure of Laelius the Wise. However, ultimately the Sage is merely a guiding concept, planted in all of our minds by Nature – an *image* of the goal of life. Arguably, by refusing to unequivocally identify the Sage with any historical individual, the Stoics avoided turning their philosophy into a sect that worshipped Zeno or Socrates.

Focus Points

The main points to remember from this chapter are:

* 'Natural affection' and philanthropy are fundamental to Stoicism: the Sage is free from irrational passions but full of rational love and to love others is more valuable than to be loved by them in return.

* The Stoic loves others in the knowledge that they are mortal and autonomous beings, accepting the inevitability of change and loss as determined by Nature as a whole.

* The Stoics contemplated the hypothetical ideal of a perfect philosophical Sage or wise man, as well as countless exemplars of relative 'wisdom' and 'virtue' from history.

Next Step

The concept of the ideal Sage helps to guide the Stoic in the right direction in life, and the desire to achieve this goal unites all of her actions. Love and friendship are natural and healthy emotions that bridge the gap between the Stoic theory of irrational 'passions' and appropriate action, or between psychological therapy and ethical conduct. So we're now ready to consider the Stoic discipline of action in more detail.

The discipline of action (Stoic philanthropy)

In this chapter you will learn:

▶ *How Marcus Aurelius defined the Stoic 'discipline of action' in terms of three specific clauses, attached to every intention*

▶ *How to undertake any action with a 'reserve clause', having serene detachment from the outcome*

▶ *How actions are undertaken 'for the common welfare', in the service of mankind, and with a unified sense of purpose*

▶ *What the Stoics meant by action 'in accord with value', and the role of prudence and justice in selecting 'preferred' outcomes*

They [the Stoics] say that the good man experiences nothing contrary to his desire or impulse or purpose on account of the fact that in all such cases he acts with a 'reserve clause' and encounters no obstacles which are unanticipated. (*Anthology*, 2.115)

This is what you will see skilful ball players doing. None of them cares about the ball, as if that were something good or bad, but only about throwing it and catching it. [...] But if we throw or catch the ball with anxiety and fear, what fun is left, how will a player be in good form, and how will he keep his eye on the progress of the game? One will say 'throw', another will say 'Don't throw', and a third, 'You've had your turn'. That wouldn't be a game but a brawl. (Epictetus, *Discourses*, 2.5)

Self-assessment: Stoic attitudes and the discipline of action

Before reading this chapter, rate how strongly you agree with the following statements, using the five-point (1–5) scale below, and then re-rate your attitudes once you've read and digested the contents.

1. Strongly disagree, 2. Disagree, 3. Neither agree nor disagree, 4. Agree, 5. Strongly agree

1 'The best way to undertake any action is to completely accept from the outset that things may not turn out as planned.'

2 'All actions should ultimately be undertaken in the service of the common good, for the benefit of mankind.'

3 'Actions should be guided by the natural value we place on external things, although this is not the most important thing in life.'

What is the 'discipline of action'?

How can Stoics reconcile the discipline of desire's emphasis on acceptance with the need for action in life? Doesn't accepting things just make us into passive 'doormats'? How can action be undertaken in the real world, especially in complex human affairs, without compromising our serenity? These are some of the questions addressed by the Stoic 'discipline of action'.

Hadot calls Epictetus' *second* discipline, 'action in the service of mankind'. He interprets it as the virtue of living in harmony with other humans, the essence of Stoic 'philanthropy' or 'love of mankind.' In a more technical sense, Epictetus says that the 'discipline of action', deals with specific cases of our impulses to action (*hormê*), meaning our intention to seek or avoid certain things in life. He adds that, in general, it concerns the Stoic's duty or 'appropriate action' (*kathêkon*), and acting 'in an orderly fashion, upon good reasons, and not carelessly' (*Discourses*, 3.2).

As noted earlier, he adds that this means 'I ought not to be unfeeling [*apathê*] like a statue, but should maintain my relations, both natural and acquired, as a religious man, as a son, as brother, a father, a citizen.' In other words, it entails psychological exercises and strategies designed to help the Stoic student 'do the right thing' consistently, throughout the specific situations that arise in different areas of life, and in their relationships with other people, without compromising their commitment to virtue or their serenity. As Hadot concludes, Marcus Aurelius often seems to equate the discipline of action with the virtue of 'justice' (Hadot, 1998, p. 219). It must also be related to the process of 'appropriation' (*oikeiôsis*) that allows us to live in greater concord with the rest of mankind.

Marcus appears to place greater emphasis than Epictetus on acting with justice and benevolence towards the rest of mankind, although he may have known more of his teachings than we do today. When discussing the three disciplines he adds a very specific formula regarding the discipline of action, which he seems to attribute to Epictetus although it's not in his surviving *Discourses*. We should guard our 'impulses' to action attentively, being mindful that all our intentions are as follows:

1 I intend to do such-and-such '*with a reserve clause*' (*hupexairesis*), meaning that I add the caveat 'as long as nothing prevents me' or 'fate permitting', and undertake action with a 'philosophical attitude' towards the outcome, calmly accepting from the outset that things may not turn out as I planned.

2 I intend to do this *'for the common welfare'* of mankind (*koinônikai*), meaning that all of my actions, throughout life, are dedicated to a single external target, serving a common purpose or at least not conflicting with it, which was ultimately harmony and friendship among the community of mankind and their collective flourishing and Happiness.

3 I intend to do it 'in accord with value' (*kat' axian*), meaning with practical wisdom and justice, dealing fairly with others by selecting those 'preferred' external things that are reasonably judged to be most appropriate under these specific circumstances.

Hadot likewise summarizes the rules governing 'appropriate actions' or Stoic duties, and the discipline of action, as follows (Hadot, 1998, p. 183):

1 We must act in the service of all Nature or, in theological language, of God, by accepting our fate as ordained by the universe – this is really the essence of the Stoic 'reserve clause'.

2 We should aspire to love all of mankind, seeing ourselves as all merely different limbs of a single organism.

3 In our actions, we must respect the rational hierarchy of values which determine the appropriate thing to do.

These notions are all found in Epictetus but Marcus alone draws them together into such a clearly-defined *formula* for action. We've touched on the concept of acting 'in accord with value' in previous chapters. It means understanding the natural value of different external things in life, while distinguishing this from the supreme 'good' found in virtue. So we'll focus on the two remaining clauses below. Of these, the first is perhaps the most important, because *without* the 'reserve' clause no action can be undertaken securely.

Philanthropic actions have to be carried out magnanimously, in other words, with enough detachment from the outcome to maintain our sanity and peace of mind, rather than allowing ourselves to become frustrated when our desires are inevitably thwarted by external circumstances. 'To be in the world but not of the world', as Christians put it. Stoics would naturally *'prefer'* to live in Zeno's ideal Republic, among a community of enlightened friends, while *accepting* that the real world is more like the metaphorical 'festival' or 'public bathhouse', full of rough and tumble, unsavoury characters, noise and distraction.

Case study: James Stockdale in Vietnam

'On September 9, 1965, I flew at 500 knots right into a flak trap, at tree-top level, in a little A-4 airplane – the cockpit walls not even three feet apart – which I couldn't steer after it was on fire, its control system shot out', wrote James Stockdale. After being forced to eject over North Vietnam, as he descended towards the village below and certain incarceration as a prisoner of war, his last thought as a free man flashed across his mind: 'Five years down there, at least. I'm leaving the world of technology and entering the world of Epictetus!' (Stockdale, 1995, p. 189).

At the outset of US involvement in the Vietnam War, Stockdale was captured by a mob of 15 angry villagers who beat him to within an inch of his life. They snapped his leg, leaving him permanently lame, just like the crippled slave, Epictetus, whose ancient *Handbook* of Stoic philosophy Stockdale had devoured after studying philosophy as a masters student at Stanford University. He was then taken prisoner by the North Vietnamese army and transported to Hanoi where, as the highest-ranking US naval officer, he became the leader of a community of captured soldiers which, at its largest, numbered in excess of 400 men. Stockdale was imprisoned in an old French colonial 'dungeon' which formed part of a large communist prison called Hao Lo, nicknamed the 'Hanoi Hilton'. American POWs there were subjected to continual attempts at psychological reprogramming by prison officers and professional torturers.

Stockdale spent seven and a half years there, four of which were in isolation, two in leg irons. He was tortured 15 times by a brutal method called 'taking the ropes'. However, throughout his time in captivity, he was aided by the many passages from Epictetus that he had learned by heart and memorized, calling them his 'consolation' and 'secret weapon' during captivity. On his release, he became a military hero, one of the most highly-decorated officers in US Naval history, and reached the rank of Vice Admiral. He began lecturing others on the relevance of Stoic philosophy to modern military life and a collection of his talks and essays was published in the book *Thoughts of a Philosophical Fighter Pilot* (Stockdale, 1995).

His remarkable story shows ancient Stoicism being applied successfully to maintain psychological resilience in the face of some of the most gruelling adversity imaginable in the modern world. In situations like this, Stoics have to reconcile their natural wishes, or perceived duties, with the fact that little of their external environment may be under their direct control. Nevertheless, they always have enough freedom to maintain their integrity, or virtue, which remains their supreme goal.

Remember this: Acting 'in accord with value'

We discussed the Stoic theory of 'indifferents' earlier, and their concept that there exists a hierarchy of values derived from our animal nature. This begins with the self-preservation instinct, and extends through the natural 'affinity' we have for our offspring, to our family, friends and the rest of mankind. Although external things are of no value with regard to *eudaimonia*, living wisely requires dealing 'appropriately' with our body, and with property, money, and other people.

Undertaking action with a 'reserve clause'

One of Epictetus' *Discourses* is entitled: 'How can concern coexist with greatness of soul?'. He means: How can we reconcile our wish to act appropriately in life, and do the right thing, with the detachment required to maintain Stoic serenity? The discipline of action, which often requires an effort to *change* the world, in the name of justice, presents a challenge for the discipline of desire with its focus on *acceptance* and emotional 'indifference'. Epictetus' answer is that we should approach life somewhat as if it were a game. We are like men playing dice for enjoyment, whose goal is to play well, fairly and in good spirits, in accord with the rules. It makes no difference, ultimately, whether we win or lose. However, we must accept whatever roll of the dice falls to us by chance and make the best of it. We try to win the game, in order to be good players, but winning is not ultimately important and, to use the cliché, it's the 'taking part' that counts. The spirit in which we 'take part' in life, and fulfil our role, is likewise more important than the fate we meet, in terms of external success or failure. When things do not turn out as he might prefer, the Stoic might therefore say to himself:

> 'My intentions were good, and that's what really counts. Destiny has decided otherwise. I must accept its will and resign myself; the virtue I must practise now is not justice but the virtue of consent. I must switch from the exercise of the discipline of action to that of the discipline of desire.' (Hadot, 1998, p. 209)

The Stoics employed a clever psychological strategy that allowed them to interact with external events, including other people, without compromising their principle of only choosing to seek what is within their sphere of control. They refer to action being undertaken 'with a reserve clause, meaning that a caveat is added such as 'fate permitting', 'God willing' or 'if nothing prevents me'. It resembles the saying: 'Do what you must; let happen what may.' I cannot rationally *demand* that my actions must be successful in terms of their intended outcome, so I embark on every journey with an open mind, prepared to accept either victory or defeat with total equanimity.

All actions are therefore to be undertaken with mindfulness and complete acceptance of the fact that the outcome may not turn out as planned. However, this idea isn't only found in Stoicism. Christians used to write 'D.V.' or '*Deo Volente*' ('God willing' in Latin) at the end of letters to attach the same caveat. '*Insha'Allah*' (Arabic for 'God willing') means something similar in Islam. The New Testament actually contains a pretty clear description of this concept in a passage that sounds like something the Stoics might have written:

> Now listen, you who say, 'Today or tomorrow we will go to this or that city, spend a year there, carry on business and make money.' Why, you do not even know what will happen tomorrow. What is your life? You are a mist that appears for a little while and then vanishes. Instead, you ought to say, 'If it is the Lord's will, we will live and do this or that.' (*James*, 4.13-15)

Likewise, Jesus is portrayed as exclaiming 'My Father, if it is possible, may this cup be taken from me. Yet not as I will, but as you will' (*Matthew*, 26.39). The Stoic version can take different forms but the underlying concept and attitude remains the same. For instance, Seneca discusses the Stoic 'reserve clause' very clearly, in several writings, defining it as the formula:

> 'I want to do such and such, as long as nothing happens which may present an obstacle to my decision' (*On Peace of Mind*, 13)

Elsewhere he gives the example: 'I will sail across the ocean, if nothing prevents me.' The Sage therefore expects that something can always oppose his plans. He chooses to think this way, according to Seneca, because the emotional distress caused by failure is necessarily lighter for someone who has not promised success to himself beforehand.

> This is the reason why we say that all goes well with him, and that nothing happens contrary to his expectation, because he bears in mind the possibility of something happening to prevent the realization of his projects. It is an imprudent confidence to trust that fortune will be on our side. The wise man considers both sides: he knows how great is the power of errors, how uncertain human affairs are, how many obstacles there are to the success of plans. Without committing himself, he awaits the doubtful and capricious issue of events, and weighs certainty of purpose against uncertainty of result. Here also, however, he is protected by that 'reserve clause', without which he decides upon nothing, and begins nothing. (*On Benefits*, 4.34)

The Stoic student therefore employs a psychological strategy throughout life, which involves qualifying every intention by introducing a distinction between her will and external factors beyond her control, similar to Chrysippus' dichotomy of living in accord with both internal and external *nature*.

The *Handbook* of Epictetus says that Stoic students should completely withdraw both desire and aversion from external events, ceasing to judge them either 'good' or 'bad', accepting them in accord with the discipline of desire. However, we're nevertheless told the discipline of action requires us to continue 'selecting' external targets and appropriate actions, albeit 'lightly and without straining', and with the addition of the 'reserve clause'. (*Enchiridion*, 2)

We should also mentally rehearse any potential challenges of the day ahead, and the specific precepts required to cope wisely with them. When planning any activity, even something trivial like visiting a public bath (perhaps intended as a metaphor for the rough and tumble of life in general) imagine beforehand the type of things that could go wrong or hinder your plans. Then tell yourself: 'I want to do such-and-such and at the same time to keep my volition in harmony with Nature', by willingly accepting whatever happens (*Enchiridion*, 4). That way if your actions are later obstructed you can say: 'Oh well, this was not all that I had willed but also to keep my volition in harmony with Nature and I cannot do so if I am upset at what's going on.' In other words, 'living in agreement with Nature' means yielding to external events, when our fate demands it.

Marcus Aurelius specifically mentions action 'with a reserve clause' (*hupexhairesis*) about five times, citing Epictetus as one of his sources but adding a different perspective. Human consciousness has a kind of unlimited flexibility; he says, it can always adapt itself to whatever befalls us in life, and this is one of the most precious gifts of Nature. It needs nothing external to flourish because in the pursuit of all of its 'preferred' things in life, it can use the 'reserve clause', preparing itself to convert whatever external fortune befalls us into an opportunity for virtue and therefore fuelling our progress towards *eudaimonia*. The ancient Stoics believed the mind was composed of a fine material substance that resembled fire. So Marcus says that action with a 'reserve clause' allows the mind to make good use of *whatever* befalls us, 'just as fire when it gets the mastery of what is cast upon it' (*Meditations*, 4.1).

In the following dialogue, Marcus appears to be imagining a debate with the hypothetical ideal of a Stoic Sage acting as his mentor, or possibly recalling a conversation with a real Stoic teacher:

[Sage:] Action by action, you must build up your life, and be content, if each act attains its end; nobody can prevent you doing this.

[Marcus:] But surely something external will impede this!

[Sage:] No one can stop you from undertaking action with justice, self-discipline, and practical wisdom.

[Marcus:] But what if some other aspect of the activity is prevented?

[Sage:] Well, yes, but if you adopt an attitude of serene acceptance with regard to such an obstacle, and if you know how to return prudently to that which you are able to do, then another action will replace it, and it will fit in with the harmonious life we are talking about. (*Meditations*, 8.32)

Stoics should never be overly attached, in other words, to a particular outcome or course of action. If someone obstructs our attempts to act justly and benevolently towards others, in accord with the discipline of action, they just provide an opportunity for us to exercise the virtues of self-discipline and courage instead, in accord with the discipline of desire.

Key idea: 'with a reserve clause'

In the Stoic texts, particularly Epictetus and Marcus Aurelius, we find the technical Greek term *hupexhairesis* meaning to act 'with a reserve clause', 'with reservation', or 'with an exception' in mind. In Seneca the same concept is referred to in Latin as *exceptio*. This means acting with a kind of *detached* attitude towards the outcome, which is made *exempt* or treated as an *exception* from what is desired. The basic concept is that the Sage always undertakes action with this reservation in mind, so that he thinks: 'I will do such-and-such, fate permitting' or 'if God wills it', etc.

The Sage's intentions are therefore never thwarted because he only wishes to do what nothing prevents him from achieving. By contrast, irrational passions, such as 'craving' cannot be undertaken with a reserve clause because they seek to obtain something outside of our direct control. However, actions are judged 'good' or 'evil', vicious or virtuous in Stoicism, based purely on the intention underlying them, regardless of their consequences (Cicero, *De Finibus*, 3.32).

Try it now: Acting with the 'reserve clause'

Pick a task to undertake with the 'reserve clause' in mind. Focus on your intention to act with integrity, while accepting the outcome with equanimity. Follow these steps:

1 Plan something that you're going to do later today, with regard to external events.
2 Try to imagine the various obstacles that could get in your way and willingly accept that things could go against your wishes.
3 Rehearse saying to yourself, 'I will do such-and-such', adding the caveat, '...if nothing prevents me' or 'fate permitting'.
4 If things don't turn out as you may have wished, focus your attention on accepting the outcome anyway, as taught by the discipline of *desire*.

Try to do this more and more, until you're able to approach most situations with the same attitude, willing yourself to accomplish any task you're engaged in with a 'reserve clause', and keeping your will in harmony with events.

The Stoic archer

Cicero's 'Cato' explains the Stoic theory of action by using the wonderful metaphor of an archer. The archer can notch his arrow and draw his bow to the best of his ability, but once the arrow has flown he can only wait to see if it hits the target. An unexpected gust of wind could blow it off course or the target (perhaps a wild animal) could move. The intention is under his control, as is the initial 'impulse' or act of setting the arrow in motion, but the result is ultimately down to 'fate' – or external variables beyond his control.

The Stoics sometimes distinguish between the 'target' (*skopos*) pursued in an action, literally the mark we fix our gaze upon, and the action's 'end' or purpose (*telos*), literally its 'completion' or 'fulfilment'. 'Cato' presents this as a metaphor for the distinction between 'preferred' external things and the goal of life. Although the Stoics seek many of the same things in life as the majority of other people, such as physical health and friendship, they do so in a subtly *detached* manner. The true 'goal' of life is practical wisdom, or virtue, and this consists in the 'art of living', the way we go about doing things in the world, regardless of the outcome.

The external 'target' of an action, for example, might be to benefit friends by educating them and encouraging them towards virtue, as Socrates did. However, whether that succeeds or not is partly in the hands of fate, as Socrates' less reputable students demonstrate. The goal of a Sage would not be to benefit others, which is beyond his control, but rather simply to do his best to benefit them. Like the archer firing his arrow, his work is complete if he has done his best, acting with the virtues of justice and benevolence, whether or not he actually succeeds in hitting his target.

The target we fix our gaze on (*skopos*), the outcome of any action, is always essentially in the future. By contrast, our *intention* to achieve it exists in the present moment. If we set out with the right attitude, as it were, we have already attained the end (*telos*) of virtue, from the very start of our endeavours. As we've seen, Epictetus makes a similar comparison between life and playing a game of ball. Although we try to possess and pass the ball, we don't consider it to be of any intrinsic value – it's just a game. What matters is that we play *well*, in a sportsmanlike (virtuous) manner, and that often means not being upset when the game is going against us.

We might also compare life to dancing or singing for pleasure, the goal of which is achieved in the performance, by dancing or singing well, rather than some external outcome. However, a physical performance can be interrupted, whereas our moral intention is complete from the outset and cannot be broken into parts. This is important to the Stoics because it means we can never be obstructed from achieving virtue – it happens in the blink of an eye, as soon as a virtuous decision is made, in the 'here and now'. Epictetus therefore asked his students: 'Can you find me a single man who cares how he does what he does, and is interested, not in what he can get, but in the manner of his own actions?' (*Discourses*, 2.16). It's the way we go about things that matters, not whether we succeed or not. As Seneca puts it: 'In short, the wise man looks to the purpose of all actions, not their consequences; beginnings are in our power but Fortune judges the outcome, and I do not grant her a verdict upon me' (*Letters*, 14).

Key idea: 'Impulses' and 'appropriate actions'

'Impulses' (*hormê*) are basically the beginning of voluntary actions, in Stoic psychology. They're somewhere between what we mean by an 'intention' and a voluntary 'action', and they're based on acts of 'assent' to particular impressions. For example, we're told 'impulses' can take the form of 'purpose', 'effort', 'preparation', 'choice', 'wish' and 'wanting'. Passions, such as fear and desire or suffering and pleasure, are a particularly important form of impulse. When our intentions are in accord with reason and the natural value of things, our actions are judged 'appropriate' to the circumstances.

Zeno coined the term 'appropriate actions' (*kathêkonta*), because of its similarity to the expression 'applying to certain people' (*kata tinas hêkein*), to refer to the right things for specific individuals to do in *specific* situations. Often this can only be judged on the basis of probability, as what it seems reasonable to 'prefer', such as whether it is appropriate to lend someone money or not on a particular occasion. By contrast, we can grasp with certainty that it is 'good' to have virtue and an intention ('impulse') to act in accord with justice. The Stoic technical jargon distinguishes between *kathêkonta*, 'appropriate actions' which anyone can accomplish, and *katorthômata*, 'perfect actions', which are only accomplished by the Sage (Long, 2002, p. 257). Any fool can do the right thing but the Sage acts both appropriately and with insight, on the basis of perfect knowledge, wisdom and virtue.

Remember this: The Sage undertakes everything with the 'reserve clause'

Marcus lists the 'reserve clause' first when describing the three clauses that define the Stoic discipline of action (*Meditations*, 11.37). Without adding this caveat to every intention, the Stoic cannot securely live in accord with virtue while interacting with the world of 'indifferent' things and other people. In theological language, he wills what is naturally preferred for himself, his friends, and the community of mankind, but only as long as God wills the same thing. If events turn out otherwise, the Stoic must accept the fact, and adapt accordingly, rather than feeling frustrated. So, as Seneca puts it, even a perfect Sage employs this strategy when planning any action in life.

Undertaking action 'for the common welfare' of mankind

We know the Stoics placed great importance on contemplating the hypothetical ideal of the Sage, as a guide in life, but could the hypothetical ideal of a *community* of Sages, the dream of an ideal Stoic 'Republic', have served a similar function? Marcus Aurelius wrote in his journal: 'Don't wait for Plato's Republic! Rather, be content if one tiny thing makes some progress, and reflect on the fact that what results from this tiny thing is no tiny thing at all!' (*Meditations*, 9.29). As we've seen, Marcus also claimed that Epictetus' 'discipline of action' involved adding the clause 'for the common welfare' (of mankind) to every intention.

One way of interpreting this, arguably, would be that the discipline of action requires us to dedicate every action, from the outset, to a single underlying target, the ideal 'Republic' or enlightened philosophical community. Despite being Emperor of Rome, the most politically and militarily powerful Stoic who ever lived, Marcus appears to be satisfied even if his individual actions are only 'tiny' steps in this general direction. Indeed, throughout the *Meditations*, he continually reminds himself to dedicate his actions to the common welfare of mankind, as fellow-citizens of the cosmos.

However, it's probably not literally Plato's *Republic* that he has in mind. Roman authors tend to refer loosely to *any* philosophical account of the ideal society as 'Plato's Republic'. For example, the Roman statesman Cicero criticized his friend Cato, another statesman and a famously *uncompromising* Stoic, for acting as if he were already living in 'Plato's Republic' rather than being willing to play *realpolitik*. The founding text of Stoicism was Zeno's *Republic* (*Politeia*), which contrasted sharply with

Plato's book of the same name and contained many criticisms of the Platonic ideal society. Marcus and Cicero are therefore speaking loosely and it's more likely to be the Stoic ideal that they have in mind. One key difference was that Plato's *Republic* was notoriously hierarchical and divided into three broad social classes, harmony depending upon each individual knowing his place, whereas Zeno's *Republic* apparently treated all citizens as equal. It seems that there would be no need for money, weapons, law courts, or temples in the ideal Stoic Republic and men and women would all wear the same kind of clothing.

Marcus elsewhere defines the supreme goal of life, which is to live as a faithful citizen of the greatest 'City or Republic', the whole of Nature, obeying its laws and following its guidance, in even the least of our actions. This means seeing the physical city or country in which we live as merely one small region of the Universal City, the whole of Nature, which takes precedence. Epictetus therefore asks 'What is a man?'

> A part of a city. If the first city, that is, which is made up of gods and men; then of that which is so called in order to come as close as possible to it, and which is a tiny image of the whole. (*Discourses*, 2.5)

For the Stoics, when we come to realize that all of mankind are essentially kin, we come to view ourselves as merely parts of a greater community. As Cicero's 'Cato' puts it, from the fact that we are all perceived as parts of a single Universal City, it follows naturally that we should value the common good more than our own.

In a sense, we all already live in the cosmic Republic, although only the Sage can truly become a citizen, because he obeys its laws by 'living in agreement with Nature'. Nevertheless, by living as aspiring Stoics, we all make progress towards a better world, an ideal community. Epictetus' aim of having the 'tiny city' in which we live, our actual community, comes as close as possible to the realization of the ideal Stoic Republic would presumably have to be classed as a 'preferred indifferent', because its attainment depends on other people, and is always necessarily outside our direct control. It could only be pursued with the 'reserve clause', the caveat 'fate permitting'.

As in Cicero's metaphor of the archer, Marcus uses the term *skopos* to describe the external 'target' of improving the common welfare of mankind and that of the political state. He says we cannot live consistently, in agreement with Nature, unless we always have the same target in view, and that target needs to be clearly defined: 'We must we set before ourselves as our target the common welfare and the welfare of the political state.' An important aspect of the discipline of action that the Stoic aspires to is to act in a unified nature, dedicating all of her actions to a single underlying purpose in life. However, this can be understood to consist of *two* elements: the internal 'goal' of acting with justice, and the corresponding external 'target' of benefitting the rest of mankind, by taking even miniscule steps towards the realization of the ideal Stoic Republic. We're likewise told Chrysippus held that even the Sage, rather than withdrawing from the world of men, 'will take part in politics, *if nothing hinders him*', so as to promote good and restrain evil among his fellow citizens.

Key idea: Zeno's 'dream' of an ideal Stoic Republic

According to Plutarch, Zeno wrote the *Republic* 'picturing as it were a dream or image of a philosopher's well-regulated society', in other words the *Republic* encouraged its readers to imagine the hypothetical ideal of a perfectly harmonious society (*On the Fortune of Alexander*, 329a). He says that the *Republic*, which was widely-admired, centred on the doctrine 'that we should arrange our households and live our lives, not as members of different nations or political states, but viewing others as fellow-citizens of the world, having one way of life, like that of a herd grazing together and nurtured by a common law.'

Most intriguingly, in stark contrast to the common image of Stoics as unemotional, it seems Zeno's ideal community was based on *love*. We're told Zeno wrote in the *Republic* that 'Eros is a god which contributes to the city's security' because he is a god of 'friendship and freedom', who provides harmony between people (*Athenaeus*, 561c). Although *erôs* normally means sexual love, Zeno was possibly influenced by the concept of 'Platonic love', a non-sexual love based on the perception of beauty as residing in the *soul* or character of others rather than their physical appearance.

The Stoics also tried to think of all mankind as a single community of rational beings – all children of Zeus and citizens of the same universe. Although none of us, strictly-speaking, possess true wisdom and virtue, Marcus and other late Stoics appear to view it as their duty to love the rest of mankind despite their imperfection, because the mere fact they possess reason gives them the *potential* for virtue. Wishing to live in friendship and harmony with those people among whom fate has set us, might be seen as a first tiny step towards the perfectly enlightened community of the ideal Stoic Republic. The early Stoics studied Zeno's *Republic* and the Stoa itself may have been intended as a small community of friends somehow modelled on that ideal.

Try it now: Dreaming of the ideal Stoic Republic

Take some time to contemplate what the ideal Stoic society would be like and try to picture it in your mind, as a kind of utopian fantasy. Imagine a city populated by men and women even wiser and more honourable than someone of Socrates' calibre, for example.

1 Just begin from the premise that it consists of a community of perfectly wise and just individuals, Stoic Sages, who are naturally friends with one another.

2 What room would there be for conflict? How would they handle property or money?

3 What would their attitude to one another be like, and how might they interact?

4 How would they handle marriage and care for their children? According to the Stoics, children are incapable of genuine practical wisdom or virtue, until they grow old enough to develop reason and self-control. Consider how an ordinary 'imperfect' adult would be treated in the ideal Republic, someone who lacks practical wisdom, like a child compared to the Sage. Try to relate this thought-experiment to your own life, by thinking of the community of people closest to you, your friends and family, as a potential microcosm of the Stoic Republic.

Try it now: Dedicating action to 'the common welfare' of mankind

Committing all of your actions to serve the common welfare of mankind might seem like a pretty tall order! However, there are some small initial steps that you should begin by taking and, as Marcus puts it, be content with tiny steps in a positive direction, 'and reflect on the fact that what *results* from this tiny thing is no tiny thing at all!' (*Meditations*, 9.29).

1 Throughout the day, before undertaking any action, ask yourself with regard to your internal attitude and your intentions: 'How does this accord with practical wisdom and moral excellence?' and 'How does this contribute to Happiness and fulfilment?'

2 Also ask yourself, in terms of the external outcome you anticipate: 'How does this action serve the community of mankind?'

3 Even if some actions don't appear to serve this higher purpose, at least they may be approved if they don't *conflict* with the common welfare of mankind.

The awareness that all of your actions consciously refer back to a single underlying purpose can be a very powerful thing, and this is undoubtedly part of what the early Stoics meant by saying that the supreme goal of life was 'living in agreement' or living consistently.

Remember this: 'Living in agreement'

Zeno originally defined the supreme goal of life as 'living in agreement', and this was expanded into 'living in agreement with Nature', perhaps by one of his successors. However, the Stoics generally appear to have understood *eudaimonia* and wisdom to require consistency in life, in the sense that one's life is structured around a unifying sense of purpose. Marcus repeatedly says that this comes from acting with wisdom and justice, referring every action somehow to the common welfare of mankind, and doing nothing at random or without consideration. This consistency is an important part of the discipline of action.

Focus Points

The main points to remember from this chapter are:

* According to Marcus Aurelius, Epictetus' discipline of action instructs Stoics to continually ensure that all their actions and intentions are 'with a reserve clause', 'for the common welfare', and 'in accord with value'.

* Even the Sage undertakes no action without anticipating potential obstacles and failure, in accord with the 'reserve clause' – 'I will do this, as long as nothing prevents me'.

* When actions are thwarted or events turn against us, the Stoic accepts external things as ultimately 'indifferent', in accord with the discipline of desire.

Next Step

The discipline of action naturally leads us into the subject of Stoic 'premeditation', or the anticipation of planned actions and their potential outcomes. Epictetus makes it clear that anticipating setbacks allows us to ensure that we undertake action 'with a reserve clause', in conformity to the discipline of action, but also gives us greater scope, through mental imagery, to practise the discipline of desire and Stoic acceptance.

7

Premeditation of adversity

In this chapter you will learn:

▶ *How to use one of the best-known resilience-building techniques of ancient Stoicism: the* praemeditatio malorum *or 'premeditation of adversity'*

▶ *How to prevent philosophical premeditation from turning into unhelpful worry*

▶ *How different psychological processes can be employed during philosophical premeditation*

Whoever it was who said, 'Fortune, I have made a pre-emptive strike against you, and I have deprived you of every single loophole,' was not basing his confidence on bolts, locks and fortifications, but on principles and arguments which are available to anyone who wants them. [...] For if the mind is self-indulgent, and takes the easiest courses all the time, and retreats from unwelcome matters to what maximizes its pleasure, the consequence is weakness and feebleness born of lack of exertion; but a mind which trains and strains itself to use rationality to conceive an image of illness and pain and exile will find that there is plenty of unreality, superficiality and unsoundness in the apparent problems and horrors each of them has to offer, as detailed rational argument demonstrates. (Plutarch, *On Contentment*, 467c)

Keep before your eyes day by day death and exile, and everything that seems catastrophic, but most of all death; and then you will never have any abject thought, nor will you crave anything excessively. (*Enchiridion*, 21)

Self-assessment: Stoic attitudes towards future adversities

Before reading this chapter, rate how strongly you agree with the following statements, using the five-point (1–5) scale below, and then re-rate your attitudes once you've read and digested the contents.

1. Strongly disagree, 2. Disagree, 3. Neither agree nor disagree, 4. Agree, 5. Strongly agree

1 'It's important to anticipate setbacks and remove the sense of shock or surprise from them.'

2 'Rather than avoiding thinking about future problems we should train ourselves to face the worst with composure.'

3 'If I face my fears patiently in my imagination, for long enough, my anxiety will eventually reduce.'

Why is anticipating future 'misfortunes' important?

What's the worst that could happen to you in life? How would you cope? How prepared are you for the typical setbacks that befall other people? In this chapter, we'll explore one of the most powerful tools in the Stoic armamentarium: *foresight*. Indeed, when asked what he'd learned from philosophy, Diogenes the Cynic reputedly said, 'To be prepared for every fortune'. Epictetus actually goes so far as to say that studying Stoic philosophy necessarily means 'preparing yourself for future events'. Seneca likewise says we should harden ourselves in advance against the troubles that may befall even the most powerful in life, remembering it is always possible a robber or an enemy could 'hold his sword to your throat'.

As noted earlier, modern English, we speak of someone being 'philosophical' in hard times, something synonymous with being 'stoical' in the popular sense: calm in the face of adversity. Horace likewise wrote: 'Remember to keep a calm and balanced mind in the face of adversity' (*Odes*, 2.3). The Stoics trained themselves to maintain equanimity and freedom from emotional suffering in the face of seeming 'misfortunes' by regularly visualizing and preparing to cope with them long in advance.

This well-known psychological technique was called the 'premeditation of adversity' by Seneca (*praemeditatio malorum*, in Latin). Irvine describes this as 'the single most valuable technique in the Stoics' toolkit' (Irvine, 2009, p. 68). He coined the term 'negative visualization' to refer to Stoic premeditation and this is fairly close to the literal meaning of *praemeditatio malorum*. However, for the Stoics, the key point is that the apparent or so-called 'misfortunes' being imagined are not actually *'negative'* at all, but completely *indifferent*. It's fundamentally this indifference to feared 'catastrophes' that the Stoic seeks to strengthen, through *prospective* meditation involving exposure to them in mental imagery. Neither worrying about feared 'catastrophes' nor avoiding thinking about them but rather facing them calmly, rationally, and patiently, while maintaining a 'philosophical attitude'.

Modern authors like Irvine and Burkeman are particularly attracted to Stoicism because they see it as providing a more psychologically credible alternative to the superficial tactic of 'positive thinking', which is so common nowadays. 'Applying their stringent rationality to the situation, the Stoics propose a more elegant, sustainable and calming way to deal with the possibility of things going wrong: rather than struggling to avoid all thought of these worst-case scenarios, they counsel actively dwelling on them, staring them in the face' (Burkeman, 2012, p. 32).

In the ancient world, people were less likely than we are today to assume that 'positive thinking' is healthy, and they were probably correct. The goal of philosophy is to cultivate *rational* and *realistic* beliefs, not 'trying to think positively'. Recent psychological research tends to show that people who are able to accept unpleasant thoughts and feelings, without being overwhelmed by them, are more resilient than people who try to distract themselves or avoid such experiences, through strategies such as positive thinking (Hayes, Strosahl, & Wilson, 2012; Robertson, 2012).

Although, as we shall see, modern research can identify several psychological mechanisms underlying mental imagery techniques of this kind, the Stoics believed that premeditation was mainly an opportunity to develop virtue by rehearsing the core maxims of their philosophy. Hadot therefore says that through premeditation of adversity, philosophers wanted not merely to soften the 'shock of reality', and achieve greater tranquillity, but also to steep their minds in the principles of Stoicism and assimilate them more deeply (Hadot, 2002, p. 137).

Other psychological processes may help but the chief goal in Stoicism must be to grasp virtue and thereby to attain Happiness and wellbeing (*eudaimonia*). A well-known fable of Aesop expresses a similar notion very nicely: A wild boar was sharpening his tusks against a tree when a fox came by and asked him why he was doing this. 'I don't see the reason,' remarked the fox, 'there are neither hunters nor hounds in sight; in fact right now I can't see any threat at all.' The boar replied, 'True, but when danger does arise, I'll have other things on my mind than sharpening my weapons.' In times of peace, prepare for war. For the Stoics, this preparation was lifelong, and both physical and mental:

> It is in times of security that the spirit should be preparing itself to deal with difficult times; while fortune is bestowing favours on it then is the time for it to be strengthened against her rebuffs. In the midst of peace, the soldier carries out manoeuvres, throws up earthworks against a non-existent enemy and tires himself out with unnecessary toil in order to be equal to it when it is necessary. If you want a man to keep his head when the crisis comes, you must give him some training before it comes. (Seneca, *Letters,* 18)

Antisthenes said that 'Virtue is a weapon of which man cannot be deprived' (*Lives,* 6.1) and for the Stoics and Cynics life resembled warfare. We can therefore think of the Stoic virtues and precepts as 'weapons', and premeditation as training in preparation for battle.

> The exercise of meditation allows us to be ready at the moment when an unexpected – and perhaps dramatic – circumstance occurs. In the exercise called *praemeditatio malorum* [by Seneca], we are to represent to ourselves poverty, suffering and death. We must confront life's difficulties face to face, remembering that they are not evils, since they do not depend on us. This is why we must engrave striking maxims in our memory, so that, when the time comes, they can help us accept such events, which are, after all, part of the course of nature; we will thus have these maxims and sentences 'at hand'. What we need are persuasive formulae or arguments (*epilogismoi*), which we can repeat to ourselves in difficult circumstances, so as to check movements of fear, anger, or sadness. (Hadot, 1995, p. 85)

In other words, philosophy, rational arguments, and the precepts that follow from them, were seen as our greatest defence against the vicissitudes of Fortune.

Seneca is the Stoic who has most to say about the premeditation of adversity as a form of moral and emotional resilience training. For example, he responds to a terrible calamity suffered by one of his friends with the advice that we should project our thoughts ahead of us at every turn, and anticipate every possible setback, not just ordinary events, but catastrophes such as exile, torture, warfare and shipwreck. This was approached, quite systematically, as a routine contemplative exercise by Stoics. However, Seneca proceeds to emphasize that Stoic contemplation of the transience of things should moderate our distress.

Rather than worrying about these things in an anxious manner, Stoics proceed calmly and contemplatively, patiently evaluating the perceived threat, particularly whether or not it is truly 'evil' or catastrophic. Facing up to perceived 'catastrophes', these blows of circumstance, we become aware that the reality is 'never as serious as rumour makes it out to be' (*Letters*, 91). The general precept of Stoic ethics should be the basis of premeditation: That some things are under our control and others are not, and that external things, outside our volition, are fundamentally indifferent to us. Hadot therefore describes it as 'a kind of examination of conscience in advance'.

No matter what 'catastrophes' the Stoic imagines befalling her, in this thought experiment, the result is always the same: external events are neither 'good' nor 'bad', only our responses to them are. The majority of us are like small children who are frightened of people wearing scary masks but immediately reassured when they are removed. We will come to see that anticipated 'catastrophes' are really indifferent to us through calm, rational contemplation of their true nature.

We should therefore prove to ourselves that we have genuinely understood the nature of misfortunes we have often heard about by thinking 'of anything that can happen as going to happen'. As Epictetus put it, the Stoic philosophy works like the magical Wand of Hermes: every 'misfortune' it touches turns into true *good* fortune, when used wisely. While contemplating perceived 'disasters' such as bankruptcy or physical injury we might literally say, as he advises: 'Non-volitional, [therefore] not bad!'

Training herself to remember the Stoic definition of the good, and related precepts, while rehearsing every possible 'misfortune' that might realistically befall her in life is the basis of the Stoic's emotional resilience or invulnerability to fortune. In the absence of real adversity, she seeks out challenges in her imagination, by confronting future hardships well in advance. Not only is she thereby prepared for whatever life will throw at her but she also has infinite opportunity for training herself in Stoic endurance and self-discipline, by not confining herself to the challenges of the present moment. She'll have undertaken what Epictetus called a 'winter training', the kind of intensive military training undertaken by ancient armies in preparation for a decisive battle.

As the ultimate 'misfortune' with which Stoicism is concerned is one's own death, the technique of premeditation also leads into the broader concept of contemplating one's own mortality. Stoics must have the courage to think the unthinkable, and to repeatedly confront 'catastrophic' events in their mind that the majority of people shy away from, in order to firmly grasp their 'indifferent' nature. As Hadot observes, the premeditation of adversity links the discipline of desire to the discipline of action, by encouraging us to overcome our anxiety in advance, while anticipating obstacles and planning appropriate actions, with the 'reserve clause' in mind. Indeed, the technique of premeditation seems to resemble certain aspects of the morning meditation routine described by some Stoics. For instance, Marcus Aurelius appears to describe a practice resembling premeditation of adversity, to be carried out after awakening each day:

> Say to yourself at daybreak: I shall come across the meddling busy-body, the ungrateful, the overbearing, the treacherous, the envious, and the antisocial. All this has befallen them because they cannot tell good from evil. (*Meditations*, 2.1)

So it appears that in addition to contemplating the fact that external events are neither good nor evil but indifferent, the Stoic may also anticipate frustrations caused by other people, in a similar manner, but perhaps with the additional observation that their actions are caused by their own lack of wisdom, their ignorance of the true nature of 'the good' and the indifference of the external things they concern themselves with. Epictetus says that when someone appears to disagree with us or we find ourselves in conflict, we must recognise that he simply wants what he assumes is right, and tell ourselves: 'It seemed so to him' (*Enchiridion*, 42).

Key idea: Praemeditatio malorum

Philosophers of different traditions, but especially the Stoics, most notably Seneca, refer to the value of a psychological exercise that involves repeatedly imagining future 'catastrophes' as if they're happening right now. In the classical literature, examples such as exile, illness, poverty and bereavement are commonly employed, but also one's own death. This is done, according to the Stoics, to strengthen the mind, exercising the virtues and the judgements upon which they are based, particularly the principle that such external events can never truly be 'bad' but are merely indifferent with regards to one's essential nature as a rational being.

Human beings can excel, in other words, in the face of unjust persecution and even death, as the examples set by Stoic heroes show, such as Hercules, Socrates, Diogenes and Cato. Prospective meditation upon future 'catastrophes', allows us to rehearse adopting a 'philosophical attitude', reminding ourselves that nothing external is intrinsically bad. The Stoics also emphasize that by anticipating possible setbacks in life we take the sting out of them by removing the irrational sense of surprise or shock experienced if they do occur. Premeditation involves temporarily imagining events as if they were happening *right now*, but you may remember that Stoics only attribute 'selective value' to *future* events. So premeditation must have involved viewing 'dispreferred' events as if they were *completely* 'indifferent' ones, and no longer negative in any sense.

Remember this: External 'negative' events or 'misfortunes' are indifferent in Stoicism

Irvine calls this 'negative visualization' (Irvine, 2009). However, the word 'negative' is potentially misleading and risks missing the point of the exercise. The basic principle of Stoicism, and this exercise, is that so-called external 'misfortune' isn't really *negative* at all. According to

Stoicism, external events are neither intrinsically good ('positive') nor bad ('negative'), but merely indifferent. Hence, the purpose is to rehearse placing more importance upon one's responses to events rather than events themselves. As Hadot says, the Stoic rehearses future setbacks 'remembering that they are not evil' (Hadot, 1995, p. 85) or, as modern psychologists say, that they are not genuinely 'catastrophic'. Epictetus even taught his students to respond to thoughts about feared events by saying quite bluntly: 'this is *nothing* to me!' It is not even a 'negative event' to me.

Case study: The execution of Seneca

There is perhaps no better example of Stoic premeditation than the famous account of Seneca's death (65 AD) recorded in the *Annals* of the Roman historian Tacitus. Seneca was appointed personal tutor and advisor to Nero when, aged only 17, he became Emperor in 54 AD. However, as he grew older and rose in power, Nero became increasingly paranoid and unpredictable. He ordered several brutal murders, including his own brother and mother, and is now remembered as one of the most tyrannical and corrupt of Roman emperors.

A plot, involving about forty people, called the Pisonian conspiracy, was therefore formulated to murder Nero and replace him with the statesman Gaius Calpurnius Piso acting as emperor. When the conspiracy was exposed, Nero jumped at the opportunity to accuse Seneca of treason and a tribune was sent to give him notice of Nero's allegations. Seneca insisted he had no involvement and when the tribune returned this news Nero angrily asked if the Stoic was suitably afraid of his impending death. The officer reported that: 'he saw no signs of fear, and perceived no sadness in his words or in his looks', which simply infuriated Nero. The Emperor sent him back to deliver the death sentence to Seneca.

When the centurions came knocking at his door, Seneca was 'quite unmoved' and merely asked for tablets to inscribe his will, which were cruelly refused. Seneca turned to his gathered friends and family and quipped that the most valuable thing he possessed was, in any case, his pattern of living in accord with Stoic philosophy, which nobody could prevent him from bequeathing them by example. Execution, typically for that period, was by forced suicide. Tacitus described in gory detail how Seneca used a dagger to cut the arteries of his arms and then of his legs.

For some reason, this took too long, so Seneca drank some poison as well but this didn't work. Finally, he asked his friends to help him into a bath of scalding hot water, which helped to end his life. However, as he was dying, seeing the others weep, Seneca urged them to remain calm. He said: 'Who knew not Nero's cruelty?' and 'After a mother's and a brother's murder, nothing remains but to add the destruction of a guardian and a tutor.' In other words: any fool could have seen this coming. He repeatedly asked: 'Where are your maxims of philosophy, or the preparation of so many years' study against evils to come?'

The maxims of Stoic philosophy were apparently what helped Seneca face his execution with equanimity along with 'many years' preparation, presumably of the kind he had described throughout his letters and essays, as *praemeditatio malorum*.

How do Stoics premeditate adversity?

The 20th-century French philosopher, Michel Foucault, discussed the psychological exercises found in classical philosophy at length in one of his last lectures. He describes the Stoic *praemeditatio malorum* as consisting of three distinct components (Foucault, 1988, p. 36).

1 Rather than imagining the most likely future, the Stoic practises imagining the worst-case scenario, even if it's unlikely to actually happen.

2 The Stoic pictures the feared scenario as if happening now, rather than in the future, e.g., not that she will one day be exiled but that she is in exile already.

3 The primary rationale is for her to rehearse freedom from irrational distress (*apatheia*), by calmly persuading herself that these external 'misfortunes' are really indifferent, and to be accepted as merely situations calling on us to exhibit virtue and strength of character.

The Stoics list typical targets for premeditation such as exile, poverty, frailty in old age, illness, bereavement, etc. However, as Foucault writes, 'The meditation on death is the culmination of all these exercises.' Seneca asked the rhetorical question:

Why is it necessary to ruin the present by anticipating such calamities? Most people would assume that it's best not to worry about these things until they actually happen, thereby avoiding feelings of anxiety about the future. Seneca says Stoics follow a 'different path' to freedom from care than the majority of people, though, by imagining that what we fear might happen is definitely going to happen and examining it in our mind, until we can view it with detachment. Concentrating on our worst fears rather than trying to avoid thinking about them might sound paradoxical but the Stoics weren't alone in adopting this strategy.

Another famous 20th-century philosopher, Bertrand Russell, described a similar method of overcoming anxiety, worth quoting in detail. He begins by noting that many people are plagued by fear and worry, which can cause fatigue and stress. However, they tend to avoid doing the very thing that's most likely to help them:

> Probably all these people employ the wrong technique for dealing with their fear; whenever it comes into their mind, they try to think of something else; they distract their thoughts with amusement or work, or what not. Now every kind of fears grows worse by not being looked at. The effort of turning away one's thoughts is a tribute to the horribleness of the spectre from which one is averting one's gaze; the proper course with every kind of fear is to think about it rationally and calmly, but with great concentration, until it becomes completely familiar. In the end familiarity will blunt its terrors; the whole subject will become boring, and our thoughts will turn away from it, not, as formerly, by an effort of will, but through mere lack of interest in the topic. When you find yourself inclined to brood on anything, no matter what, the best plan always is to think about it even more than you naturally would until at last its morbid fascination is worn off. (Russell, 1930, p. 60)

Russell provides the following explanation of the technique itself:

> When some misfortune threatens, consider seriously and deliberately what is the very worst that could possibly

happen. Having looked this possible misfortune in the face, give yourself sound reasons for thinking that after all it would be no such very terrible disaster. Such reasons always exist, since at the worst nothing that happens to oneself has any cosmic importance. When you have looked for some time steadily at the worst possibility and have said to yourself with real conviction, 'Well, after all, that would not matter so very much', you will find that your worry diminishes to a quite extraordinary extent. It may be necessary to repeat the process a few times, but in the end, if you have shirked nothing in facing the worst possible issue, you will find that your worry disappears altogether, and is replaced by a kind of exhilaration. (Russell, 1930, pp. 59–60)

Russell's version of premeditation involves facing our worst fears in imagination, patiently, and persuading ourselves that they are not as catastrophic as first assumed. For the Stoics this is made simpler by the fact that their basic doctrine declares that nothing can be truly bad or awful except moral ignorance or vice.

However, both Russell and the Stoics appear to recognize that avoidance also maintains anxiety and that by confronting our fears in the right way, we naturally reduce the distress they cause. This is one of the most important findings of modern psychotherapeutic research on anxiety. Indeed, several psychological mechanisms are believed to come into play in this type of mental imagery technique and it's worth distinguishing carefully between them:

1 Habituation

2 Decatastrophizing

3 Modelling and rehearsing coping skills

4 Eliminating surprise

5 Reversing hedonic adaptation

The sections below will briefly explore each of these processes in turn.

> **Remember this:** Premeditation and the
> 'reserve clause'
>
> As premeditation, by definition, relates to future events, we do not yet
> know for certain what their outcome will be, or how much control we will
> have over things. For that reason, premeditation will generally involve the
> use of the Stoic 'reserve clause', because any action or outcome that you
> will must be accompanied by the caveat: 'fate permitting'. This may help
> to prevent premeditation turning into worry, which often takes the form
> of frustrated attempts at problem-solving and what psychologists call
> 'intolerance of uncertainty'. In premeditation, a central focus should be
> your willing *acceptance* of many things as being outside of your control,
> and determined by Nature as a whole. However, even your attempts to
> cope or act in some way should be accompanied by rational acceptance
> of the fact that events may intervene and thwart your goals.

Habituation and imaginal exposure

The psychological process called 'habituation' is the basis
of the most well-established behaviour therapy for anxiety,
known as 'exposure therapy'. In short, when people face
anxiety-provoking situations in reality, or to a lesser extent in
imagination, there's a natural tendency for anxiety to simply
reduce over time, as long as the 'exposure' is sufficiently
prolonged, repeated, and certain other factors do not interfere.
Curiously, the Stoics refer to passions as being based on 'fresh'
impressions. We don't know much about what they meant by
this term but it's quite possible they recognized something akin
to the process of habituation. When we've grown bored with a
mental image, through prolonged exposure, its emotional power
tends to wear off, and perhaps we could say that it's no longer
'fresh' in our minds. Seneca and other ancient authors definitely
appear to recognize that simply imagining feared events
systematically can 'blunt' or 'dull' anxious arousal, perhaps
even turning it into mere boredom.

> They do not bend under the blows of fate, because they
> have calculated its attacks in advance. For of the things
> that happen against our will, even the most painful are

alleviated by foresight. Then thought no longer encounters anything unexpected in events, but the perception of them is dulled, as if it were dealing with old and worn-out things. (Philo of Alexandria, *On the Special Laws*, 2.46)

Stoic premeditation is actually quite similar to certain forms of or exposure to *imagined* events, or 'imaginal exposure', the most common and perhaps most important 'mental imagery' strategy found in CBT for anxiety. Imaginal exposure typically takes 15–30 minutes at a time, every day, for a couple of weeks in cases of clinically severe anxiety. So it's not necessarily a quick fix for emotional disturbance, although for most people it's a one of the more reliable and lasting 'fixes' available. Aaron Beck, the founder of cognitive therapy, describes a similar type of technique, 'repeatedly reviewing' mental imagery, which particularly resembles the examples in Stoic literature:

> By reviewing what he fears, the patient is able to start to accept the possibility of the feared event. In the reviewing process, he is counteracting his avoidance tendency. At the start of one review, the patient, who was afraid of growing old, though, 'It's too terrible to face. I can't believe this is happening.' Later she was able to imagine directly, with minimal anxiety, what it would be like to be old. The reviewing process gets the patient to face the reality of the situation and makes it easier to accept. (Beck, Emery, & Greenberg, 2005, p. 250)

Again, they observe that this could easily be confused with morbid rumination or worry. The crucial difference is that this mental process is deliberate and involves concrete imagery rather than abstract verbal thoughts and circular 'What if?' questions.

Remember this: Premeditation is the opposite of worry

Contemplation and worry are two different things. When we contemplate future adversities, we may feel anxiety, but the Stoic steps back from his initial feelings, acknowledges them, and is not 'carried away' by them into fully-fledged passions such as worry. This is important to remember as people who are prone to morbid worrying or rumination may find it difficult to employ Stoic premeditation. It takes patient practice to learn to confront troubling situations with courage and restraint, enduring them long enough to develop a deeper sense of conviction that they are neither 'bad' nor 'harmful', and that only our misplaced value judgements made them appear so. Stoics don't allow themselves to be 'carried away' by distressing thoughts but pause and survey the situation rationally instead, staying with the objective facts.

Key idea: Rehearsing classic 'misfortunes'

There's something to be said both for rehearsing the same 'misfortunes' discussed by the ancient Stoics and for rehearsing setbacks more likely to be encountered in your own life, in the modern world. To begin with, read one of the classic examples of a philosopher in adversity: torture, warfare, shipwreck, imprisonment, exile, bereavement, execution, etc. For example, read about the last days of Socrates, particularly in the *Apology* of Plato; or look up Tacitus' account of Seneca's execution online; or read about the Stoic hero Cato the Younger's experience of watching helpless as the Republic fell to the tyrant Julius Caesar in the Great Roman Civil War. Seneca actually said that we should begin by conquering our fear of *death* first, which is why a whole extra chapter of the *ebook* is dedicated to that subject, and second we should free ourselves from the fear of *poverty*, i.e., the craving for wealth and property.

Decatastrophizing imagery

In cognitive behavioural therapy approaches, the judgement that the anticipated event is truly 'awful' or 'catastrophic' is challenged in a number of ways, most crudely by repeatedly asking 'So what if that happens?', 'Would it really be the end of the world?' Focus is shifted onto developing 'coping plans' and re-evaluating how you might handle the situation best. The pioneer of this 'decatastrophizing' approach in modern therapy was Albert Ellis, the founder of Rational Emotive Behaviour Therapy (REBT), the main precursor of CBT, who was particularly influenced by his reading of Stoic philosophy. The basic imagery technique employed in REBT was called 'Rational-Emotive Imagery' (REI), which Ellis describes as follows:

> Use rational-emotive imagery to vividly imagine unpleasant activating events before they happen; let yourself feel unhealthily upset (anxious, depressed, enraged, or guilty) as you imagine them; then work on your feelings to change them to appropriate emotions (concern, sadness, healthy anger, or remorse) as you keep imagining some of the worst things happening. Don't give up until you actually do change your feelings. (Ellis & MacLaren, 2005, pp. 125–126)

This is similar to the premeditation technique of Stoicism, although the Stoics use their fundamental definition of the nature of the good to challenge the judgement that external events can ever be truly 'bad' or 'harmful'.

Try it now: Premeditation of external events (decatastrophizing)

Make a list of the four or five worst catastrophes that could realistically befall you in life. Whether you're rehearsing classic examples or situations closer to home, place them roughly in rank order of difficulty, and start with the least difficult, moving on to the harder examples as soon as you feel ready. The Stoics assume your own death is typically one of the hardest and most important future events to contemplate with a calmly 'philosophical' attitude.

1   You might find it helps to write what modern therapists call a 'catastrophe script', describing the event in as much detail as possible. Eliminate any emotive language or value judgements and just describe the facts of the situation in a detached, objective manner, as if they were happening to someone else.

2   Close your eyes and imagine the 'catastrophe' happening right now. Do this patiently and you will tend to find distress naturally reduces over time. Continue until anxiety has reduced by at least 50 per cent.

3   Ask yourself 'So what if this happens?' Is it really as 'catastrophic' as it seems? Remind yourself of the basic principles of Stoic philosophy: That the essence of the good is human virtue and that external events are indifferent with regard to our wellbeing (*eudaimonia*).

4 Also ask yourself: 'What happens next?' How long will the 'catastrophe' last? What is most likely to follow? Focusing on the temporary nature of most adversities can make them easier to endure. Repeat this daily. This takes patience and you may grow bored but that's often a sign of progress in overcoming the distress caused by hypothetical catastrophes. More distressing events might need to be reviewed for 15–30 minutes every day for a week or more. However, five minutes per day is often sufficient to contemplate typical 'misfortunes' without undue anxiety. What do you learn by carrying out these exercises? How can you ensure that you retain what you've learned and apply it to real situations when they arise in life?

Modelling and rehearsing coping skills

Other behaviour therapy approaches adopt what's called a 'coping skills' approach. They focus on using repeated exposure to stressful situations, in reality or imagination, as an opportunity for rehearsing new behavioural strategies. In other words, both skill and confidence in responding to adversity are developed through repeated emotional 'fire-drills'. Some ('emotion-focused') coping skills such as muscle relaxation are used to manage emotional responses, whereas other ('problem-focused') skills such as assertiveness are used to address the external situation. For example, an early form of cognitive behavioural therapy called 'Stress Inoculation Training' (SIT), developed by the psychologist Donald Meichenbaum, provides a systematic approach to anticipating future setbacks and rehearsing coping skills (Meichenbaum, 1985).

Stress inoculation is a flexible approach to building psychological resilience by repeatedly rehearsing a variety of distressing situations, in reality, role play, or in imagination, while practising more rational and constructive ways of coping. As in Stoicism, a broad range of situations are rehearsed, so that general emotional resilience can be developed, through a process explained by analogy with viral *immunization*. By exposing yourself to small doses of stress in a controlled way, sometimes in imagination, you can build up stronger defences and become less vulnerable when confronted with a real-life problem. Psychological resilience tends to 'generalize', though, so that even situations that are neither anticipated nor directly rehearsed may be experienced as less overwhelming, as long as a wide variety of other adversities have been anticipated and coped with resiliently.

Clients in SIT rehearse both coping statements (e.g., 'I can handle this') and coping skills, e.g., controlled relaxation or assertiveness. Likewise, Stoics rehearse philosophical maxims ('What's outside my control is indifferent to me') and appropriate actions, such as acting with acceptance and courage, in order to progress towards virtue and *eudaimonia*. Coping skills approaches often involve modelling (or emulating) the behaviour of others who show emotional resilience in similar situations. The Stoics refer extensively to the notion of modelling the resilient behaviour of the ideal Sage and of others who have endured 'misfortunes' with wisdom and courage, and Seneca makes it clear he views this as part of Stoic premeditation.

Key idea: Stress inoculation training (SIT)

Stress inoculation training (SIT) is a cognitive behavioural therapy (CBT) approach designed to build psychological resilience, which was developed by psychologist Donald Meichenbaum in the 1970s. Its efficacy is supported by a wealth of clinical and experimental research evidence, for a wide range of problems and populations. It's one of the modern psychological therapies most resembling the Stoic technique of premeditation. In SIT, the individual is trained to cope better with stress across a variety of situations, often by rehearsing imagined threats or setbacks that may be encountered in the future. By practising coping with a range of real and imaginary problems, a general sense of resilience or 'self-efficacy' can be developed.

Try it now: Contemplation of Stoic exemplars (modelling)

Seneca recommends that we should set up each of the worst misfortunes that can possibly befall someone and 'summon as supporters those who scorned them'; in other words, contemplating wise men and heroes who provide models worthy of emulation, having coped with similar situations themselves. This resembles the Stoic practice we've called 'Contemplation of the Sage', although it extends to anyone worthy of emulation. Stoic literature is full of examples of wise men and heroes who have faced exile, persecution, bereavement, poverty, death, and other classic 'misfortunes' with a philosophical attitude. Reading about these examples is therefore a good starting point, although you may also be able to identify any number of examples of your own, including more contemporary figures, or even your own friends and family.

1 Take time to study written accounts of how a Stoic hero (such as Socrates or Cato) coped in the face of adversity or imagine how a perfect Stoic Sage might handle things.

2 What virtuous attitudes or actions might help them? What do they do that's worthy of emulation?

3 Imagine being the person you're modelling, facing the events they did in the way they did, putting yourself in their shoes, as if it's happening to you right now.

4 Now apply that to your own life, mentally-rehearsing similar 'misfortunes' that you might realistically face at some point, trying to emulate what seems most helpful and appropriate from their example.

Again, you may find it helpful to write this down, like a short script or story describing your model's way of coping. Review and revise it periodically, so that it becomes ready-to-hand in your memory as an example you can learn to emulate in your own life.

Eliminating surprise

The Stoics also emphasized the notion that by anticipating possible future adversities we can learn to take away the sense of 'surprise' or 'shock' that often accompanies their occurrence, seeing them instead as something natural and in some cases inevitable in life. 'Whatever has been long anticipated comes as a lighter blow' (Seneca, *Letters*, 78). The Stoics were particularly concerned with the psychological impact of irrational 'surprise' at undesirable events, but this way of thinking isn't really an explicit emphasis of *modern* psychological therapies. For example, Epictetus said that being able to tell yourself that it was 'not unexpected' when some such misfortune happens 'will be the first thing to lighten the burden' (*Discourses*, 3.24).

Likewise, Seneca writes that we should contemplate events in advance so that nothing ever takes us by surprise in this way, as 'What is quite unlooked for is more crushing in its effect, and unexpectedness adds to the weight of a disaster' by magnifying the distress experienced (*Letters*, 91). He goes on to say that we should therefore 'project our thoughts ahead of us' and imagine every conceivable setback so that we may 'strengthen the mind' to cope with them, or as we put it today, to develop psychological resilience in the face of adversity.

In other words, premeditation is one of the main ways to prevent this sense of irrational surprise at life's 'misfortunes'. Seneca elsewhere writes that although we cannot escape the blows of fate we can learn to look down upon them 'if by constant reflection you have anticipated future happenings'.

> Everyone faces up more bravely to a thing for which he has long prepared himself, sufferings, even, being withstood if they have been trained for in advance. Those who are unprepared, on the other hand, are panic-stricken by the most insignificant happenings. We must see to it that nothing takes us by surprise. And since it is invariably unfamiliarity that makes a thing more formidable than it really is, this habit of continual reflection will ensure that no form of adversity finds you a complete beginner. (*Letters*, 107)

Plutarch likewise seems to point to irrational thoughts of surprise as the cause of much anxiety:

> The point is that, if anything happens which may be unwelcome, but is not unexpected, this kind of preparedness and character leaves no room for 'I couldn't have imagined it' and 'This isn't what I'd hoped for' and 'I didn't expect this', and so stops the heart lurching and beating fast and so on, and quickly settles derangement and disturbance back on to a foundation. Carneades [the skeptical Platonic philosopher] used to remind people who were involved in important affairs that unexpectedness is the be-all and end-all of distress and discontent. (*On Contentment*, 474e)

He adds that such distress can best be avoided, therefore, 'by the beneficial practice of training oneself to gain the ability to look straight at fortune with open eyes.'

Try it now: Premeditation of virtue (coping)

Modern therapists talk about writing a detailed 'coping plan' describing how you might best handle anticipated 'catastrophes'. Likewise, the Stoics contemplated how they might act with prudence, courage, and self-discipline in the face of adversity. So consider what else you could do to cope well with the situation you've been imagining. What faculties or strengths has Nature given you to deal with situations like this?

1 If possible, take time to write down a coping plan, based on your understanding of Stoic philosophy; it's okay if this just starts as a few bullet points because you may want to revise it periodically until it develops into a more detailed plan or a story about how you would cope.

2 How would emulating Stoic heroes help you? What can you learn from the example of others? What would a Sage with perfect practical wisdom and self-mastery do?

3 How would the Stoic philosophy help you? In particular, what would happen if you focused on the basic principle that only our own actions can be truly 'good' or 'bad' and that external things are ultimately 'indifferent'?

4 What specific faculties or strengths has Nature given you to cope with this situation and how can you best apply them? What virtues does the situation call for or demand?

Again, you might want to develop a detailed coping plan by reviewing it daily and revising it in the light of your contemplations. How 'catastrophic' does this situation seem when you imagine coping to the best of your ability? What's more important, the external events that happen to you, or the ways in which you voluntarily choose to respond?

Reversing 'hedonic adaptation'?

To these standard processes found in CBT, Irvine adds the concept of 'hedonic adaptation'. He claims that by picturing misfortunes that involve the loss of cherished things we can prevent ourselves taking them so much for granted that they cease to give us pleasure (Irvine, 2009). Picturing future loss then becomes a way of enhancing current pleasure. Although there may be some trace of this notion in the literature it perhaps flies in the face of the essential Stoic philosophical premise: that external things and the pleasure they bring are 'indifferent' with regard to true Happiness and wellbeing (*eudaimonia*).

Rational joy comes from the contemplation of praiseworthy, or virtuous, actions, not from maximizing sensory pleasures, according to Stoicism. Indeed, the notion of enhancing pleasure in this way might appeal more to the rival Epicurean school. For the Stoics, imagining the possibility of going bankrupt in the future, as if it's happening now, isn't meant to make us take more pleasure in our current wealth. The point is to prize our ability to respond with wisdom and virtue more highly than our material possessions or external situation.

Focus Points

The main points to remember from this chapter are:

* The basis of Stoic premeditation is the underlying principle that no external 'misfortune' can truly be 'bad' or 'harmful' because everything outside our sphere of volition is 'indifferent'.
* Anticipating every possible form of adversity helps the Stoic to rehearse her principles, strengthen her character, and develop greater emotional resilience rather than worrying about things.
* The element of 'surprise' is also removed from 'misfortune' in this way, making events easier to handle when they occur.

Next Step

Stoic premeditation was concerned with a variety of 'misfortunes' but the most important was undoubtedly considered to be one's own death, a subject that gets its own chapter in the *ebook*. However, it's time we proceeded to discuss the role of Stoic Logic in relation to the 'discipline of judgement' and the practice of Stoic mindfulness, to complete our survey of the three basic Stoic topics and disciplines.

8

The discipline of judgement (Stoic mindfulness)

In this chapter you will learn:

▶ *About the practical discipline of judgement, or 'assent', and how it relates to the wider theoretical topic of Stoic Logic*

▶ *How to use the psychological exercise of 'physical definition' to develop what the Stoics called an 'objective representation' of events*

▶ *How to use mindfulness and 'cognitive distancing' to avoid being 'carried away' by impressions*

People are not disturbed by events, but rather by their judgements about events. For example, death is nothing terrible (otherwise it would have appeared so to Socrates). But rather the judgement itself concerning death, explaining it as terrible: that is the thing that's terrible. (Epictetus, *Enchiridion*, 5)

Therefore train yourself without hesitation to say in response to every harsh appearance that 'you are [merely] an appearance and in no way the thing appearing.' Next examine it and evaluate it against these the [philosophical] rules and standards which you have, but first and foremost this, whether it concerns things that are up to us or it concerns those things not up to us. And if it concerns something that is not up to us, have ready-to-hand the answer: 'It is nothing to me.' (*Enchiridion*, 1)

Self-assessment: Stoic attitudes and the discipline of judgement

Before reading this chapter, rate how strongly you agree with the following statements, using the five-point (1–5) scale below, and then re-rate your attitudes once you've read and digested the contents.

1. Strongly disagree, 2. Disagree, 3. Neither agree nor disagree, 4. Agree, 5. Strongly agree

1 'We should respond to troubling impressions by reminding ourselves they are just events in the mind and not the things they represent.'

2 'I should step back from strong desires or emotions and postpone acting on them until they've settled down and I can evaluate them properly.'

3 'It's helpful to remind yourself that it's our judgements about things that upset us rather than things themselves.'

What is the 'discipline of judgement'?

How do we turn philosophy from something we read about in books into a *practical* discipline, that permeates our daily routine?

Without the help of a wise teacher to point out our vulnerability to misguided desires and emotions how are we meant to spot them before it's too late? Socrates famously said that the unexamined life is not worth living. How does a philosopher begin to rationally 'examine' her own life – her thoughts, feelings and actions? As we'll see, the Stoics practised a psychological exercise called *prosochê* (attention to one's mind) that resembles Buddhist 'mindfulness'. This provides the answer to many of these questions about applying philosophy to our daily lives.

I'll call Epictetus' third Stoic discipline that of 'judgement', for the sake of simplicity. He referred to it more specifically as the discipline of 'assent' (*sunkatathesis*), which means agreeing with or saying 'yes' to some initial idea or impression. This discipline is all about granting or withholding 'assent' in response to impressions that impose themselves on us in daily life, particularly those involving value judgements that might lead to irrational 'passions', such as troubling fears or desires. Hadot claimed that it entails several psychological exercises that, as a lived philosophical practice, correspond with the broader theoretical field of Stoic 'Logic'.

However, it is grounded in the basic exercise of adopting an *objective* perspective on life. In a nutshell: 'The discipline of assent consists essentially in refusing to accept within oneself all representations which are other than objective or adequate' (Hadot, 1998, p. 101). Hadot therefore interpreted this discipline as a means of living in harmony with reason, which the Stoics view as our essential nature. It can be linked to the cardinal virtue of 'wisdom' or truthfulness. In fact, according to Epictetus, Zeno also defined the chief doctrine of Stoicism as the view that man's highest good, wisdom, consists in the 'correct use of impressions'.

One way that Stoics therefore interpreted their most famous doctrine, to 'live in agreement with Nature', was by sticking with the facts and describing events to themselves in a 'natural' and objective manner, without confusing their value judgements about things with external reality. 'My dog has died', is a fact, a physical description; 'My dog has died and that's *awful*' is a value judgement that goes beyond the facts. Our value judgements exceed the objective facts of any given situation and thereby bring us into conflict with external nature.

The objective representation of things seems to be a point at which Stoic Logic overlaps with Physics or 'natural philosophy'. In a similar way, the modern scientific method seeks to know facts about 'Nature' by viewing it in an objective manner, suspending value judgements or emotive rhetoric in favour of impartial observation and description. However, in Stoicism this becomes a spiritual and psychotherapeutic exercise.

Marcus Aurelius said that the discipline of judgement requires us to learn the 'true practical art' or technique of assent. Before we can begin disputing our own thoughts, through dialectic and logic, we have to be able to spot them, take a step back from them, and view them as if they were hypotheses that are at least 'up for debate'. That's what they mean by 'withholding assent' from our impressions. This involves adopting an impartial or objective attitude in order to rationally evaluate impressions, before deciding whether they deserve to be accepted or rejected. It's a *pre-requisite* of any serious philosophical self-examination. Epictetus therefore says the discipline of assent, is particularly concerned with both 'the avoidance of error and rashness' in our thinking (*Discourses*, 3.2):

1 Freedom from 'rashness', meaning we must train ourselves first to actually spot our initial impressions when they occur, and to suspend our 'assent' to problematic value judgements rather than being 'carried away' by them into unhealthy passions, such as irrational fear or excessive desire.

2 Freedom from 'error', meaning we must then learn to examine and evaluate these impressions rationally, particularly by reference to our philosophical doctrine about what is good, bad and indifferent, and ultimately with the aid of formal Stoic Logic.

Epictetus makes it very clear that the most important question to ask in examining our thoughts is whether they relate to things that are 'up to us' or not, something we'll return to in the next chapter. In this chapter, we'll focus on the first task: avoiding rashness in 'assenting' to, or going along with, our initial impressions. We can view this as a central skill in developing 'Stoic mindfulness'.

Epictetus emphasized that the third discipline should only be pursued when students have made sufficient progress in the disciplines of desire and action. It's possible he simply meant that the aspect of this discipline that involves advanced training in Stoic Logic should be postponed until later, as this serves mainly to strengthen our knowledge of basic principles. However, as Hadot notes, some aspects of this discipline appear to be necessary from the very outset, particularly the ability to free oneself from granting assent too rashly and being carried away by initial impressions, something Epictetus can be seen repeatedly warning his students to avoid.

The key element here is therefore the practical exercise of spotting our irrational passions developing and nipping them in the bud by withholding assent from the impressions they're based upon. Epictetus says that at first we must resist being swept off our feet by the vividness of the initial impression, but rather say: 'Wait for me a little, impression; allow me to see who you are, and what you are an impression of; allow me to put you to the test'. The opening passage of the *Enchiridion* similarly describes how, in general, Stoics should catch problematic impressions early and respond to them by saying: 'You are just an impression and not at all the thing the impression is of', then examine and evaluate them according to their philosophical principles.

Judgement is the core of our being as rational creatures, and the locus of our freedom. To be aware of our judgements moment-by-moment, is to be profoundly *self-aware* and this appears to be one way in which the Stoics interpreted the Delphic maxim: 'Know thyself'. Hadot therefore talks about the discipline of assent as constituting the 'Inner Citadel' of the Stoic (Hadot, 1998, p. 101). Marcus refers several times to the practice of retreating to this invulnerable fortress within all of us. We're told the early Stoics referred to 'Logic' metaphorically as resembling the bones and sinews of an animal's body, the shell of an egg, and, as we've seen, the protective wall surrounding a garden or orchard. The message appears to be that the study of Stoic

Logic is what makes us strong and protects us from the external world. However, retreat to the inner citadel is something always available to even the novice Stoic because to begin with it only requires that we notice our judgements and step back from them, rather than allowing them to sweep us away. By truly knowing ourselves, being continually mindful, remaining attentive to the core of our being as rational creatures, observing our thoughts and value judgements, we allow ourselves to stand back from the world and rise above external events, through a kind of detachment or purification of the mind. By avoiding 'rashness' in assenting to our initial impressions we increasingly realise that we are not upset by external things, after all, but by our own judgements about them.

Case study: The anxious musician (cithara-player)

In his discourse 'On anxiety', Epictetus provides the example of a musician, a singer accompanying himself on the cithara, who suffers from what we would call 'stage fright' (*Discourses*, 2.13). The musician performs perfectly when alone and feels no anxiety until he enters the theatre and stands before an audience. Epictetus astutely interprets this as evidence that the anxiety is caused by the musician's perception of the situation, his desire to please the audience and fear of being criticized by them.

According to Epictetus, when Stoics see someone who appears anxious they should generally ask: 'What does this person want?' Anxiety, he says, is ultimately caused by wanting either to obtain something or avoid something outside of our direct control. Even if the performer has a fine voice and plays the cithara well, he may still make himself anxious, 'for he wants not only to sing well, but to gain applause'. As this is always uncertain and beyond his direct control, he is bound to feel unsure of himself, conflicted, and anxious, being trapped by a fundamental error of judgement. He has unwittingly given his assent, and allowed himself to be 'carried away' by his false impression that the audience's reaction is intrinsically more important than his own character or performance.

Though he may have mastered the art of performing he is not a master of the art of living, and lacks practical wisdom, which would liberate him from such fears. A Stoic cithara player, by contrast, might have trained himself, over a lifetime, to pause for thought when anxious feelings arise and remember the Stoic doctrine that we are not upset by events but by our judgements about them. He would ask himself whether the audience's reaction was under his direct control and, as it is not, he would respond to his anxiety by saying 'Their applause is nothing to me.' He would remind himself that external things are 'indifferent' and that what's truly important in the situation is his ability to realize this and accept whatever happens with magnanimity. However, developing this ability may require longer and more demanding training than learning to play a musical instrument.

Remember this: Passions are impressions

Remember that for the Stoics all 'passions' are basically 'impressions' of a certain kind, with irrational value judgements attached. The impressions they're most interested in spotting, not being 'carried away' by, and learning to re-evaluate are the 'passions', irrational fears and unhealthy desires. Postponing responding to a fear would mean abandoning avoidance, not running away, standing your ground. Postponing responding to a craving would mean not giving in to it and indulging in the thing desired. In other words, 'endure and renounce' in the words of Epictetus' famous slogan. Avoiding being 'carried away' by your initial impressions of fear and desire will require the cardinal virtues of courage and self-discipline.

Stoic psychology and theory of knowledge

We need to pause to review some aspects of Stoic psychology briefly. The Stoics believed that bodily sensations create an internal 'impression' (*phantasia*) of external events, an 'appearance' of things, distinct from the thing itself. This mental representation occurs in the *hêgemonikon*, or 'ruling faculty' of the mind, the seat of consciousness and volition. We can ask whether the impression we receive is accurate and objective, as a representation of the external world. We can also ask how the impression affects our mind, whether it's distressing, or evokes strong desires or aversions. We can also form impressions through memory or imagination, constructing new or composite images, such as the image of the ideal Sage and comparing these to reality. So, although *phantasia* is often misleadingly translated as 'external impression', it's a much broader concept than this, encompassing different kinds of mental representation, including what people today refer to as 'thoughts' and 'feelings' (Long, 2002, p. 133; p. 214).

These initial impressions are associated with inner discourse and an interpretation placed on them, using language and abstract concepts, which give events their meaning. Whereas external impressions are imposed on us by sensation, the meaning attributed to them through language is an activity of the 'ruling faculty' of the mind, although these two things become intimately fused together in our daily experience. According to Hadot, it is strictly speaking this verbal meaning to which we give or withhold our conscious 'assent', although the Stoics typically refer to assenting to our 'impressions'. It's only when we give our voluntary assent to an impression, and agree that it is what it appears to be, that it becomes experienced as a fully fledged 'perception' of external events.

Crucially for the Stoics, some impressions may impose themselves on us, and are not under our control. Psychologists nowadays might say that they are 'automatic' rather than 'voluntary' thought processes. By contrast, our conscious 'assent' to impressions is free and voluntary, giving adult humans the ability to self-consciously question their own impressions, in a way that infants and animals cannot.

Even the Sage is affected by involuntary impressions of danger, and may be initially startled and alarmed by a sudden noise. However, an anxious person will continue to worry, going along with the initial impression, whereas the Sage will step back and evaluate things rationally, restoring his equanimity if he judges the impression false. For example, suppose an external event, such as someone criticizing me, is communicated to my mind by the senses of sight and hearing. According to Hadot's analysis, the subsequent process of 'assent' in Stoicism typically consists of the following stages (Hadot, 1998, pp. 103-104).

1 **'What happened?'** A 'primary' internal impression occurs, through which the event is automatically represented in the

mind, and this begs for a response by implicitly posing the question: 'What is this?'

2 **'Someone criticized me.'** We naturally respond by using language and reason to describe the event. This is the initial judgement that the Stoics refer to as an 'objective representation', because it just *echoes* the self-evident facts of the situation, literally 'agreeing with Nature'.

3 **'He has wronged me!'** We may then go on to add a value judgement (*hupolêpsis*). The Stoics, however, trained themselves to temporarily suspend judgement rather than adding the evaluation that what happened is 'good' or 'bad', 'helpful' or 'harmful', etc.

Epictetus and Marcus Aurelius provide several fairly clear examples where this sequence of psychological events is spelled-out as a kind of inner dialogue between the individual and her impressions.

> He was sent to jail. [The initial impression that comes from our senses.]
>
> What happened? [Which calls for us to make a judgement or interpretation.]
>
> He was sent to jail. [We reply with an objective verbal judgement, which simply echoes the self-evident facts.]
>
> But 'He is unhappy' [an *unnecessary* value judgement] is added by oneself. (*Discourses*, 3.8)

Marcus Aurelius writes in his journal that we should entertain 'nothing but what you get from first impressions', stick with these, don't extrapolate, and no harm can befall us (*Meditations*, 8.49). The examples he gives are:

> That someone has insulted you, for instance.
>
> That – but not that it's done you any harm.
>
> The fact that my son is sick – that I can see.
>
> But 'that he might die of it,' no.

Stoics therefore try to remain with their 'objective representations', in accord with nature, without adding further value judgements or inferences because these form the basis of irrational 'passions'. However, often value judgements sneak in, fused with our external impressions, whether through habit or for some other reason. We are either rashly 'carried away' into irrational passions by going along with these impressions or we pause, step back, and withhold our assent temporarily, until we've had a chance to evaluate things philosophically.

Key idea: 'Objective representation'

Phantasia katalêptikê is one of those notoriously tricky-to-translate Stoic technical terms that cause a headache for scholars. The Stoics believed that some mental impressions were self-evident and could be grasped with certainty. By contrast, their opponents, the Academic Skeptics refused to admit that any impressions could grasp reality with certainty and so they criticized the Stoics, calling them 'the Dogmatists'. There's a complex and (very) long-running philosophical debate here but for our purposes it will suffice to note that many people conclude philosophical skepticism is a bit of a dead-end as the basis for a philosophy of life. (The Platonic Academy itself abandoned Skepticism by about 90 BC and moved to a position somewhat closer to the Stoics, known as 'Middle Platonism'.)

The Stoic position is also closer to the common-sense view that we can *generally* trust our senses. A *phantasia* is an impression, a mental representation or thought that claims to represent something, such as the mental images we have of external reality – it can be true or false, accurate or inaccurate. By contrast, a *phantasia katalêptikê* is an impression that is certain and reliable, one that 'grasps' or 'seizes' upon events accurately. Hadot translates it as 'objective representation' because value judgements are suspended and things are grasped in terms of their physical properties.

Key idea: Zeno's clenched-fist

Zeno famously employed a series of hand gestures to symbolize different levels or stages of knowledge:

1 An impression [*phantasia*] is symbolized by the right hand being held open, with the fingers spread out, as if the impression is resting loosely upon it.

2 Assent [*sunkatathesis*] is like the fingers being closed loosely, as if holding on to the impression.

3 Certainty [*katalêpsis*] resembles the hand being clenched tightly into a fist, from which the expression 'to grasp' an impression is derived – this comes from perceiving certain impressions very clearly and distinctly, and grasping their nature with complete objectivity.

4 Knowledge [*epistemê*] is symbolized by this clenched right-fist being enclosed tightly in the palm and fingers of the left hand.

The Stoics said that true knowledge is possessed only by the perfect Sage, and that virtue is such knowledge about what is good, bad and indifferent. However, knowledge is founded upon firmly grasped impressions, and this kind of certainty is attainable by everyone. It becomes true knowledge when it is supported by reason, and thereby integrated with other clearly perceived impressions.

'Objective representation' and 'physical definition'

The Stoic term *phantasia katalêptikê* literally means 'an impression that grips us', apparently meaning one that seizes the mind as being self-evident. Hadot translates it as an 'objective' or 'adequate representation'. 'An objective or adequate representation is one which corresponds exactly to reality, which is to say that it engenders within us an inner discourse which is nothing other than the pure and simple description of an event, without the addition of any subjective value judgement' (Hadot, 1998, p. 104). Like a scientist or natural philosopher, someone having 'kateleptic' impressions also lays hold of and grips the objective nature of things, unclouded by value judgements. By 'firmly grasping' the natural appearance of things, in this way, we prevent ourselves being 'carried away' by the passions. (You could say we try to 'get a grip' on reality once more!) Epictetus therefore advises his students to challenge their impressions as follows:

> Let's see some identification! Do you have the sign from nature which every impression must have, in order to be approved? (*Discourses*, 3.12)

He appears to mean that we should check whether the impression is a true 'objective representation' of events. Otherwise, we should withhold our assent from it, particularly if it contains value judgements of the kind associated with the passions.

The concept of a *phantasia katalêptikê* therefore provides the basis of something that is best described as a verbal or psychological exercise in Stoicism, called the practice of 'physical definition' by Hadot (Hadot, 1998, pp. 104–105). There are many examples of this throughout *The Meditations*.

> One must always make a definition or description of the object which is presented in an impression, so as to see it in itself, as it is in its essence, in its nakedness, in its totality, and in all its details. One must say to oneself the name which is peculiar to it, as well as the names of the parts which compose it, and into which it will be resolved. (*Meditations*, 3.11)

Marcus gives a variety of specific examples:

> How important it is to represent to oneself, when it comes to fancy dishes and other such foods: 'This is the corpse of a fish, this other thing the corpse of a bird or a pig.' Similarly, 'This [expensive] Falernian wine is just some grape juice,' and 'This purple [imperial] robe is some sheep's wool dyed in the juices of shellfish.' When it comes to sexual union, we must say, 'This is the rubbing together of abdomens, accompanied by the spasmodic ejaculation of a sticky liquid.' How important are these [objective] impressions which reach the thing itself and penetrate right through it, so that one can see what it is in reality. (*Meditations*, 6.13)

He is speaking of his own emperor's robes and the expensive purple dye used to make them, which, ironically, was made from notoriously disgusting and foul-smelling *murex* shellfish extracts. This dye was actually the cargo that Zeno lost in his shipwreck, so it may have been a Stoic byword for something apparently highly-precious but objectively quite worthless and even disgusting. The Emperor Napoleon likewise reputedly said something much like Marcus: 'A throne is only a bench covered in velvet.'

When we stick to the facts like this and describe events in a value-free and objective manner, we're doing something that resembles the kind of neutral observation required in the physical sciences. So the process of 'physical definition' also forms part of the psychological exercises drawn from Stoic *Physics* or natural philosophy. 'In the last analysis, then, the discipline of assent appears as a constant effort to eliminate all the value judgements which we bring to bear upon those things which do not depend upon us, and which therefore have no moral value' (Hadot, 1998, pp. 111-112). In other words, it's the continual practice, throughout the day, of Stoic *mindfulness* and *objectivity*. This mindful self-awareness of our value judgements, forms our 'ruling faculty' into an Inner Citadel, and constitutes the basis of practical wisdom, the central virtue, and therefore the essence of *philosophy* itself.

Try it now: The exercise of 'physical definition'

This exercise employs the Stoic practice Hadot calls 'physical definition', which attempts to focus attention on 'objective representations', without imposing value judgements on our experience.

* Think of an event that you find *mildly* upsetting, not something overwhelming.
* Close your eyes and imagine that you're in that situation right now, as if it's actually happening.
* See if you can sum up the essence of things objectively in a brief label or description, such as 'Someone said something that I disagreed with.'
* Try also to describe the physical properties of the situation in as much detail as possible, naming each of the ingredients that go together to compose the total situation in a 'matter of fact' way. Take your time and do this slowly.
* Avoid any value judgements, or inferences, just stick to the raw data, the facts of the situation. Try to prevent yourself from adding anything to the initial impression you have of the physical situation, don't go any further by judging it 'good' or 'bad', but just view it with Stoic indifference.

Take your time doing this and be patient; you'll probably find that your feelings reduce gradually. Focus on trying to penetrate beyond your value judgements, your fears and desires, to grasp the objective nature of the situation as it is in itself.

Cognitive distancing in Stoicism

Epictetus repeatedly emphasized to his students that evaluating their impressions according to Stoic philosophical doctrines presupposes a more basic psychological strategy. Although this is of great practical importance to Stoicism it's often overlooked by modern commentators. Before we can begin to question our own impressions, we must first spot them happening. This is harder than it sounds because we naturally view our thoughts as facts about the world and only in moments of reflection do we place them in question, viewing them *as* thoughts, that is as judgements or hypotheses that may be true or false. Modern CBT explicitly acknowledges the same dilemma.

We can only evaluate our automatic thoughts or change our response to them once we've 'caught' them and taken a step back from them, a process technically referred to as gaining '*cognitive distance*'. This doesn't mean distancing ourselves from events emotionally, by suppressing our feelings or distracting ourselves from things, but rather something more subtle and fundamental: distancing our thoughts from *reality* by viewing them as merely mental representations.

This is often illustrated by the analogy of wearing coloured spectacles. Normally we view the world 'through' the lens of our positive or negative judgements, like someone looking at the world through 'rose-tinted' spectacles or through gloomy dark glasses. We may forget we're wearing glasses, though, and assume that's just the way external things look in themselves and how they appear to everyone else. Cognitive distancing is like the process of taking off the glasses and looking *at* them, rather than *through* them. Or, more accurately, it's like simply realizing that you're wearing glasses and that the colours you see are coming from the tinted lenses rather than the world itself.

In early forms of CBT, particularly Albert Ellis' Rational Emotive Behaviour Therapy (REBT), clients were actually taught the famous quotation from Epictetus to illustrate this notion: 'Men are disturbed not by things, but by the views which they take of them'. Hence, clients in CBT often begin by being taught to spot automatic thoughts, write them down, and view them *impartially*, with a rational 'scientific' attitude. They practise treating their own thoughts as if they were 'hypotheses' that deserve to be evaluated rationally and tested empirically, rather than simply facts about the world. Indeed recently researchers have argued that training in strategies such as 'cognitive distancing' may be one of the most important processes in psychotherapy.

Virtually the same psychological technique was emphasized in the ancient Stoic literature. Epictetus repeatedly says that we should stop ourselves being 'carried away' by our initial impressions, when unhealthy passions begin to develop, by reminding ourselves of the Stoic principle, quoted in REBT, that we're upset not by things but by our judgements about them. For example, he advises his students as follows:

▶ Do not be carried away by the impression of someone else's good fortune, if they achieve wealth or status; instead remind yourself that the only good that can befall you is freedom and that is within your own power to achieve, if you can look down on external things with indifference (*Enchiridion*, 19).

▶ Even if you witness a bad omen, like a raven croaking, do not be swept away by the appearance of prophesied misfortunes; remind yourself that misfortunes can only be predicted for your body or your property but your mind is always available to turn it into good fortune by responding with virtue (*Enchiridion*, 18).

▶ When you see someone else in misery (and for the Stoics, this includes characters in the famous tragedies) do not be swept along by the impression that some catastrophe has befallen him; remind yourself that it is not the thing itself but his judgement that upsets him otherwise others would be affected in the same way (*Enchiridion*, 16).

▶ When someone seems to insult or offend you, aim from the outset not to be carried away by such impressions; remind yourself that it is not their behaviour but your judgement that affronts and provokes you (*Enchiridion*, 20).

As Hadot points out, Epictetus refers to stepping back from an initial 'harsh' or 'troubling' appearance, which means one that already contains the value judgement 'This is troubling', rather than a *phantasia katalêptikê* or objective representation of events. Indeed, paradoxically, for the Stoics, the only true 'danger' or harm that can befall us lies in foolishly giving our assent to impressions like these. For this reason, they say that it is not death that is the greatest evil but the *fear* of death, meaning the *impression* that death is an evil.

Key idea: The concept of 'cognitive distance' in CBT

The term 'distancing' or gaining 'cognitive distance' was employed by Aaron T. Beck, the founder of cognitive therapy and has become an increasingly important aspect of modern CBT. It refers to the ability to see our thoughts *as* just thoughts, hypotheses about reality, rather than confusing them with facts. For example, it's the difference between saying to yourself 'This situation *is* awful' and 'I'm having the *thought* "this situation is awful"'. This is Beck's definition: 'Distancing' refers to the ability to view one's own thoughts (or beliefs) as constructions of 'reality' rather than as reality itself' (Alford & Beck, 1997, p. 142). This necessarily *precedes* the disputation techniques used in cognitive therapy, such as weighing up the evidence for and against a thought. Another group of researchers experimented with an approach that placed greater emphasis on this initial step, calling it '*comprehensive* distancing', which later developed into a new therapy called Acceptance and Commitment Therapy (ACT). Likewise, other 'mindfulness and acceptance-based' therapies, sometimes called the 'third-wave' of CBT, have generally placed increasing importance on psychological strategies like 'distancing'.

Remember this: It's not events that upset us but our opinions about them

Epictetus repeatedly advises his students to avoid being 'carried away' by their initial impressions, when toxic 'passions' are emerging. They were to remind themselves that it's their own value judgements upsetting them rather than external events. This is a famous Stoic strategy and it's clearly fundamental to Epictetus' *Handbook*. A similar strategy involves reminding yourself that other people might view the same event differently, perhaps with 'indifference', and your own thoughts and judgements are responsible for your distress. Remember that gaining 'distance' from impressions is *not* the same as trying to avoid or suppress them. In fact it's a form of acceptance. It means accepting the presence of disturbing thoughts, while viewing them in a more detached manner.

Key idea: 'Cognitive distancing' strategies in CBT

Throughout his writings, Beck described a variety of strategies designed to encourage cognitive distancing, such as the following:

1 Spotting fleeting, automatic thoughts and writing them down concisely on a self-monitoring record, so they can be viewed in a detached manner.
2 Carefully distinguishing emotions from the thoughts and beliefs that underlie them, so the thoughts can be viewed as representations of reality that could be true or false.
3 Writing thoughts up on a flipchart or board and literally taking a step back to view them from a distance as something 'over there'.
4 Referring to your thoughts in the third-person, e.g., 'I notice that Donald is beginning to feel angry and thinking to himself that this person has insulted him...'.
5 Using a counter or keeping a tally to track the frequency of particular automatic thoughts or feelings, throughout the day, thereby viewing them as habitual and repetitive, like reflexes rather than rational conclusions.
6 Shifting perspectives and imagining being in the shoes of other people who might view the same events differently, and perhaps exploring a range of different perspectives on the same situation.

The practice of mindfulness meditation, inspired by the Buddhist approach, has become central to several third-wave therapies and can be seen as employing a process that is essentially the same as 'cognitive distancing'. When an automatic thought intrudes during meditation, we're advised to view it in a detached manner and let go of it, as if it were an autumn leaf floating past on a stream, rather than engaging with it. As we'll see, most of these techniques are consistent with Stoic practices and, indeed, resemble psychological strategies that can be found in the ancient Stoic literature. This similarity between ancient Stoic therapy and modern cognitive therapy is important because a considerable body of scientific evidence now supports the efficacy of 'distancing' strategies.

Try it now: Gaining cognitive distance in Stoicism

We can perhaps expand upon some of Epictetus' advice in the *Handbook* by combining it with elements of modern CBT as follows. When you spot an irrational fear or excessive desire arising, or any kind of unhealthy passion, pause and do not allow yourself to be swept along by the impressions it contains, particularly the value judgements about what is good or bad, helpful or harmful. Practise withholding your assent, viewing the impression in a detached way, and saying in response to it such things as:

* 'You are just an appearance and not at all the thing you claim to represent.'
* 'We are upset not by things but by our judgements about things.'
* 'External and bodily things are fundamentally 'indifferent' with regard to becoming a good person.'
* 'The Sage would rise above this, viewing it as 'nothing' with regard to his wellbeing or *eudaimonia*.'

Particularly focus on viewing the impression as a mental representation, containing the judgement that something is 'good' or 'bad'. Remember that it is just an impression or appearance, something distinct from the thing itself that it claims to represent.

Try it now: The leaves on a stream meditation

This is an exercise adapted from a modern 'third-wave' form of CBT called Acceptance and Commitment Therapy (ACT) (Hayes, Strosahl, & Wilson, 2012). It provides a good way to practise some of the psychological skills that the Stoics appear to have valued.

1 Close your eyes and sit in a comfortable position, take a moment to relax and settle down as you begin to observe your stream of consciousness more closely.

2   Picture a slowly-flowing stream or river; this can be a memory or an image you've made up. Imagine that it's autumn and there are a few leaves falling in the river and being slowly swept past you and off downstream. Imagine you're observing things from a distance, from high up on the bank or a bridge overhead. This gives you something to keep bringing your attention back to.

3   It's natural that from time to time, your attention will wander or other thoughts and feelings will spontaneously pop into your mind. Rather than interpreting these as distractions and struggling to prevent them, just accept your automatic thoughts (or 'impressions') as normal and harmless, and incorporate them into the exercise as follows.

4   When a thought intrudes, or your mind wanders, just catch it as early as possible, and bring your attention back gently to the image of the river.

5   Turn the thought into an object. For example, if words cross your mind, imagine they're written down on a slip of paper; if a memory or image pops into your mind, turn it into a photograph; if a feeling or bodily sensation grabs your attention, picture it as a colour or shape.

6   Now place that object on one of the leaves, 'out there', at a distance from you, on the river, and just let go of it, and allow it to drift naturally downstream, until it eventually disappears from view.

7   Keep catching your automatic thoughts or impressions early, turning them into objects, putting them on leaves, at a distance, and letting go of them, in this way. Even if the same thoughts or feelings keep popping back into your mind, that's absolutely fine, just keep responding in the same way.

It's important that you don't approach this as a way to avoid or 'get rid' of your automatic thoughts. Rather, your goal is to focus on acknowledging and accepting anything that enters your stream of consciousness, with a sense of cognitive distance. Ideally, you're neither grabbing onto these thoughts nor trying to push them away, but allowing them to fade naturally from the mind, in their own time. The Stoics believed that 'impressions' occur automatically in the mind and that these are inherently 'indifferent' but that our response to them is the most important thing in life. The foundation of wisdom and virtue, according to Epictetus, is to make the 'correct use of our impressions', and this begins with our being able to spot them without being 'carried away' by them, often postponing any response until later.

Remember this: You need to spot impressions before you can challenge them

As Beck observed, we need to be able to spot our automatic thoughts and take a step back from them (gaining 'cognitive distance') before we can even begin to change them by evaluating the evidence, etc. Put another way, we need to be able to view our impressions of events as 'hypotheses' capable of being disputed, as thoughts rather than facts, before we can dispute them. The Stoics seem to have arrived at a similar finding. Epictetus repeatedly tells his students that they must avoid being 'carried away' by their initial impressions, slow down, and remind themselves that they are just appearances and not themselves the things they claim to represent, before checking out their validity, philosophically, according to Stoic doctrine. Sometimes this is done after a 'cooling down' period, postponing any evaluation until later, when the impressions are no longer 'fresh' and our passions have calmed down, so that we can think more calmly and clearly. He says the main question we should pose is whether they are about things that are 'up to us' or not, something we'll return to in the next chapter.

Focus Points

The main points to remember from this chapter are:

* The discipline of judgement, or 'assent', is linked to Stoic Logic and involves avoiding rashly being 'carried away' by our initial impressions and then evaluating them in terms of our Stoic principles.
* The Stoic technique Hadot calls 'physical definition', entails stripping away value judgements and sticking with a firmly-grasped objective representation (*phantasia kataléptikê*) of events.
* Epictetus repeatedly advises us to gain what modern therapists call 'cognitive distance' from disturbing impressions, e.g., by saying 'You are just a mere appearance and not at all the thing itself appearing' or reminding ourselves that we are upset by our own value judgements rather than by external events.

Next Step

As we've seen, Epictetus appears to say that the discipline of judgement consists in two basic steps. Having looked at the initial step of gaining 'cognitive distance', we're now going to look at the following step: evaluating the impression in accord with Stoic principles. He tells us that this mainly consists in examining whether it relates to things that are 'up to us' or not, which I refer to as the 'Stoic fork', as this dichotomy is absolutely central to Stoic practice, particularly in the teachings of Epictetus.

9

Self-awareness and the 'Stoic fork'

In this chapter you will learn:

▶ *How Stoics practise mindfulness or 'attention' to their ruling faculty, and the art of distinguishing between what is 'up to us' and what is not*

▶ *How to use the ancient strategy of postponement, by delaying your responses to initial impressions until you can evaluate them calmly*

▶ *How the Stoics assimilated morning and evening contemplative practices from the Pythagoreans, to help maintain self-discipline and a structured daily routine of philosophical practice*

When you relax your attention for a little while, do not imagine that whenever you choose you will recover it, but bear this in mind, that because of the error you made today, your condition must necessarily be worse as regards everything else. For, to begin with – and this is the worst of all – a habit of not paying attention is developed; and after that a habit of deferring attention; and always you grow accustomed to putting off, from one time to another, serene and appropriate living, the life in accord with nature, and persistence in that life. (Epictetus, *Discourses*, 4.12)

Never allow sleep to close your eyelids, after you went to bed,

Until you have examined all your actions of the day by your reason.

In what have I done wrong? What have I done? What have I omitted that I ought to have done?

If in this examination you find that you have done wrong, reprove yourself severely for it;

And if you have done any good, rejoice.

Practise thoroughly all these things; meditate on them well; you ought to love them with all your heart.

It is those that will put you in the way of divine virtue. (*The Golden Verses of Pythagoras*)

Self-assessment: Stoic attitudes towards self-examination

Before reading this chapter, rate how strongly you agree with the following statements, using the five-point (1–5) scale below, and then re-rate your attitudes once you've read and digested the contents.

1. Strongly disagree, 2. Disagree, 3. Neither agree nor disagree, 4. Agree, 5. Strongly agree

1 'It's essential to be continually mindful of your value judgements throughout the day.'

2 'The most important thing to evaluate is whether upsetting impressions are about things under my control or not.'

3 'Each morning we should plan our actions, and review them in the evening, evaluating whether we have lived wisely or not.'

How is self-awareness developed in Stoicism?

Many people today are drawn to Oriental traditions such as Buddhism because they provide guidance on the art of living. One of the best-known aspects of Buddhist practice is the emphasis on cultivating 'mindfulness' during meditation and throughout daily life. As we've seen, ancient Stoicism places considerable importance on very similar concepts and practices. The closest thing the Stoics have to a technical term for 'mindfulness' is *prosochê*, or 'attention', which refers to the continual self-monitoring of one's thoughts and actions, as they happen, in the here and now.

> Attention (*prosochê*) is the fundamental Stoic spiritual attitude. It is a continuous vigilance and presence of mind, self-consciousness which never sleeps, and a constant tension of the spirit. Thanks to this attitude, the philosopher is fully aware of what he does at each instant, and he *wills* his actions fully. (Hadot, 1995, p. 84)

Stoics weren't cultivating mindfulness of their body or breathing but specifically their conscious 'ruling faculty' (*hêgemonikon*), the central and most important function of the mind. Epictetus said that a good philosopher 'has so many eyes', when it comes to minding his ruling faculty, 'that you will say Argus was blind in comparison with him' because 'here is concentrated his earnest attention (*prosochê*) and energy' – Argus Panoptes, the 'all-seeing', was a mythic giant with a hundred eyes (*Discourses*, 3.22).

In a sense, Stoic Ethics *inevitably* leads to greater mindfulness. Once we accept that the true nature of the supreme 'good' is virtue, which resides within us, we *naturally* seek to pay attention to its source, as it's the most important thing in the universe. Stoic practice is essentially an exercise in contemplating the good and therefore an exercise in mindfulness of our own voluntary judgements and actions. Moreover, for the Stoics our conscious 'ruling faculty' is the essence of our true self. Being more self-aware means being more aware of our innate freedom and, in a sense, more alive. Epictetus frequently reminds his students that Nature has entrusted them with a divine spark, this faculty of reason, which it is their sacred responsibility to continually guard and protect from harm in every circumstance. The three Stoic disciplines of desire, action and judgement entail a kind of 'mindfulness' of the three functions of the 'ruling faculty', over which we can acquire voluntary control.

Epictetus delivered a whole discourse entitled 'On attention' (*prosochê*), which is about this concept of 'Stoic mindfulness' (*Discourses*, 4.12). He poses the rhetorical question: 'What thing is done better by those who are inattentive?' He also asks his students very specifically: 'What things therefore is it necessary for me to pay attention to?' The answer lies in two 'general principles' of Stoicism we should constantly have ready-to-hand in every situation:

1 Nobody is master of another's volition or moral purpose.

2 But in this alone are to be found one's good and evil.

In other words, Stoics should continually be mindful of their volition (*prohairesis*). Their voluntary thoughts and actions are, by definition, the only things completely under their control.

We are to watch ourselves like a hawk, particularly what is most 'helpful' or 'harmful' with regard to the good life, and attaining perfect Happiness (*eudaimonia*). The famous Daoist scripture *Dao de Jing* said that the wise man is 'cautious like someone crossing a winter stream'. Epictetus likewise says that just as someone walks very cautiously when he has to take care not to step on a sharp object or sprain his foot, the Stoic is always cautious, in his every act, not to harm the 'ruling faculty' of his own mind by lapsing into folly or vice.

It is impossible to be completely faultless in our actions but, says Epictetus, it is within our power to make a commitment to trying and we can be satisfied if we escape a few faults 'by never relaxing our attention'. Musonius Rufus likewise said very bluntly that we should never relax our attention because 'to let one's mind go lax is, in effect, to lose it' (*Sayings*, 52). To abandon mindfulness is, in a sense, to become *mindless*.

Epictetus therefore stresses that it is never completely within our power, once our attention has wandered, to recall it. We effectively give up being philosophers, and Stoics, when we act on autopilot. If we say 'Tomorrow I will pay attention' we effectively tell ourselves that today we are willing to sacrifice our sense of discretion and caution, to allow ourselves to be upset by the actions of others, to become angry, to be overcome by envy. As Epictetus elsewhere explains, we can view this as a kind of financial transaction, where we exchange self-awareness for something else. However, it is never 'profitable' to relax our attention because we always sell ourselves short in any transaction that involves sacrificing freedom and virtue. The Gospel of Mark employs similar language: 'For what shall it profit a man, if he shall gain the whole world, and lose his own soul?' (*Mark*, 8.36).

Training in mindfulness and philosophical 'self-examination' is therefore integral to Stoicism. For example, Stoics seem to have 'bookended' their daily practice of self-monitoring with a formal morning and evening meditation, derived from the much older philosophy of Pythagoreanism. It's unclear whether the lines from *The Golden Verses* quoted above came from Pythagoras himself or, perhaps more likely, evolved over centuries among his followers. Marcus Aurelius' physician, Galen, said that to master our passions we should contemplate *The Golden Verses* at least twice per day as an adjunct to moral reflection under the supervision of a wiser and more experienced mentor. Galen recommends first reading the verses then reciting them aloud, at dawn before beginning our daily tasks, and then again each evening before we go to sleep. Both Seneca and Epictetus taught others to use the Pythagorean technique of evening meditation as part of their Stoic practice, but they do not go into much detail about the procedure.

Fortunately, we gain more information from subsequent 'Neoplatonic' philosophers, who were particularly interested in ancient Pythagoreanism. According to Iamblichus, Pythagoreans arose before daybreak to contemplate and worship the rising sun, perhaps as part of a 'cosmological' meditation. Pythagoras instructed them never to do anything without rationally evaluating it first and discussing it with others, forming a plan of action each morning. Then at night, they reviewed all of the preceding day's actions, which served a *dual* purpose, both strengthening their memory and allowing them to evaluate their own conduct. Iamblichus' teacher, Porphyry, provides a more detailed description, saying that Pythagoras advised that special attention should be paid to two times of the day: when going to sleep we should review our past actions, accounting for them to ourselves, and when awakening in the morning those that are yet to come, planning them wisely. Like Galen, he recommended actually reciting *The Golden Verses*, and repeating the following words before falling asleep:

> Nor suffer sleep to close thine eyes
>
> Till thrice thy acts that day thou has run o'er;
>
> How slip? What deeds? What duty left undone? (Porphyry, *Life of Pythagoras*)

On awakening, though, we are to recite the lines:

> As soon as ere thou wakest, in order lay
>
> The actions to be done that following day.

As we'll see, centuries earlier, Stoics used the same lines as part of their contemplative practice. This is a mental training routine and clearly, like any *physical* exercise regime, it requires self-discipline to patiently rehearse the day ahead each morning and to review one's conduct critically each evening. However, this Pythagorean tradition clearly provided an important framework for daily Stoic practice.

Case study: Zeno meets King Antigonus

What would the ideal Stoic Sage do to avoid stage-fright if he found himself in the shoes of the cithara player mentioned earlier? Epictetus says he would have trained himself in advance to firmly grasp the indifference of external things and so 'he would never feel hindered, never feel restrained, and never feel anxious' (*Discourses*, 2.13). He refers to the example of Zeno, who had some intensive training in overcoming his own social anxiety when he first began to study philosophy, under the famous Cynic Crates. We're told that after his shipwreck, as he wandered Athens penniless, he was anxious about what others thought of him.

So one day Crates asked him to carry a clay pot full of lentil soup through the busy crowds in the potters' district. This sort of thing was actually a common Cynic exercise in developing 'shamelessness'. Zeno was worried about looking foolish and tried to conceal the pot under his cloak. When Crates spotted this he smashed it with his staff, splattering the soup all over Zeno's body, so it ran down his legs. 'Courage my little Phoenician', said Crates, 'it's nothing *terrible*, only soup!'

Similar 'shame-attacking' exercises, such as walking around a shopping centre with a banana on a leash, are sometimes used as part of modern CBT, to help people overcome their sense of shame about looking foolish in public.

It seems training in exercises like these eventually cured Zeno of his self-consciousness. Epictetus therefore advises us to contemplate his exemplary lack of anxiety, several decades later, when meeting the Macedonian king Antigonus II Gonatas, a powerful military and political leader. Antigonus sought the company of Cynic and Stoic philosophers, travelling to Athens several times to listen to Zeno teach at the *Stoa Poikilê*. We're told Zeno was completely unconcerned when first meeting him because Antigonus had power over absolutely nothing that Zeno saw as important in life, and Zeno desired nothing that Antigonus possessed. Antigonus was more anxious about meeting Zeno, because he desired to make a good impression on the philosopher, although that was beyond his direct control.

There's a similar legend, almost certainly a myth, that Alexander the Great once visited Diogenes the Cynic, whom he greatly admired, and asked if he could do anything for him. Notoriously, Diogenes was said to have replied: 'Yes, could you step aside, you're blocking the sunlight right now.'

In both these stories, a great king, despite his material wealth and power, is suddenly reduced in status when faced with a penniless philosopher's complete 'indifference' to external things. It's said that Antigonus became a great admirer of Zeno, perhaps considering himself an aspiring Stoic. We're told he later wrote pleading with Zeno to travel to Macedonia and become his personal tutor but by that time he was too old and frail for the journey so he sent one of his finest students, Persaeus, instead (*Lives*, 7.6). Antigonus reputedly wrote Zeno a letter saying: 'While in fortune and fame I deem myself your superior, in reason and education I own myself inferior, as well as in the perfect Happiness [*eudaimonia*] which you have attained.'

Key idea: Stoic mindfulness

The word *prosochê*, literally means 'attention' to one's conscious 'ruling faculty', which we could describe as 'Stoic mindfulness'. This word is actually not used frequently in the surviving literature but it clearly refers to a central aspect of Stoic practice, and we do have an entire discourse by Epictetus that was explicitly dedicated to the concept (*Discourses*, 4.12). Because we naturally pay attention to what seems most important, it follows that the Stoic Sage will continually attend to the source of virtue, his voluntary judgements and actions, which renders him unusually self-possessed in any given situation. One of the 'healthy passions' cultivated in Stoicism, called *eulabeia*, meaning 'caution' or 'discretion', can also be seen as a form of mindfulness. It's defined as a rational feeling of aversion towards lapsing into folly or vice, a kind of healthy *self-consciousness* that keeps us from being 'carried away' by unhealthy fears and desires.

The 'Stoic fork' or 'sovereign' precept

As we've seen, Stoic mindfulness is rooted in the central doctrine that only what is under our control can be 'good' or 'bad' and that everything external is 'indifferent'. The opening section of the Stoic *Handbook* (or *Enchiridion*) compiled from Epictetus' lessons by his student Arrian, provides the definitive account of this doctrine and its relationship with Stoic practice. This is one of the most important passages in the surviving Stoic literature, particularly for applying Stoicism to daily life, and therefore worth summarizing:

- ► Some things are 'up to us', or under our direct control, while others are not.

- ► Our judgements are 'up to us', particularly *value judgements* about what is 'good' and 'bad' or 'helpful' and 'harmful', as are our voluntary 'impulses' or intentions to act, the desires and aversions based on these, and in a word whatever are our own voluntary actions.

- ► By contrast, our body is not 'up to us', and neither are property, reputation, social or professional status, and in a word, whatever is not our own voluntary action.

- ► What is 'up to us' is our own true self, and naturally free, unhindered and unimpeded; while what is not up to us is weak, slavish, hindered, and alien to us, being not truly our own.

- ► Remember therefore that if you confuse these things and think what is naturally slavish to be free, and that which is not your own to be your own, then you will be hindered, grieve, be distressed, and you will angrily blame mankind, resent life and even hate the gods.

- ► By contrast, the promise of philosophy is that if you think only what is your own to be your own, and what is not your own to be not your own, just as it actually is, then nobody will ever force you to do anything nor prevent you doing anything. You will neither blame nor criticize anybody, nor will you do anything against your will. You will not have any enemy, nor will you be harmed, for nothing genuinely harmful will be able to reach your true self.

- ► Therefore with such ambitious goals, remember that you must hasten yourself to undertake them without reservation, for you cannot serve two different masters. You will have to completely abandon some of your goals in life and set aside others for the time being. For if you wish to have both Happiness and also to have social status and wealth it may be your misfortune to lose out on the latter, because you aim at wisdom and virtue. More importantly, you will definitely fail to attain wisdom and virtue, which alone produces freedom and Happiness (*eudaimonia*).

▶ Therefore train yourself without hesitation to say in response to the impression underlying every troubling passion that 'you are merely an appearance and in no way the thing appearing'.

▶ Next examine it and evaluate it against these the philosophical rules and standards which you have, but first and foremost this, whether it concerns value judgements about things that are 'up to us' or about things not up to us. And if it concerns something that is not up to us, judging it 'indifferent' with regard to achieving virtue and Happiness, have ready-to-hand the answer: 'It is nothing to me'.

This fundamental distinction between what is 'up to us' or under our direct control and what is not, is therefore presented as the basis of Epictetus' whole *Handbook* of Stoic practice. I've described it as the 'Stoic fork' because it refers to such a clear-cut and sharp division. This is a recurring theme throughout Epictetus' writings, repeated in many forms in countless passages. It is the essence of Epictetus' Stoicism and its practical application is straightforward:

> What, then, is to be done? To make the best of what is in our power, and take the rest as it naturally happens. (*Discourses*, 1.1)

The *Serenity Prayer, which we came across earlier,* expresses virtually the same idea – to do what we can, and serenely accept what we cannot change – and has all the marks of being derived from Stoicism itself (Pietsch, 1990).

Key idea: The 'Stoic fork'

The focus of Stoic mindfulness is the basic distinction between what is 'up to us', or within our control, and what is not. This is so central to the Stoicism of Epictetus that it's set forth in the very first sentence of the *Enchiridion*: 'Some things are up to us, whereas others are not' (*Enchiridion*, 1). Shaftesbury likewise described it as the 'sovereign' dogma of Stoicism (Shaftesbury, 2005, p. 233). As we've seen, this basic dichotomy is quite well expressed in the modern *Serenity Prayer*.

> God, grant me the serenity to accept the things
> I cannot change,
>
> The courage to change the things I can,
>
> And wisdom to know the difference.

However, for the Stoics, the only things entirely 'up to us', or under our control are our own *voluntary* judgements and intentions to act. Our fears and desires, false pleasures and emotional suffering, are ultimately based on these and so we have to assume responsibility for the 'passions' also. Epictetus' three disciplines of desire, action, and judgement, therefore correspond with the three faculties that are potentially 'up to us'. By contrast, bodily and external things – health, wealth, and reputation – are *not* completely 'up to us', nor are the outcomes of our actions in general, as these things are always ultimately in the hands of fortune. Stoic Ethics and the therapy of the passions require us to continually recall this distinction, applying it to each specific situation, and meditating deeply on its implications. It can also be understood as a way of drawing a clear and distinct boundary around the 'inner citadel' of the true self.

Remember this: Four strategies for dealing with passions

Epictetus gives his students several options for dealing with irrational fears and unhealthy desires, etc. These presuppose you've managed to catch them early and gain 'cognitive distance' from your impressions, rather than allowing troubling desires or emotions to spiral out of control.

* **Postponement**. If you're feeling overwhelmed by your feelings, try simply to do nothing, take a 'time out', and postpone responding until you've cooled off and had time to think things through rationally.
* **Modelling**. If you're not sure what to do, contemplate the hypothetical example of the ideal Sage, or consider exemplary individuals from real life or fiction, whom you could imitate. What would they do under the same circumstances? What would they advise you to do?

❊ **Coping**. Ask yourself what resources or virtues Nature has given you that might help you to deal with the problem, e.g., consider whether the situation calls for you to be prudent, benevolent, courageous, or restrained, etc.

❊ **Philosophical disputation**. Try to apply Stoic philosophical doctrines to your initial impressions, particularly by asking yourself whether things you're judging to be important ('good' or 'bad', 'helpful' or 'harmful') are actually under your direct control or not. If not, then tell yourself: 'This is nothing to me' or 'What is not 'up to me' is ultimately indifferent to me.'

These are similar to strategies commonly used in modern CBT and so we now have empirical evidence proving that, done *right*, they can be healthy ways to respond to negative or unhelpful feelings.

Postponement: not getting 'carried-away'

Throughout the *Discourses* and *Enchiridion*, as we've seen, Epictetus repeatedly refers to the threat of being 'carried away' by our passions by allowing them to seize control of our mind. For example, the discourse entitled 'How we struggle against our impressions', deals with our ability to take a step back from our initial impressions rather than being swept away into worry and distress (*Discourses*, 2.18). Epictetus begins by explaining that, just like physical abilities, the passions tend to become more habitual and automatic the more we indulge them, until we don't even notice them anymore because they've become part of our character.

> In general, therefore, if you want to do something make a habit of it; if you want not to do something, refrain from doing it, and accustom yourself to something else instead. (*Discourses*, 2.18)

For example, by habitually indulging unhealthy sexual cravings or lust for money they take root as lasting 'infirmities' of the mind. However, when reason is applied to the corresponding impressions, it can function as a 'remedy'. Sex and money are neither good nor bad, according to Stoicism, but excessive attachment or aversion to either is toxic. When we firmly grasp that external things are 'indifferent' and that only our own character and actions really matter, the strength of these problematic feelings is undermined and they become manageable. The first step in the Stoic therapy of the passions is to engage in what therapists now call 'self-monitoring' of symptoms. Epictetus gives the example of counting the days on which you've been angry and recording your progress in reducing this over time. If we can go thirty days without anger, he says, we should rejoice. He suggests it might take two or three months, though, to change the underlying character trait. Stoic practice therefore require us to train in these exercises, like athletes, otherwise we will simply be indulging in 'philosophical quibbles', all talk and no action.

In addition to this self-monitoring, Epictetus advises his students to aim from the outset not to be 'carried away' by unhealthy impressions, because if we simply 'gain time and respite' we more easily command our own mind (*Enchiridion*, 20).

At the start of Stoic training, presumably, or when our feelings appear overwhelming, we're to *postpone* responding to them, and do nothing, until they've settled down. We can then evaluate the underlying impressions calmly and rationally, with a 'philosophical' attitude, at a later time. We should stop picturing the future outcome of our fears or desires, until we can do so calmly and rationally. In particular, we should stick with the objective facts and refrain from adding any further value judgements such as that someone is a 'happy man' because he has something we do not. This simple ability to 'postpone' responding to passionate impressions is the very basis of virtue and self-mastery. The sagacious advice that no important decision should be taken when in the grip of a disturbing passion was also attributed to the ancient Pythagoreans:

> If however at any time any one of them fell into a rage, or into despondency, he would withdraw from his associates' company, and seeking solitude, endeavour to digest and heal the passion. Of the Pythagoreans it is also reported that none of them punished a servant or admonished a free man during anger, but waited until

he had recovered his wonted serenity. They use a special word, *paidartan*, to signify such [self-controlled] rebukes, effecting this calming by silence and quiet. (Iamblichus, *Life of Pythagoras*)

Similar 'postponement' or 'time-out' techniques are employed in modern therapy to control impulses by nipping them in the bud before they have a chance to spiral into more serious episodes of anger, worry, or depression. For example, there's direct evidence from modern psychological research, that by postponing thinking about problems until a specified time, the intensity and duration of worry can be reduced by about half and this 'postponement' strategy has therefore become an important component of several modern forms of CBT for Generalized Anxiety Disorder.

Epictetus suggests that when we're calm enough to address our troubling impressions rationally, perhaps after postponing them, there are several strategies we can use. We should 'withdraw to the society of the good and excellent men' and compare our conduct with the ideal standard of the Sage or what we consider praiseworthy in others. When such passions arise in the future, if we're ready to confront our initial impressions with the 'beautiful and noble' examples set by exemplary people, we will weaken and not be 'carried away' by them (*Discourses*, 2.18). Likewise, we should ask ourselves what mental resources or potential virtues Nature has given us to match each event that befalls us. For example, does a situation call for 'patience', and is patience more likely to lead to *eudaimonia* than indulgence? What would be the more *praiseworthy* course of action? Rather than following our initial impressions, and being led astray by irrational passions, we should praise ourselves for the very act of resisting or rising above our initial thoughts and impulses, as this response is the basis of virtue. In fact, Epictetus says that, ultimately, the secret of not being 'carried away' by fears and desires is simply to have completely grasped the core of Stoic Ethics. That means being persuaded that the most important thing in the world is our own flourishing and fulfilment (*eudaimonia*), which comes from achieving virtue.

Try it now: Stoic self-monitoring and postponement

Throughout the day, try to be continually mindful of your thoughts and feelings, particularly how you respond to them. The ancient Stoics employed basic self-monitoring techniques, to help them do this. Modern students of Stoicism might find it helpful to use a *modified* CBT self-monitoring form, like the one below to record information such as:

1 Where and when did problematic feelings arise, such as anxiety, anger or unhelpful desires? (Unlike cognitive therapy, Stoicism groups both emotions and desires together as forms of 'passion'; it treats anger as a *desire* for someone to be harmed.)

2 What emotions or desires ('passions') did you experience? Also note any 'early-warning signs' that disturbances were beginning to develop, such as physical tension or bodily sensations.

3 What specific thoughts or judgements were these feelings based on? (Try to spot any questionable *value judgements* that might be the source of unhealthy emotions or desires.)

4 What did you actually say or do? What, if anything, did you avoid doing? Try to record these things as soon as you notice the feelings. To begin with, simply practise self-monitoring and using the discipline of writing things down patiently and concisely to help you learn greater 'cognitive distance' from your initial upsetting impressions. When you spot the early-warning signs of an unhealthy 'passion' arising, rather than allowing yourself to be swept along by it, remind yourself that it is just the 'impression' that upsets you and not the thing itself. Do nothing else, if possible, and postpone responding until your feelings have subsided – especially when confronted by a seemingly overwhelming desire or emotion. This may take an hour or longer, perhaps even until the following day. Say to yourself 'I'll come back to this later, when I'm in the right frame of mind', rather than allowing your automatic impressions to dictate where and when you think about them.

When you're ready to do so more calmly, examine and evaluate your impressions, employing your philosophical principles. It helps to set aside a specific time and place to do so, perhaps during your morning or evening meditation. Apply the 'Stoic fork' first, by asking whether you're making value judgements, or experiencing 'passions', regarding things under your control or not. Remind yourself of the arguments meant to persuade Stoics that bodily and external things are neither good nor bad, but 'indifferent' regarding *eudaimonia*. Also consider what the ideal Sage would do and try to emulate his example. Perhaps ask yourself what inner resources Nature has given you to cope with the challenge you face?

With practice, you'll find that you're able to respond calmly to upsetting thoughts and feelings without the need to postpone things. Memorizing short 'laconic' statements helps. For example, Epictetus taught his students to respond to 'indifferent' things by telling themselves: 'This is nothing to me', or 'non-volitional = not evil'. You should formulate your own maxims and coping statements, using them frequently, until they become habitual and familiar responses.

Date/Time/Situation	Feelings (Passions)	Thoughts (Impressions)	Actions (Impulses)
3/4/2013 – 1.30pm A woman was pushing past me while I was trying to help my toddler in the hotel lobby after she spilt a cup of water all over herself and the floor.	Anger Noticed I was tensing my shoulders, beginning to frown.	'Are you an idiot?' 'Why can't you see what I'm doing?' (What she's doing is bad; she's getting in the way of me doing what I have to.)	Glared at her angrily but didn't do or say anything else. Didn't ask her to wait until we'd finished because I felt too angry.

Remember this: How to postpone responding to passions

Epictetus repeatedly advised his students to *postpone* responding to unhealthy impressions and passions. Similar strategies have been found effective in research on modern CBT, as long as they're not abused as a form of emotional suppression or avoidance. Think of this in terms of three stages:

1 **Spotting passions:** Epictetus says we should keep a tally of our toxic passions, or we could keep a more detailed record like the one above, particularly looking out for the 'early warning signs' of irrational fears and desires; this helps to raise awareness and increase 'cognitive distance' from automatic impressions.

2 **Postponing responses:** If they're potentially overwhelming, avoid being 'carried away' by disturbing passions by withholding assent from the impressions underlying them, rather than going along with them; 'gain time and respite' by delaying taking further action until you've calmed down, and the impressions are no longer

'fresh' in your mind; gain 'cognitive distance' by reminding yourself that these are just impressions and not the things they claim to represent, and that you are upset by your own value judgements rather than things themselves.

3 **Philosophical examination:** When you're able to do so calmly and rationally, begin to apply your Stoic doctrines to the impressions that trouble you; first and foremost examine whether you are making value judgements that conflict with the basic doctrine that only what is 'up to us' can be truly 'good' or 'bad'; you might also consider how an exemplary person or the ideal Sage would respond to the same situation; you might ask yourself what faculties or potential virtues you might have that would allow you to cope better with the situation.

Why meditate morning and night?

THE MORNING MEDITATION (PROSPECTIVE CONTEMPLATION)

Epictetus said that Stoics should rehearse the day ahead upon rising in the morning and then review their progress again at the end of the day. At daybreak we should ask ourselves, 'What do I still lack in order to achieve freedom from passions [*apatheia*]?', 'What to achieve tranquillity?' (*Discourses*, 4.6). Then we should ask a question based on the famous inscription at the Delphic Oracle of Apollo: 'Know Thyself.' For the Stoics, we continually risk alienation from our true nature, and descent to the level of mindless wild beasts or cattle, by allowing our attention to slip. We should therefore ask 'What am I?'

Stoics try to develop greater affinity with their essential nature as *rational* animals, rather than identifying themselves with their body, property or reputation, as the majority of people do. We can then ask what nature demands of us, as *rational* animals, and rehearse appropriate actions for the day ahead, aspiring to greater reason and virtue, in preparation for reviewing our progress at the end of the day. Marcus Aurelius likewise says:

> At daybreak, when reluctant to rise, have this thought ready in your mind: 'I am getting up to do a human being's work.' (*Meditations*, 5.1)

He also focused his preparations on living in harmony with the rest of *mankind*, saying to himself that in the day ahead he shall come across meddling, ungrateful, overbearing, treacherous, envious and antisocial people, anticipating the worst that can happen as if it were inevitable (*Meditations*, 2.1). However, he has his Stoic principles ready-to-hand, reminding himself that they are acting this way because they lack wisdom, and do not know the true nature of 'good' or 'evil'. All that ultimately matters is that he has grasped the true nature of the 'good' himself. He also reminds himself that those who oppose him and do wrong are fundamentally akin to him 'not of the same blood or birth as me, but the same mind', sharing a spark of divine reason. He carefully rehearses the Stoic precepts that nobody can truly harm him, nor implicate him in their vice, and that he cannot feel the passions of anger or hatred towards them when he recognizes his affinity with them, and that conflict is unnatural. 'We were born to work together like feet, hands, and eyes, like the two rows of teeth, upper and lower.'

Marcus also mentioned the fact, as noted above, that the ancient Pythagoreans would meditate each morning on the stars and rising sun, perhaps introducing elements of philosophical cosmology to his morning contemplations.

> Look, said the Pythagoreans, at the sky in the morning, that we may recall those hosts of heaven that ever follow the same course and accomplish their work in the same way, and their orderly system, and their purity, and their nakedness; for there is no veil before a star. (*Meditations*, 11.27)

Stoics may therefore have potentially rehearsed 'living in agreement with Nature' at three levels, an attitude of harmony and natural affection towards reason, their own essential nature, towards the brotherhood of mankind, and towards Nature, or the cosmos, as a whole.

As we've seen, Iamblichus also said that the Pythagoreans' mental preparation in the mornings involved 'forming a plan of what was to be done later' in the day. These deliberations, like those of the Stoics, apparently took account of any possible catastrophes which might befall them, in order to cultivate a stoical sense of being resilient and 'ready for anything'.

It was a precept of theirs that no human casualties ought to be unexpected by the intelligent, expecting everything which is not in their power to prevent. (*Life of Pythagoras*, 31)

As we've seen, when planning any action, or presumably the whole day ahead, Stoics add the 'reserve clause', a caveat such as 'fate permitting'. Whatever plans we make, fortune may intervene, and the only certainty is that our body will eventually be destroyed, and we shall lose everything.

Try it now: How to awaken like a Stoic

When you awaken each morning, take a few moments to compose yourself and then spend 5–10 minutes patiently rehearsing the day ahead. How can you progress a few steps closer towards the ideal of the Stoic Sage? How can you take appropriate action in the world, while accepting things beyond your control?

1 Marcus alludes to the ancient Pythagorean practice of walking in solitude to a quiet place at daybreak and meditating upon the stars and the rising sun, while developing mindfulness of one's reasoning faculty in preparation for the day ahead. You might have to make do with setting aside a particular place at home for doing this, such as sitting on the end of your bed, or standing in front of the mirror in your bathroom. However, you can still think of the sun rising against a backdrop of stars – we'll discuss more 'cosmological' meditations like this later.

2 Pick a specific philosophical precept that you want to rehearse and repeat it to yourself a few times before imagining how you could adhere to it more fully during the rest of the day. To begin with, choose the general principle: 'Some things are under our control whereas others are not'. Keep this idea ready-to-hand as you practise placing more importance upon your own character and actions and viewing external events as indifferent.

3 Alternatively, you might pick a specific virtue that you want to cultivate and mentally rehearse your day ahead, in broad outline, while trying to imagine how you would act if showing more wisdom, justice, courage, or self-discipline, etc.

Once you've got into the habit of doing this, try imagining greater challenges, difficult people, etc., as discussed in the chapter on premeditation of future adversity. As we've seen, some Stoics also recall their own mortality while planning the day ahead. For instance, Seneca actually recommends that when we awaken each morning we should tell ourselves: 'You may not ever sleep again'.

Key idea: The evening and morning meditations

The Stoics adopted the Pythagorean practice, described in *The Golden Verses*, of contemplating the events of the day patiently, perhaps three times, before retiring to sleep. The famous questions from *The Golden Verses*, quoted by Epictetus, were: 'Where did I go wrong? What did I do? What duty is left undone?' For Stoics, these questions all refer to their supreme goal and so Epictetus specifically recommends asking where we went wrong with regard to living a 'smoothly flowing' and harmonious life, in accord with wisdom and virtue. Stoics might also examine whether they're actually living in harmony with their own rational nature, with the rest of mankind, and with Nature as a whole – the *threefold* sense of 'living in agreement with Nature'.

One of the fundamental questions a Stoic should ask when planning the day ahead is presumably: 'How can I progress closer towards becoming a perfect Sage?' This is undoubtedly influenced by what he learned about his own weaknesses during the preceding evening contemplation. What is required to overcome any irrational fears and desires that remain? Do I lack courage, self-discipline, or some other virtue that life demands of me? Epictetus compares this to an athlete or a vocal-coach, planning a training regime and putting it into practice. Fundamentally, the Stoic also prepares, upon awakening, to apply the general precept that says external things are indifferent to us and that our chief good lies in excelling in terms of what is 'up to us', our own character and actions, and this overlaps with the more general technique of 'premeditation of adversity', discussed earlier.

THE EVENING MEDITATION (RETROSPECTIVE CONTEMPLATION)

Seneca described a method of evening meditation taught by the Roman philosopher Quintus Sextius, who combined Pythagoreanism and Stoicism. He says that for our minds to flourish as nature intended, we must continually train ourselves by posing questions such as the following before retiring to sleep:

1 What bad habit have you put right today?

2 Which fault did you take a stand against?

3 In what respect are you better?

This philosophical and therapeutic self-examination is compared to a courtroom trial: 'every day I plead my case before myself as judge'. Our passions will calm down and we will achieve more control over them, he says, when they know they must answer before a judge each evening in this way. In other words, this routine contributes to mindfulness throughout the day. Also, rather than fuelling worry, Seneca says that it is conducive to sounder sleep – which can be taken as an indication that the practice is being used correctly.

> When the lamp has been removed from my sight, and my wife, no stranger now to my habit, has fallen silent, I examine the whole of my day and retrace my actions and words I hide nothing from myself, pass over nothing. For why should I be afraid of any of my mistakes, when I can say: 'Beware of doing that again, and this time I pardon you'? (*On Anger*, 3)

Seneca's examples of self-reproaches clearly illustrate that rather than indulging in morbid self-criticism he adopted the attitude towards himself of a friend providing wise and benevolent counsel:

> In that discussion you spoke too aggressively: do not, after this, clash with people of no experience; those who have never learned make unwilling pupils. You were more outspoken in criticizing that man than you should have been, and so you offended, rather than improved him: in the future have regard not only for the truth of what you say but for the question whether the man you are addressing can accept the truth: a good man welcomes criticism, but the worse a man is, the fiercer his resentment of the person correcting him. (*On Anger*, 3)

It's said the Pythagoreans practised reviewing the sequence of events that happened during the day as a method of improving their memory. The Stoics prefer to focus on its potential as a method of ethical and therapeutic self-analysis. However, Epictetus quotes the relevant lines from *The Golden Verses* to his students, saying that we should keep them 'on hand to use', applying them to our daily lives; unlike Seneca he sticks with the standard Pythagorean questions.

1 Where did I go wrong?

2 What did I do (right)?

3 And what duty's left undone?

The past is ultimately indifferent. Nevertheless, we can learn from our mistakes and perhaps there is a sense in which we can 'rejoice in what we did well', as Epictetus puts it. We should desire to do what's left undone, 'fate permitting'. The morning and evening meditation routines therefore appear to complement each other, forming stages in a cyclical process of reflection, learning, and mental preparation for action.

Try it now: How to sleep like a Stoic

At night, before going to sleep, take 5–10 minutes to calmly review the events of your day, picturing them in your mind if possible. Try to remember the order in which you encountered different people throughout the day, the tasks you engaged in, what you said and did, etc. Although this may exercise and improve your memory, for Stoics the most important aspect is that you question whether you could have lived more consistently in the service of wisdom and *eudaimonia*.

1 'What did you do badly?' Did you do allow yourself to be ruled by fears or desires of an excessive, irrational or unhealthy kind? Did you sacrifice *eudaimonia* for the sake of something external?

2 'What did you do well?' Did you make progress towards wisdom and virtue? Did you act 'appropriately', in accord with your principles?

3 'What did you omit?' Did you fail to do what was 'appropriate' or your duty? Did you overlook any opportunities to exercise practical wisdom, justice, courage or self-discipline?

4 Consider how anything done badly or neglected could be done differently in the future. What would the perfect Sage do?

5 Praise yourself for anything done well.

You are rehearsing the role of a friend and wise counsellor towards yourself, and that relationship should be kept in mind. In addition, Seneca says that we should tell ourselves each evening 'You may not wake up', before going to sleep. Remember that all of these events are in the past that therefore strictly-speaking 'indifferent' to you, and accept them as determined to happen as they did by fate. You may find it helpful to rehearse exercises in a journal at this time also, paraphrasing Stoic precepts, like Marcus Aurelius does in his *Meditations*.

Remember this: Problems sleeping and waking-up

It's going to take some trial and error to find the best morning and evening routines, so you'll need to adopt a flexible approach. It's probably not best to try doing these exercises while actually lying drowsily in your bed but better if you sit or stand upright and awake. It would take you about 16 hours to either plan or review your whole day in 'real-time' so, of course, you'll be going over things in broad outline, picking out key events. Avoid worrying about things that appear troubling, especially if that's likely to interfere with your sleep. Morbid worry and rumination are the *opposite* of what you should be doing. Always remind yourself that things beyond your control are to be judged 'indifferent', in Stoic terms.

Focus Points

The main points to remember from this chapter are:

- Many people find the concept of 'mindfulness' in Buddhism appealing but a similar practice, called *prosochê* or 'attention' to one's conscious 'ruling faculty', was central to ancient Stoicism.
- Epictetus' Stoic *Handbook* opens with the fundamental practice of evaluating our impressions using the 'Stoic fork', the distinction between what's 'up to us' and what isn't, reminding ourselves that external things are inherently 'indifferent' with regard to virtue and *eudaimonia*.
- Planning the day ahead and reviewing the day gone by can help you maintain a structured routine of living wisely, and following Stoic principles.

Next Step

We've now covered the theory of Stoic Ethics and the basic practices involved in the three disciplines of Epictetus, as well as the notion of a morning and evening routine, giving structure to philosophical self-examination. We're now going to look at some of the most dramatic and challenging Stoic contemplative exercises.

10

The view from above and Stoic cosmology

In this chapter you will learn:

▶ *That the ancient study of Nature, or philosophical 'Physics', was linked to important psychological exercises*

▶ *How to contemplate life as a 'festival', an ancient Pythagorean metaphor adopted by the Stoics*

▶ *How to practise a Stoic meditation modern scholars call 'the view from above'*

▶ *How to contemplate time and the transience of all individual, material things, adopting a 'cosmological' perspective on life*

Take a bird's-eye view of the world, as seen from above: its numerous gatherings and ceremonies, many voyages in calm and storm, and the different ways things come into being, take part in it, and cease to be. Reflect also on the life lived long ago by other men, and the life that shall be lived after you are gone, and is now being lived in foreign lands, and how many have never even heard your name, and how many will very soon forget it, and how many who now perhaps praise, will very soon blame you, and that neither memory nor fame nor anything else whatsoever is worth anything. (*Meditations*, 9.30)

How tiny a fragment of boundless and abysmal time has been appointed to each man! For in a moment it is lost in eternity. And how tiny a part of the universal substance! How tiny of the universal soul! And on how tiny a clod of the whole Earth do you crawl! Keeping all these things in mind, think nothing of moment except to do what your nature leads you to do, and to bear what the universal nature brings you. (*Meditations*, 12.32)

Self-assessment: Stoic attitudes towards cosmology

Before reading this chapter, rate how strongly you agree with the following statements, using the five-point (1–5) scale below, and then re-rate your attitudes once you've read and digested the contents.

1. Strongly disagree, 2. Disagree, 3. Neither agree nor disagree,
4. Agree, 5. Strongly agree

1 'Imagining events as if seen from a bird's-eye perspective can help me achieve tranquillity and a rational perspective.'

2 'Life is like a festival or pageant, lasting a short time, which we should be grateful for attending.'

3 'When I think of the brevity of life in terms of the history of the universe, I'm reminded to value my own actions more than my possessions.'

Why is contemplating Nature important?

What happens if you take a step back from your life and look at it from a different point of view? What's the bigger picture? These are the sort of questions that underlie some basic *perspective-shifting* exercises the Stoics employed as a form of philosophical contemplation. This chapter looks in particular at meditations related to Stoic Physics, designed to stretch our imaginations, encouraging detached acceptance of events, in accord with the Stoic 'discipline of desire' and therapy of the passions. They train us to enlarge our consciousness, while diminishing the perceived importance of external things.

This notion of expanding our minds is related to another important virtue called 'magnanimity' (*megalopsuchia*, a 'mega psyche'), which literally means 'greatness of soul' or 'greatness of mind' – having a *big* soul. It's defined as the quality that allows us to remain superior to and detached from anything that happens to us in life, whether judged 'good' or 'evil' by the majority, i.e., the ordinary objects of fear and desire. Zeno wrote that magnanimity by itself is sufficient to 'raise us far above all things' and that because it is an essential part of all virtue, the Sage will necessarily 'look down upon all things that appear troublesome' and attain Happiness or *eudaimonia* regardless of his external circumstances.

Although, this might seem peculiar to modern readers, Seneca argues that because Stoics believe every true good resides in the mind, rather than in external or bodily things, it follows that whatever strengthens, elevates, or enlarges the mind is good for us. Virtue, in the form of 'magnanimity', raises the mind *above* 'indifferent' things and *enlarges* it far beyond their influence. By contrast, attachment to such bodily and external things as 'weigh down' the mind and weaken it or perhaps bloat it with emptiness, rather than allowing it to flourish, grow, and expand naturally. When we become absorbed in petty things, like the pursuit of wealth or reputation, in a sense our souls shrink and are dragged down into a narrow perspective in life.

Expanding the mind, in accord with wisdom and virtue, was therefore an important feature of Stoic Physics, and the discipline of desire. One of Marcus Aurelius' major themes in his *Meditations* is the vastness of time and space and how minute our bodies and the span of our lives are by comparison. The mere experience of *reading* these passages, which recur again and again, is enough to evoke a sense of expanding consciousness for many people. Marcus says that 'nothing is so conducive to greatness of mind', or magnanimity, as the practice of exercises derived from Stoic Physics. For example, making a detailed study of the processes of Nature, the 'mutual change of all things' one into another, and viewing all things objectively, stripped of value judgements, and within the context of the whole of Nature (*Meditations*, 10.11; 3.11). It's as though the universe granted us the gift of consciousness precisely so that we could expand our minds in this way.

> Wisdom is a great and extensive thing; it needs space; one must learn about matters, divine and human, about the past and future, about transient and eternal matters, about time. (Seneca, *Letters*, 88)

The Stoics were basically pantheists for whom 'Nature' and 'God' (or 'Zeus') were virtually synonymous terms. Zeus is an immortal animal, who is perfectly rational, completely Happy, stands aloof from anything bad, and looks after the whole cosmos, but he is *not* 'anthropomorphic', i.e., he does not resemble a man with a beard, perched on a cloud. The other gods are simply manifestations of him, in different guises. His body is the whole of Nature and his will is the vast chain of causation, called 'Fate', which naturally determines the outcome of all events. For Marcus, then, contemplating the universe as a single organism, of which we are all individual limbs, becomes an important psychological exercise: 'meditate often on the intimate union and mutual interdependence of all things in the cosmos' (*Meditations*, 6.38).

In addition to contemplating the ideal *mortal* Sage, therefore, Stoics contemplated the perspective of the ideal, perfectly wise and virtuous, *immortal* being, Zeus, by contemplating the whole of Nature in its totality. They imagined that Zeus must be aloof from worldly concerns in the same way and completely at peace within himself. They sought to envisage life from his godlike perspective, encompassing the whole of his creation in a single vision. By employing Stoic Physics as a kind of mind-expanding contemplative exercise they hoped to emulate the perfect serenity and magnanimity of the gods themselves.

According to Cicero, the three theoretical topics of philosophy typically begin with Physics, the contemplation of the stars and the nature of the universe, particularly of life and death, and the impermanence and mutability of all things, in accord with the laws of causal determinism. By becoming 'immersed night and day in these meditations' on the Nature of the cosmos, we make progress towards wisdom and rational joy, until we can look down serenely on the concerns of daily life, which seem petty by comparison. Both Cicero and, later, Epictetus, therefore appear to suggest that Stoic Physics, or the discipline of desire, functions as a kind of therapy for the passions, which students of philosophy must master first, in order to attain the tranquillity and magnanimity required to embark securely upon the second branch of philosophy, the study of Ethics, and the discipline of action. However, these contemplations were not just for novices.

Although, paradoxically, he stands aloof from all external things, the Stoic Sage becomes more firmly rooted in the whole of Nature and more at one with the cosmos, and genuinely at home here. Epictetus liked to remind his students that, when asked to what country he belonged, Socrates would say, 'I am a Citizen of the Universe', something echoed by Diogenes the Cynic and subsequently the Stoics, 'cosmopolitans' in the original, philosophical sense of the word. Marcus likewise says the goal of philosophy is to live according to Nature and thereby 'no longer an alien in your fatherland' but a true Citizen of the Universe, which means neither depending on external things nor being surprised by them.

Through the discipline of desire, the Stoic identifies herself with Nature, as a part to the whole – in a sense, the whole is the foundation of her being, therefore, and her own true identity – not an Athenian or a Roman but a cosmopolitan, in her very essence.

In this chapter we'll look at two Stoic contemplative practices. The first is based on a very ancient Pythagorean metaphor, which encourages philosophers to view life as a 'festival' or pageant. The second was named the 'view from above' by Pierre

Hadot, who called it the 'very essence of philosophy' and found repeated examples of it occurring throughout classical literature, in a variety of forms, across every school of ancient philosophy. It involves picturing life on earth as if seen from high overhead and it naturally leads into a widening perspective on space and time, which overlaps with Stoic cosmological meditations.

Although they're quite different exercises at first glance, they arguably served a similar purpose. Life is a spectacle and opportunity to be enjoyed, albeit briefly, as a gift from Nature but nevertheless from the detached perspective of a visitor passing through. Both of these exercises can therefore give us glimpses of magnanimity, 'rising above' or remaining detached from the hustle and bustle of ordinary life, and the illusion of conventional values.

Case study: 'The Dream of Scipio'

Scipio Aemilianus (185–129 BC) was renowned as a cultured Roman, later known as Scipio Africanus the Younger after his adoptive grandfather, a highly revered general. He surrounded himself with intellectuals, the 'Scipionic Circle', including his Stoic friend Laelius the Wise, whom we met earlier, and the scholarch Panaetius. *The Dream of Scipio*, from Cicero's *Republic*, is a famous vignette about his early career, and one of the most iconic examples of the 'view from above'.

It is the start of the third Punic War (149–146 BC) and the mighty armies of Rome are laying siege to the ancient city of Carthage in North Africa. On his arrival, as a young officer, Scipio seeks the hospitality of King Masinissa of Numidia. They converse late into the night about Africanus the Elder, an old friend of the King, who was supposed by Romans to have attained a godlike status after death in reward for his legendary victory over Hannibal at Carthage, decades earlier. Scipio falls deep asleep and experiences a strange, mystical dream, in which he ascends to meet Africanus the Elder in the outer heavens and together they look down upon the whole cosmos. Aemilianus exclaims that Earth seems tiny, adding 'I began to think less of this empire of ours, which only amounts to a pinpoint on its surface.' Yet he is filled with awe at the overwhelming beauty and harmony of the universe. Africanus the Elder shows him that the Earth and mortal life are miniscule parts of the whole cosmos and that 'the lips of mankind can grant you no fame or glory worth seeking'.

He realizes that Rome itself is but a fraction of the Earth, and that most of its surface is unpopulated, or inhabited by men who will never know of his achievements. Even those who do will soon die, and legends passed down through generations will inevitably fade over time.

Scipio Africanus encourages him to see beyond the superficial opinions of the majority and to be true to his innermost nature. 'Strive on!', the old general advises, 'Understand that you are a god.' He should forget about reputation and act purely in the service of wisdom and virtue, as a soul doing so 'will find it easiest of all to soar upwards to this place, which is its proper habitation and home'. He adds that the ascent will be easier if during life, confined by the body, it has nevertheless 'ranged freely abroad, and by visualising and meditating upon what lies outside itself, has worked to dissociate itself from the body to the greatest possible degree.'

As prophesized in the dream, Scipio's career advances at an extraordinary pace. Within a year he was made Roman consul, then placed in command of the legions in Africa. Eventually, Carthage fell to the Roman troops under his leadership, earning him the same honorific title as his grandfather: 'Africanus'. Carthage was 'torn apart, stone by stone', putting an end to Rome's greatest adversary and securing its power for many centuries to come. Even as he watched, though, Scipio reflected that one day Rome itself would likewise become extinct, all things being transient, from the perspective of the cosmos.

The Pythagorean 'festival'

Pythagoras reputedly compared the philosopher's role to that of a spectator at a busy 'festival' (*panêguris*) with various sporting events and forms of entertainment. He apparently meant they are spectators of the cosmos, seeking to contemplate the beauty and order of the whole universe. Diogenes the Cynic also reputedly said that a good man considers every day to be a festival and Epictetus subsequently taught his Stoic students to contemplate life in this way. The Stoics used this metaphor to convey a sense of gratitude for the opportunity of life, while accepting that it is temporary and will soon come to an end. The majority of people in this 'festival' or 'pageant' of life are interested purely in material gain, like cattle interested only in their fodder, whereas a handful 'attend the festival because they are fond of the spectacle' says Epictetus. These spectators are people who inquisitively ask 'What is the cosmos and who governs it?' or, as we might say, 'What does it all mean?' Being struck by this question, natural philosophers are drawn to the pursuit of knowledge, which becomes their chief goal in life – 'to study the festival before they leave it'.

Epictetus emphasized that they are therefore inevitably mocked by those who prefer to seek wealth and glory. However, philosophers should be no more disturbed by the ridicule of the ignorant than they would be if cattle could speak as, looking up momentarily from their troughs, 'they too would laugh at those who had wonder and admiration for anything but their fodder!' Although most people adopt a narrow perspective on life, absorbed in ultimately trivial pursuits, philosophers seek wisdom, above everything, through contemplation of the whole spectacle of Nature.

Epictetus uses this metaphor several times, instructing his Stoic students to regard the turmoil of life in a more detached manner as if it were merely the unavoidable hustle and bustle of a busy festival, like the Olympic Games. Nobody grumbles at the noise or jostling crowds, and everyone accepts they must leave eventually, although they would naturally prefer to stay. Epictetus says we should approach the 'festival' of life with this attitude, remembering that our life is 'on loan' from Nature and grateful for being allowed to participate in existence, albeit temporarily. The Stoics believed Zeus created mankind, and gave them the gift of consciousness and reason, precisely to enjoy the spectacle of Nature. The study of natural philosophy allows us to expand our contemplation to take in even more of creation. It is our duty to make progress towards wisdom, living in agreement with our experience of Nature, because 'God has no need of a fault-finding spectator'.

Key idea: The Pythagorean 'festival' and 'three lives'

Legend has it that Pythagoras coined the term 'philosopher' or lover of wisdom, which he reputedly explained using the allegory of human life as a crowded 'festival', like the ancient Olympic Games. There are athletes competing for glory, stallholders selling their wares for profit, and spectators who simply want to take in the whole experience that surrounds them. According to Pythagoras, these illustrate three ways of life:

1 The ambitious (competitors), who seek public acclaim and reputation as the chief good in life.
2 The greedy (traders), who cherish wealth and material gain above all.
3 The philosophers or 'lovers of wisdom' (spectators), who prize truth and knowledge, seeking to understand life in its entirety.

Philosophers stand apart from events and are not 'enslaved' by the desire for wealth or reputation, but simply rejoice in the opportunity to witness the spectacle. Epictetus emphasized that wisdom consists in being grateful for the festival or pageant of life, while accepting that it is on loan to us, and will inevitably come to an end.

Try it now: Contemplating the 'festival' of life

Imagine that you're attending a big music 'festival' like Glastonbury, a sporting event like the modern Olympic Games, or a busy exhibition in a museum or art gallery. Think of this as a metaphor for your life, as you go about your daily business. You're only a visitor, soon it will all be over, and eventually the whole site will be cleared. Think of your ticket as a gift and that you're privileged to be here, even if it only lasts a matter of days. None of this really belongs to you, the whole experience is temporary and on loan.

Your job is to 'take it all in' properly, and really appreciate the opportunity. Study the whole spectacle unfolding around you, in a detached and philosophical manner, as if seeing it all for the first time. The majority of people may be absorbed in pursuing wealth, seeking reputation, or indulging in empty pleasures. If occasionally they're rowdy or bump into you, that's inevitable – it's just part of the natural hustle and bustle. There's no point complaining, now you're here, if you don't like the programme of events – don't be a resentful or 'fault-finding' spectator. Just be where you are and take each moment as it comes. Right now, this is all there is. In a nutshell, step back from the 'rat-race' and begin to really notice life, being grateful for the 'here and now'.

Remember this: Stoic Physics as contemplative meditation

Chrysippus said that Stoic Physics or 'natural philosophy' was studied mainly to progress in Ethics, the transformation of one's character through the attainment of virtue. Although studying nature sometimes took the form of primitive philosophical and scientific speculations, it also culminated in contemplative exercises, which transform our perspective on life. 'The goal of physics as a spiritual exercise was to relocate human existence within the infinity of time and space, and the perspective of the great laws of nature' (Hadot, 1995, p. 244). Stoics considered these to have powerful therapeutic consequences, related to the discipline of desire. Hence, Marcus Aurelius wrote: 'Visions of this kind purge away the dross of our earth-bound life' (*Meditations*, 7.47).

Philosophical contemplation of Nature can take numerous forms, including contemplating the Earth seen from high above, or even the *whole* of space and time as one grand vision. Stoic Physics was employed as a way of overcoming unhealthy fears, particularly of death, and of mastering excessive desires, by viewing material things and reputation as transient and ultimately insignificant.

The 'view from above' and 'cosmic consciousness'

Zeno's lost book entitled *On the Whole* presumably set forth the conception of the universe upon which early Stoic Physics was based. As we've seen, ancient 'natural philosophy' often culminated in psychological exercises, with ethical and therapeutic implications. In particular, contemplating Nature as a whole, or on a grand scale, was often described as a powerful transformative practice. We still speak today of taking the 'long view', the 'bird's eye view', looking at 'the bigger picture', and considering how events fit into 'the grand scheme of things', etc.

Hadot coined the term 'the view from above' to describe one of the most common of these meditations. In his view, Stoic Physics as a contemplative practice begins with 'an exercise that consists in recognizing oneself as a part of the Whole, elevating oneself to cosmic consciousness, or immersing oneself within the totality of the cosmos' and 'to achieve this, we must practice the imaginative exercise which consists in seeing all human things from above' (Hadot, 2002, p. 136).

The 'view from above', like the meditation on death and contemplation of the Sage, appears fundamental to the whole practice of Stoic philosophy, because it encapsulates many important themes in a single image. Shaftesbury said we should be 'deep in this imagination' of the whole cosmos and the history of the universe, otherwise we are like children narrowly absorbed in playing with their toys, oblivious to their real surroundings (Shaftesbury, 2005, p. 19). Human affairs in general and our misfortunes in particular are bound to seem more trivial, from this perspective, he adds.

The Renaissance Neostoic Justus Lipsius described the 'view from above' as a visualization exercise involving picturing the world as if viewed from atop Mount Olympus. Indeed, it perhaps originated in the primitive notion of Zeus looking down upon mortal life in this way. Some of the most vivid descriptions of this exercise are found in Marcus Aurelius' *Meditations*. He repeatedly urges himself to recall that if he imagines looking down on human affairs from the heavens above, he naturally finds himself 'looking down' on them in the *moral* sense as well, i.e., with supreme indifference. Envisaging the vastness of the heavens and the multitude of the stars 'in one view', all things appear similarly inconsequential: 'everything identical in kind, everything fleeting' (*Meditations*, 12.24). Although these sayings do not occur in his surviving works, Marcus appears to attribute this concept to Plato, who wrote over 500 years earlier:

> Watch the stars in their courses as one that runs alongside them, and think constantly about the reciprocal changes of the elements, for thoughts on these things purify us from the mire of our earthly life.

> This saying of Plato is beautiful. Whoever would speak of mankind should survey, as from some high watchtower above, the things of earth: its gatherings during peace and war, marriages and separations, births and deaths, the noise of the law-court and the silence of the desert, foreign peoples of every kind, its feasts and mourning and markets, the medley of it all, and the harmonious order of contraries.

Review the distant things of the past and its succession of sovereignties without number. You can look forward and see the future also. For it will most surely be of the same character, and it cannot but carry on the rhythm of existing things. Consequently it is all one, whether we witness human life for forty years or ten thousand. For what more shall you see? (*Meditations* 7.47-49)

The 'view from above' and contemplation of impermanence naturally culminate in a more comprehensive perspective that has been called the 'point of view of the cosmos' or 'cosmic consciousness'. This 'cosmic perspective' perhaps came from a slightly more sophisticated and metaphysical theology, in which Zeus is everywhere and sees everything in one grand unified vision. Marcus sums this up neatly, and treats it as a regular contemplative exercise: 'Continually picture to yourself time and space as a whole, and every individual thing, in terms of space a tiny seed, in terms of time the mere turn of a screw' (*Meditations*, 10.17).

It's clear the Stoics employed this as a psychological therapy of the passions. Marcus says, for example, that we have the ability to rid ourselves of many unnecessary troubles, which exist wholly in our imaginations, if we simply plant ourselves in an enlarged space, 'embracing the whole universe in your mind and including in your survey time everlasting', observing the transience of all things, including our own lives (*Meditations*, 9.32).

One of the most remarkable descriptions of such contemplative exercises is found in the writings of Plotinus, who assimilated aspects of Stoicism into his later Neoplatonic philosophy. He says we should keep before our mind's eye an image of a *glass sphere* containing the whole universe and all living things, like a kind of cosmic snow-globe. 'Let us form a mental image of this universe,' he says, and 'entertain the shining representation of a sphere, enclosing all creation', each part envisaged as distinct but nevertheless forming a unity. We should thereby picture in a single vision all the stars of the cosmos, our sun, the earth, land and sea, and all living creatures, 'just as they would be seen within a transparent globe' (*Enneads*, 5.8).

There's another striking example of a similar exercise in an ancient text of the so-called Greek 'Hermetic' tradition, probably influenced by Neoplatonism, which it's worth quoting.

> Reflect on God in this way as having all within Himself as ideas: the cosmos, Himself, the whole. If you do not make yourself equal to God you cannot understand Him. Like is understood by like. Grow to immeasurable size. Be free from everybody, transcend all time. Become eternity and thus you will understand God. Suppose nothing to be impossible for yourself. Consider yourself immortal and able to understand everything: all arts, sciences and the nature of every living creature. Become higher than all heights and lower than all depths. Sense as one within yourself the entire creation: fire, water, the dry and the moist. Conceive yourself to be in all places at the same time: in earth, in the sea, in heaven; that you are not yet born, that you are within the womb, that you are young, old, dead; that you are beyond death. Conceive all things at once: times, places, actions, qualities and quantities; then you can understand God. (*Corpus Hermeticum*, 11.18-22)

As we've seen, stretching the mind in this way and expanding consciousness is linked to the virtue of 'magnanimity', the ability to look down with indifference on the things people mistakenly value, such as wealth, property, and social status.

Key idea: 'The view from above' and 'cosmic consciousness'

Hadot coined the name 'the view from above' for one of the main Stoic psychological exercises, which involves visualizing the world as though seen from high overhead – an 'Olympian perspective'. There are many variations of this undoubtedly very ancient exercise, which recur throughout classical literature, across all schools of philosophy. To view the world from above is to embrace the perspective of natural philosophy by seeking to contemplate creation, the physical universe, in a detached manner. A closely-related exercise, involved imagining the whole of space and time as if from the perspective of God or eternity – a 'cosmic perspective'.

This is a truly *cosmological* meditation, on the whole of Nature as a single entity. For Stoics, as pantheists, this is tantamount to glimpsing the perspective of Zeus, and his profound serenity, magnanimity, and freedom from suffering. So this exercise links natural philosophy, theology and psychological therapy. 'Never cease to think of the cosmos as one animal, possessed of a single substance and a single mind', says Marcus Aurelius, treating the concept as a kind of psychological exercise (*Meditations*, 4.40). Even if we approach this today simply as a metaphor or 'thought-experiment', we can still benefit from his advice.

Try it now: Contemplating the 'view from above' and 'cosmic perspective'

This is a big one... Take a moment to close your eyes and relax first, as this contemplation may take some patience and effort, but should be practised regularly:

1 Imagine leaving your body and rising higher upwards as you look down on yourself and things around you.
2 Picture first of all what you currently look like as if seen from the outside.
3 Now rise up higher and imagine your surroundings, as if seen from above – if you're indoors, just imagine the ceiling vanishes so that you can survey things from overhead!
4 Now rise even higher and imagine looking down on the town or city you're in, as if seen from high above; contemplate how many different people there are doing different things.
5 Rising even higher, imagine the whole country you're in, and the land or sea around it; contemplate the way some areas are populated more than others and the variety of things going on below.
6 Now imagine rising into the heavens, as it were, and viewing the whole planet Earth as if seen from space; see the polar ice caps, north and south, and the land and oceans in between.
7 Recall that your body lives down there, just one tiny occupant of a huge and diverse planet, but realize that your mind is able to grasp the concept of the whole of Nature; think of the transience and inter-action of all material things and imagine *all* things together as *one* thing, parts of the same whole.
8 Be aware of your life as part of the whole network of events on Earth below, just one of over seven billion people.

Over time, try to expand your perspective to contemplate the whole of time and space, from a more 'cosmological perspective'. If you like, try contemplating these things as if the universe were contained within a glass orb, as Plotinus describes, or experiment with other variations. What seems trivial? What seems important? How does this contemplation relate to the Stoic philosophy you've been reading about? Try to memorize what this contemplation tells you about life, perhaps by writing down some brief notes afterwards.

Remember this: You can't visualize the whole universe

Some people say it's a bit tricky to visualize the whole of space and time! That's certainly true. However, if we can talk about it, we can contemplate its meaning, and that's all that's really required. You may just think about the abstract idea more deeply, or picture fragmented images that nevertheless help you to contemplate the notion of the whole of Nature in this way. Alternatively, you might want to represent Nature schematically to yourself by drawing or visualizing a diagram of some kind, perhaps even something as simple as a circle with a tiny dot in the centre, to represent the whole of Nature as a single entity, and the infinitesimally small part of space and time occupied by your body right now.

The contemplation of impermanence and 'eternal recurrence'

Epictetus' surviving *Discourses* contain very little about Physics but even he advises his students frequently to remind themselves what the natural philosophers taught about the universe being a single entity, which changes continually. This naturally leads to contemplating the transience of your own life.

> I am not eternal, but a human being; a part of the whole, as an hour is of the day. Like an hour I must come and, like an hour, pass away. (*Discourses*, 2.5)

Change is the universal law of nature. We ourselves are continually transforming, in a sense decaying, gradually working our way to extinction along with the whole cosmos. Epictetus taught that if we consider ourselves alienated or detached from the rest of the universe we are prone to forget our mortality. However, by reminding ourselves that we are part of a vast string of intertwined causes, we're reminded of our vulnerability to factors outside of our control, which may destroy the body. This is a humbling perspective. He says that when we divorce ourselves from Nature, however, indulging in a kind of delusion of independence, we harm our essential nature, and cease to be true human beings at all.

As we've seen, Marcus, likewise, trained his mind, through natural philosophy, to contemplate the transience of material things, and their transformation, one into another, because 'nothing is so conducive to greatness of mind' (*Meditations*, 10.11). According to him, we thereby reduce attachment to the body, and eliminate fear or desire over external things. This liberates us to cultivate virtue in our actions and acceptance of whatever fate sends us. Marcus therefore reminds himself to think of Heraclitus' famous metaphor of time as a river, in which all material things flow past, constantly changing.

> Think often on the swiftness with which the things that exist and that are coming into existence are swept past us and carried out of sight. For all substance is as a river in ceaseless flow, its activities ever changing and its causes subject to countless variations, and scarcely anything stable; and ever beside us is this infinity of the past and yawning abyss of the future, wherein all things are disappearing. Is he not senseless who in such an environment puffs himself up, or is distracted, or frets as over a trouble lasting and far-reaching? (*Meditations*, 5.23)

Seneca adds that it makes no difference, from the perspective of eternity, whether we live the shortest or longest of human lives, if we try to compare the number of years a man lives with the number of years during which he does not exist, before and after his life.

> All things human are doomed to a short life and perishable, and in the boundlessness of time they take up no part at all. If we apply the scale of the universe, this earth with its cities and peoples, it rivers and surrounding sea, we may regard as a pinprick: if compared with all time, our life occupies less space than a pinprick for eternity has a greater

scale than that of the world, which, of course, renews itself so often throughout the passing of time. (Seneca, *Consolation to Marcia*, 21)

Health, wealth, and reputation seem ultimately less important when we contemplate what a fleeting portion of cosmic time they occupy. However, Stoics also believed that virtue and *eudaimonia* have a timeless quality, and their worth is not undermined by the brevity of their duration. An act of exemplary wisdom and courage that lasts a split second is still intrinsically good, whereas a split-second of pain is arguably something the majority of people would regard as quite trivial. Chrysippus said: 'If one has wisdom for one instant, he will be no less Happy than he who possesses it for all eternity.'

Contemplation of Stoic Physics was also believed to reveal the 'homogeneity', or sameness and repetitiveness, of all things. To the Sage, there is nothing new under the sun. Seneca quotes Heraclitus' ancient saying: 'One day is like every day' (*Letters*, 12).

He who has seen the present has seen everything: all that has occurred from all eternity, and all that will occur throughout infinity, for everything is homogenous and identical in form. (*Meditations*, 6.37)

Stoic Physics holds that the universe is infinitely varied and perpetually changing in terms of its physical qualities. However, from *another* perspective, what's most important in life is completely uniform. This is the perspective of Stoic Ethics and the discipline of action, for which all virtues are one and all external events are equally (absolutely) indifferent, literally 'no different' to each other, with regard to the good life. Countless generations who came before us, or will come after us, despite their many differences, all face exactly the same fundamental challenge to become good by flourishing in terms of their essential nature.

Although the majority of people are dazzled by life's seeming variety, every single moment that we encounter presents us, fundamentally, with the same moral dilemma, albeit in different guises. We skip from one external thing to another but the real decision we're continually confronted with is simply whether to place our good in internal or external things, in what is up to us or what is not.

> Each time you are elevated in this way, looking at human affairs from above, you would see the same things: uniformity and brevity. And to think that this is what men brag about! (*Meditations*, 12.24)

The Stoic Sage therefore has a consistency that is unshaken by changing circumstances. He perceives that although the body demands *countless* things, the mind needs only virtue, which is essentially the same in every situation. Grasping this hidden 'sameness' is therefore another route by which Stoic Physics leads to the discipline of desire and towards greater magnanimity.

However, the Stoics had another and perhaps more obscure perspective on time, which they may have inherited from earlier philosophers. They believed that the universe would be destroyed one day in a 'great conflagration', a vast explosion or fire. However, they also believed that it would re-create itself, in *exactly* the same form, and that this cycle would therefore repeat throughout all eternity. Probably because of their belief in causal determinism, they assumed that the whole chain of events would be *identical* each time.

It's not clear that the Stoics actually employed the concept of the 'eternal recurrence' as a psychological *exercise*. However, in the 19th century, Nietzsche made use of it for that purpose, as a means of developing what he called *amor fati*. According to the theory of eternal recurrence, although all individual events are minute and transient, when seen from a cosmological perspective, they are also timeless, in the peculiar sense that they are repeated an infinite number of times, although only once during each cycle of the universe. So each moment of your life is, paradoxically, both eternal and transient. This is certainly a mind-bending concept! Perhaps it's also a good place to end, with the revelation that you've read this book countless of billions of times before, having identical thoughts and feelings along the way, and will continue to do so, over and over again, for all eternity...

Key idea: 'Everything flows' and the 'eternal recurrence'

The doctrine of 'impermanence' is familiar to many people today as one of the cornerstones of Buddhist philosophy. However, over 500 years before the earliest Buddhist scriptures were written, the cryptic pre-Socratic philosopher Heraclitus made famous a theory called *panta rhei*, or 'everything flows'. Heraclitus said that nothing remains the same in life, which he illustrated with the well-known metaphor of the river: 'You cannot step into the same river twice because ever new waters are flowing in.'

This idea became very well-known, through the dialogues of Plato. However, Stoic Physics was apparently influenced by Heraclitus' natural philosophy. Marcus Aurelius alludes to his theories throughout the *Meditations*, citing him alongside Socrates, Diogenes, and Pythagoras as a great philosopher (*Meditations*, 6.47; 8.3). For the Stoics the doctrine that 'everything flows' is important because, as part of the 'discipline of desire', it has the psychological effect of reducing the perceived importance of external things, and our attachment (or aversion) to them.

The Stoics believed that the soul is not immortal but physical and therefore impermanent. So how can we come to terms with our mortality? They had a strange theory that offers one answer and has appealed to other philosophers, most notably Friedrich Nietzsche. The theory of 'eternal recurrence' holds that the universe will be recreated in absolutely the same form in an infinite number of cycles, beginning and ending with a cosmic conflagration. Nietzsche took this to follow from the view that the universe comes from nothing and that all things are determined by the laws of Nature. Eventually the universe will return to nothing, from which, according to this view, the whole cycle must begin again and follow exactly the same course. It's not clear if this is precisely what the Stoics meant. However, Nietzsche may have been right to view this as a psychologically very powerful idea. Perhaps we don't need to be immortal, as long as we can be *recurring*?

Try it now: Contemplating the vastness of time and eternal recurrence

This is another big one... Again, take time to settle, close your eyes, and become physically comfortable and mentally prepared before you begin.

1 Focus your attention on what you're actually doing right here and now, becoming mindful of your actions in the present moment.

2 Now gradually, broaden your perspective on time, becoming aware of the smallness of the present moment, each passing second, within the total duration of your whole waking day – if it helps, watch the second hand on a clock, and recall that there are 86,400 seconds in each day!

3 Now think of the present instant within the context of your whole lifespan, the years behind you, and ahead of you, and how these few seconds are preceded or followed by countless millions upon millions of instants, all different and yet all the same.

4 Now think of your own life as just one among many, preceded and followed by the lives of many billions of other people; think of how many famous or important people have lived and died before you ('Where are they now?') and will live and die long after you have gone.

5 Now broaden your perspective to think of the whole history of the human race, as part of the natural history of the planet Earth, and how tiny the mankind's duration is compared to the lifespan of our planet. Humans as we know them today have been around for hundreds of thousands of years but animal life has been on earth for several billion years.

6 Now think of the whole planetary history of Earth itself and how it was born from the debris of an exploding star, countless billions of years ago, and will one day be consumed by the fires of our own sun, and contemplate your own place, right now, within that vast cosmic epoch.

7 Finally, contemplate the whole history of the cosmos in its entirety, how the present moment is such an infinitesimally small part of the vast river of time, the mere turn of a screw in an incomprehensibly long cosmicera; think of the transience of all things, including your own life, and contemplate *all* things that happen throughout time together as *one* thing, as parts of a single tapestry, threads closely woven together forming the whole story of the cosmos.

If you like, also try to imagine that although each moment is transient, the whole universe will one day be destroyed and, like a phoenix, arise again in exactly the same form, an infinite number of times. So that every moment of your life has been repeated endless times before, and will continue to be repeated eternally in the future. Try to think of each moment as both transient and yet timeless, in this peculiar way. What matters isn't what happens, but how you respond. Once again, try to take away something you can remember and continue to contemplate, linking this meditation to your Stoic studies.

Remember this: It's about 'magnanimity' not trivializing everything

Some people might say that these exercises make them feel very small and insignificant in a demoralizing way. Epictetus responded to precisely this criticism, teaching his students that although our bodies are indeed a very small and transient part of the physical universe, paradoxically, we are equal to the gods in terms of our consciousness, which can reach out to encompass the vastness of Nature. As pantheists, the Stoics assumed that contemplating the whole of existence was equivalent to adopting the perspective of Zeus, who eternally contemplates his own creation. So this exercise can be seen as a means of emulating Zeus, and likewise imitating the godlike perspective of the ideal Stoic Sage.

Seneca said that as the only true good resides entirely within our mind, in the 'ruling faculty' or consciousness, we should somehow seek to enlarge that part of ourselves, because in doing so, we 'rise above' individual external things, diluting their perceived significance. We become 'bigger than' the events that trouble most people. The Stoics said that such 'magnanimity', or greatness of soul, is an essential feature of all true virtue. 'Human affairs, when seen from above, seem very tiny and puny; they are not worthy of being desired, nor does death appear as something to be feared' (Hadot, 1998, p. 173).

Returning to these perspective-shifting exercises frequently can help you to manage your emotions and desires, obtain a glimmer of tranquillity, and make progress, albeit in small steps, towards the lofty goal of Stoic *eudaimonia*.

Focus Points

The main points to remember from this chapter are:

* The Stoics believed that we can expand our minds through natural philosophy, or the study of Physics, when approached as a contemplative exercise.
* The 'view from above' and metaphor of the 'festival' were used by the Stoics to change perspective on life, and train themselves to view events with greater detachment and magnanimity.
* 'Physics' or natural philosophy was the basis of a number of contemplative exercises, employed by Stoics for psychological and moral transformation as part of the 'discipline of desire'.

Next Step

If you've bought the *eBook* edition, you'll be able to read an extra appendix with more information on the Stoic contemplation of death. However, as this is the final chapter of the main text, I think it's only appropriate to conclude with those magnificent words of Spinoza:

> If the road I have shown to lead to this is very difficult, it can yet be discovered.

> And clearly it must be hard when it is so seldom found.

> For how could it be that if salvation were close at hand and could be found without difficulty it should be neglected by almost all?

> But all excellent things are as difficult as they are rare. (Spinoza, *Ethica*, 5.42n)

Further Reading

▶ **Chapter 1**

Marcus Aurelius, *The Meditations*

Epictetus, *The Handbook*

John Sellars' *The Art of Living: The Stoics on the Nature and Function of Philosophy* (2003)

Jules Evans' *Philosophy for Life* (2012)

William Irvine's *A Guide to the Good Life: The Ancient Art of Stoic Joy* (2009)

▶ **Chapter 2**

Diogenes Laertius' *Lives* (Book 7)

Cicero's *On the Ends of Good and Evil* (esp. Book 3) and *Disputations at Tusculum* (Book 5)

▶ **Chapter 3**

Epictetus' *Handbook* (Enchiridion)

A. A. Long's *Epictetus: A Stoic and Socratic Guide to Life* (2002)

D. Robertson's *The Philosophy of Cognitive-Behavioural Therapy* (2010)

Pierre Hadot's *What is Ancient Philosophy?* (2002)

▶ **Chapter 4**

Pierre Hadot's *The Inner Citadel* (1998) (Chapter 7, 'The Discipline of Desire, or *amor fati*')

Pierre Hadot's *Philosophy as a Way of Life* (1995) (esp. Chapter 8, on the here and now)

Keith Seddon's *Stoic Serenity* (2006)

► **Chapter 5**

Epictetus' *Discourses* ('Of Natural Affection', 1.11; 'Of Friendship', 2.22; 'That we ought not to yearn for the things that are not under our control', 3.24

Cicero's *Laelius: On Friendship*

Shaftesbury's *Philosophical Regimen* (Chapter 1, 'Natural Affection')

Pierre Hadot's *Philosophy as a Way of Life* (1995) (Chapter 10, on the Sage)

Xenophon's *Symposium* and *Memorabilia* (esp. Chapter 2)

Plato's *Apology*, *Crito*, and *Phaedo*

► **Chapter 6**

Michael Shoster's *The Stoic Idea of the City* (1999)

Pierre Hadot's *The Inner Citadel* (1998) (Chapter 8, 'The Discipline of Action, or Action in the Service of Mankind')

► **Chapter 7**

Seneca's *Letters* (18, 24, and 91)

Tacitus' *Annals* (Book 15, the account of Seneca's death)

► **Chapter 8**

Epictetus' *Discourses* ('On attention', 4.12; 'How we struggle against our impressions', 2.18)

The Golden Verses of Pythagoras (See also Seneca's *On Anger*, Book 3, and Epictetus' Discourses 'In what manner we ought to bear sickness', 3.10, and 'Against those who lament over being pitied', 4.6)

► **Chapter 9**

Pierre Hadot's *Philosophy as a Way of Life* (1995) (Chapter 9, 'The View from Above')

Cicero's 'The Dream of Scipio' (from Book 6 of his *Republic*)

Boethius' *Consolation of Philosophy* (Books 4 and 5)

▶ **Chapter 10**

Seneca's *Letters* (4, 24, 70 and 82)

Seneca's *Consolations* to *Marcia*, *Helvia* and *Polybius*, and *On Earthquakes*

References

Alford, B. A., & Beck, A. T. (1997). *The Integrative Power of Cognitive Therapy.* New York: Guilford.

Aurelius, M. (2003). *Meditations: Living, Dying and the Good Life.* (G. Hays, Trans.) London: Phoenix.

Baudouin, C., & Lestchinsky, A. (1924). *The Inner Discipline.* London: George Allen & Unwin.

Beck, A. T. (1976). *Cognitive Therapy & Emotional Disorders.* New York: International University Press.

Beck, A. T., Emery, G., & Greenberg, R. (2005). *Anxiety Disorders and Phobias: A Cognitive Perspective (20th Anniversary Edition).* Cambridge, MA: Basic Books.

Beck, A. T., Rush, A. J., Shaw, B. F., & Emery, G. (1979). *Cognitive Therapy of Depression.* New York: Guilford Press.

Becker, L. C. (1998). *A New Stoicism.* NJ Princeton University Press.

Becker, L. C. (2004). Stoic emotion. In S. Strange, & J. Zupko (Eds.), *Stoicism: Traditions & Transformations.* Cambridge: Cambridge University Press.

Benson, H. (1975). *The Relaxation Response.* New York: William Morrow.

Borkovec, T. (2006). Applied Relaxation and Cognitive Therapy for Pathological Worry and Generalized Anxiety Disorder. In G. C. Davey, & A. Wells (Eds.), *Worry & its Psychological Disorders: Theory, Assessment & Treatment.* Chichester: Wiley.

Brunt, P. A. (2013). *Studies in Stoicism.* (M. Griffin, & A. Samuels, Eds.) Oxford: Oxford University Press.

Burkeman, O. (2012). *The Antidote: Happiness for People who Can't Stand Positive Thinking.* London: Canongate.

Clark, D. A., & Beck, A. T. (2010). *Cognitive Therapy of Anxiety Disorders: Science & Practice*. New York: Guilord Press.

Dubois, P., & Gallatin, L. (1908). *The Influence of the Mind on the Body*. New York: Funk and Wagnalls.

Ellis, A. (1962). *Reason & Emotion in Psychotherapy*. Secaucus, NJ: Citadel.

Ellis, A., & MacLaren, C. (2005). *Rational Emotive Behavior Therapy: A Therapist's Guide* (Second ed.). Atascadero, CA: Impact.

Engberg-Pedersen, T. (2009). Stoicism in the Apostle Paul: A Philosophical Reading. In S. K. Strange, & J. Zupko (Eds.), *Stoicism: Traditions and Transformations* (pp. 52–75). Cambridge: Cambridge University Press.

Epictetus. (1995). *The Discourses, The Handbook, Fragments*. (R. Hard, Trans.) London: Everyman.

Evans, J. (2012). *Philosophy for Life and Other Dangerous Situations*. London: Rider.

Foucault, M. (1988). Technologies of the Self. In L. H. Martin, H. Gutman, & P. H. Martin (Eds.), *Technologies of the Self: A Seminar with Michel Foucault*. Massachusetts: University of Massachusetts Press.

Gill, C. (2003). The School in the Roman Imperial Period. In B. Inwood (Ed.), *The Cambridge Companion to Stoicism* (pp. 33–58). Cambridge: Cambridge University Press.

Gill, C. (2006). *The Structured Self in Hellenistic and Roman Thought*. Oxford: Oxford University Press.

Gill, C. (2010). *Naturalistic Psychology in Galen and Stoicism*. Oxford: Oxford University Press.

Gill, C. (2011). Introduction. In M. Aurelius, *Meditations with Selected Correspondence* (R. Hard, Trans.). Oxford: Oxford University Press.

Graver, M. R. (2007). *Stoicism and Emotion*. Chicago: University of Chicago Press.

Hadot, P. (1995). *Philosophy as a Way of Life*. (A. I. Davidson, Ed., & M. Chase, Trans.) Malden, MA: Blackwell.

Hadot, P. (1998). *The Inner Citadel: The Meditations of Marcus Aurelius*. (M. Chase, Trans.) Cambridge, MA: Harvard University Press.

Hadot, P. (2002). *What is Ancient Philosophy?* (M. Chase, Trans.) Cambridge, MA: Harvard University Press.

Hayes, S. C., Strosahl, K. D., & Wilson, K. G. (2012). *Acceptance and Commitment Therapy: The Process and Practice of Mindful Change* (Second ed.). New York: Guilford.

Hierocles. (2012). Ethical Fragments Preserved by Stobaeus. In T. Taylor, *Political Fragments of Archytas, Charondas, Zaleucus, and Other Ancient Pythagoreans* (pp. 75–115). Forgotten Books.

Iamblichus. (1988). The Life of Pythagoras. In K. S. Guthrie, *The Pythagorean Sourcebook and Library*. Grand Rapids, MI: Phanes.

Irvine, W. B. (2009). *A Guide to the Good Life: The Ancient Art of Stoic Joy*. New York: OUP.

Jarrett, T. (2008, July-September). Warrior Resilience Training in Operation Iraqi Freedom: combining rational emotive behavior therapy, resiliency, and positive psychology. *US Army Medical Department Journal*, 32–38.

Kelley, K. W. (Ed.). (1988). *The Home Planet*. Boston: Addison-Wesley.

King, C. (2010). *Musonius Rufus: Lectures & Sayings*. Lulu.

Lazarus, A. A. (1981). *The Practice of Multimodal Therapy*. Baltimore: John Hopkins University Press.

LeBon, T. (2001). *Wise Therapy: Philosophy for Counsellors*. London: Sage.

LeBon, T. (2012). *Report on Exeter University 'Stoic Week'*. Retrieved from Stoicism Today: University of Exeter: http://blogs.exeter.ac.uk/stoicismtoday/files/2013/01/Stoic-Week-Report-Web.pdf

Lipsius, J. (2006). *On Constancy.* (J. Sellars, Ed., & S. J. Stradling, Trans.) Exeter: Bristol Phoenix Press.

Long, A. (2002). *Epictetus: A Stoic and Socratic Guide to Life.* Oxford: Oxford University Press.

Long, A., & Sedley, D. (1987). *The Hellenistic Philosophers: Volume 1 (Translations of the principal sources with philosophical commentary).* Cambridge: Cambridge University Press.

Marks, I. M. (2005). *Living with Fear: Understanding and Coping with Anxiety* (Second ed.). London: McGraw-Hill.

Meichenbaum, D. (1985). *Stress Inoculation Training.* New York: Pergamon.

Nussbaum, M. C. (1994). *The Therapy of Desire: Theory & Practice in Hellenistic Ethics.* New Jersey: Princeton University Press.

Pietsch, W. V. (1990). *The Serenity Prayer Book.* New York: Harper Collins.

Reivich, K., & Shatté, A. (2002). *The Resilience Factor.* New York: Three Rivers.

Robertson, D. J. (2005, July). Stoicism: A Lurking Presence. *Counselling & Psychotherapy Journal (CPJ).*

Robertson, D. J. (2010). *The Philosophy of Cognitive-Behavioural Therapy (CBT): Stoic Philosophy as Rational & Cognitive Psychotherapy.* London: Karnac.

Robertson, D. J. (2012). *Build your Resilience.* London: Hodder. & Stoughton

Roth, A., & Fonagy, P. (2005). *What Works for Whom? A Critical Review of Psychotherapy Research* (Second ed.). New York: Guilford.

Russell, B. (1930). *The Conquest of Happiness.* Padstow: Routledge.

Schofield, M. (1999). *The Stoic Idea of the City.* Cambridge: Cambridge University Press.

Seddon, K. (2006). *Stoic Serenity: A Practical Course on Finding Inner Peace.* Lulu.

Sedley, D. (2003). The School, from Zeno to Arius Didymus. In B. Inwood (Ed.), *The Cambridge Companion to the Stoics* (pp. 7–31). Cambridge: Cambridge University Press.

Seligman, M. E. (2002). *Authentic Happiness: Using the New Positive Psychology to Realize your Potential for Lasting Fulfilment.* New York: Simon & Schuster.

Seligman, M. E. (2011). *Flourish: A New Understanding of Happiness and Well-being.* Nicholas Brealey: London.

Sellars, J. (2003). *The Art of Living: The Stoics on the Nature and Function of Philosophy.* Burlington, VT: Ashgate.

Seneca. (2004). *Letters from a Stoic.* (R. Campbell, Trans.) Middlesex: Penguin.

Seneca. (2009). *On Benefits.* (A. Stewart, Trans.) BiblioLife.

Shaftesbury, A. A. (2005). *The Life, Unpublished Letters, and Philosophical Regimen of Antony, Earl of Shaftesbury.* (B. Rand, Ed.) Elibron Classics.

Sherman, N. (2005). *Stoic Warriors: The Ancient Philosophy behind the Military Mind.* New York: Oxford University Press.

Sorabji, R. (2004). Stoic First Movements in Christianity. In Strange, & Zupko (Eds.), *Stoicism: Traditions & Transformations.* Cambridge: Cambridge University Press.

Stephens, W. O. (1996, December). Epictetus on How the Stoic Sage Loves. *Oxford Studies in Ancient Philosophy,* pp. 193–210.

Still, A., & Dryden, W. (1999). The Place of Rationality in Stoicism and REBT. *Journal of Rational-Emotive & Cognitive-Behavior Therapy,* 17(3), pp. 143–164.

Stockdale, J. (1995). *Thoughts of a Philosophical Fighter Pilot.* Stanford, CA: Hoover Institute Press.

Taylor, T. (2012). *Political Fragments of Archytas, Charondas, Zaleucus, and Other Ancient Pythagoreans.* Forgotten Books. *The Stoics Reader: Selected Writings and Testimonia.* (2008). (B. Inwood, & L. P. Gerson, Trans.) Cambridge: Hackett.

Ussher, P. (2012). Stoicism and Western Buddhism: A Comparative Study of Two Philosophical Ways of Life (Unpublished Dissertation). Exeter: University of Exeter.

Wolfe, T. (1998). *A Man in Full* New York: Farrar, Straus and Giroux.

Index